D1303186

WHITE PAPER

WHITE PAPER

ON CONTEMPORARY AMERICAN POETRY

J. D. McClatchy

COLUMBIA UNIVERSITY PRESS   NEW YORK

811.09
M12w

Earlier versions of many essays in this book first appeared in *The American Poetry Review*, *The Cream City Review*, *Field*, *The Georgia Review*, *Grand Street*, *The Massachusetts Review*, *Modern Poetry Studies*, *The New Republic*, *Poetry*, *Southwest Review*; and in two collections, *Sylvia Plath: New Views on the Poetry*, edited by Gary Lane (Johns Hopkins University Press), and *James Merrill: Essays in Criticism*, edited by David Lehman and Charles Berger (Cornell University Press).

The following poems, reprinted here in their entirety, have been used by permission:

"Power" is reprinted from *The Dream of a Common Language: Poems 1974–1977*, by Adrienne Rich with the permission of W. W. Norton & Co., Inc. and the author. Copyright © 1978 by W. W. Norton & Co., Inc.

"One Art" and "The End of March" are used by permission of the publishers, Farrar, Straus & Giroux, Inc. Copyright © 1975, 1976 by Elizabeth Bishop.

"Snow" is reprinted by kind permission of Charles Wright.

"Angel," "An Urban Convalescence," "A Tenancy," and "Scenes of Childhood" are reprinted by kind permission of James Merrill.

"A Hill" is reprinted by kind permission of Anthony Hecht.

Library of Congress Cataloging-in-Publication Data
McClatchy, J. D., 1945–
    White paper: on contemporary American poetry / J. D. McClatchy.
      p.   cm.
    ISBN 0-231-06944-8
    1. American poetry—20th century—History and criticism.
  I. Title.
  PS325.M38   1989
  811'.54'09—dc19   88-36423
                                         CIP

Columbia University Press
New York   Oxford
Copyright © 1989 Columbia University Press
All rights reserved
Casebound editions of Columbia University Press books are Smyth-sewn and printed on permanent and durable acid-free paper
Book design by Jennifer Dossin
Printed in the United States of America

CONTENTS

PREFACE

The title, *White Paper*, points in two directions, and refers to the complementary purposes of this book. It should first recall *"le vide papier"* of Mallarmé, who identified it in the end with an ineffable emptiness, the Word that words embody and thereby distort. Mallarmé also meant, of course, something humbler, and at times more terrifying: the morning's blank page on the desk, the silence of possibility. Here is the problem any poet sits down to solve. The apparent problem for the creator is how to make something of nothing. The real problem for poets is how to make something new out of something else—out of traditions of experience and language they have assumed with the art. It's as if the other side of this translucently thin white paper is scrawled over with a not quite discernible writing, a sort of private anthology of one's own fragmentary starts and half-forgotten lines by others. The following essays are especially concerned with this problem, and with the various solutions proposed by the careers of several important contemporary American poets. My interest here has been in their individual achievements, the mythmaking realized and tactics deployed, and in those ways they have retrieved earlier traditions. I have wanted to explain in order to pay tribute.

A second meaning for my title is "position paper." As a statement of aims, it implies a necessarily partial and directive summary. This is an emphasis of the opening chapters, but an attitude throughout. These essays, written over a period of fifteen years, take just such a consistent and at times combative position. Though I have written, briefly or at length, about many other poets than those I discuss here, I have selected these because they seem to my mind to form a group, or the wing of one—if "group" is the word for writers of such singular and often contradictory gifts. Yet each in a different way presents a difficult and exemplary challenge to the middlebrow expectations brought to poetry over the past thirty years by critics and poets alike. By this I don't mean my choices are all knotty and severe. The styles of some may be hermetic, but others write in an entirely open and direct manner (that can at times be even harder to interpret). I am thinking here of Elizabeth Bishop's conversational ease, or of W. D. Snodgrass' candid lyrics.

I bear no ideological grudges. In fact, my brief is against those who would make American poetry over into images of any narrow critical orthodoxy. Ours is a heritage of heresies. It is still true, though, that I read these poets in the light of American and English romanticism, a line stretching from Emerson and Whitman through Dickinson and Crane to Stevens and on to the best poets now among us. And stretching back still further to Keats and Wordworth—poets for whom the imagination's own "executant power" hastens the central encounters in their work. This should not preclude either the cunning moralism of a Frost or the historical consciousness of an Auden. (Richard Howard and Robert Lowell would be this book's corresponding examples.) Autobiography, too, leads to the palace of wisdom. If the imagination is the poet's way of apprehending the past and fantasizing a future, then the autobiographical impulse that mingles facts and desires is a sure form of knowledge, and has been a dominant influence on American poetry for the past three decades. Lowell, Snodgrass, John Berryman, James Merrill, Sylvia Plath, and Anthony Hecht have all projected private dramas onto the wider screen of myth. If to help understand them I have sometimes turned to modern mythographers like Freud and Jung, that is because the poets themselves have shaped their stories into patterns that psychology had most vividly drawn for them. Some of these poets, in fact, wrote after the model (and experience) of psychotherapy, but in any case demonstrate the correspondences between psychological and rhetorical strategies. Still other poets here—John Ashbery and John Hollander, for instance—while avoiding autobiography, have set themselves the poignant task of *figuring out* the self in the play of voices and parables. Their rhetoric stands for life. And all the poets in this book have affiliated themselves to earlier poetic models that often set the course of a subsequent career, and adjust those balances— sublime to domestic, visionary to natural, abstract to specific— central to any poet's work.

Of course I have followed my own preferences, and the canny reader may wonder if there isn't a hidden program whereby I seek precedents for my own practice as a poet. That goes without saying. But it requires I say also that, like any poet, I often admire in another precisely what I cannot do myself; and that, like my essays, my poems are also *readings*. Both poetry and criticism spring from the same fascination with home truths and extravagant fictions that are part of the poet's temperament, and from the same instinct to encode and decipher. Language constitutes my most intimate relationship with myself, and my most stylized, most expressive relationship with the world. The poets in this book have challenged and enriched those relationships for themselves, but not for themselves alone. They have expanded what is possible for us all.

Roland Barthes wanted to define the "poetic" as the symbolic capacity of a form—the ability a fiction has to depart from its original intention in all sorts of directions, the better to add significance and surprising elegances to itself. Just as a poem is not a container of meaning but a context for meanings, so too the true opposite of the poetic is not the prosaic but the stereotype. The American poets I have written about in this book have all written poems that—it seemed so when you first read them, and still seems so—make just such breathtaking departures, and shimmer with meanings that continually revise and extend themselves. Their departures are into areas of experience and reaches of language we had not suspected were available to us. And these poets have also made controversial departures within their careers. I have tried to describe both moves. It is my hope that readers, when they return to the poems again, may find this book also to have been one of those crucial points of departure.

For, through that better perception, he stands one step
nearer to things, and sees the flowing or metamorphosis;
perceives that thought is multiform; that within the form
of every creature is a force impelling it to ascend into
a higher form; and, following with his eyes the life, uses
the forms which express that life, and so his speech flows
with the flowing of nature.

—Emerson, *The Poet*

Ah, but styles. They are the new friend's face
To whom we sacrifice the tried and true,
And are betrayed—or not—by. For affection's
Poorest object, set in perfect light
By happenstance, grows irreplaceable,
And whether in time a room, or a romance,
Fails us or redeems us will have followed
As an extension of our "feel" for call them
Immaterials, the real right angle,
The golden section—grave proportions here,
Here at the heart of structure. . . .

—James Merrill, *The Changing Light at Sandover*

WHITE PAPER

I
WRITING

THE ISSUE of *Poetry* for October, 1932, marked the magazine's twentieth anniversary. Its founding editor, the redoubtable Harriet Monroe, had long since felt "it would be idle to deny a certain pride." What she called the "Gopher Prairie" banalities of American poetry had by then been routed by her new poets—Ezra Pound, T. S. Eliot, William Butler Yeats, Robert Frost, Wallace Stevens, Marianne Moore, William Carlos Williams, D. H. Lawrence, Hart Crane, H. D., Edwin Arlington Robinson, and James Joyce. Pound, whose brain child the magazine had been and who was invited to boast about it in this issue, scolded it instead. The new poetry had not fostered a criticism adequate to its demands, one with "a new depth and fineness of perception and a new severity of critical expression." This, in collusion with sentimental or bewildered editors—their "dithering hands on the controls"—had made a successful poetry fatuous and dull. Its own tetrarchs could no longer recognize "that certain ideas have failed, or at least waned." (No more could Pound himself have then predicted his own collapse.) "There are limits," he mocked, "there are limits to respectable failure."

Can so little have happened during sixty years that Pound's

attack on the worthies of his day should still sting those of ours? At certain times, from our certain angle, twentieth-century poetry in English seems to have been—and we can very nearly talk about it in the past tense now, as a history of modernism, that late efflorescence of romanticism—a series of convulsive leaps ahead. The insights of psychology, physics, philosophy, linguistics, structuralism and radicalism seem to have all been anticipated or absorbed by our poets. Every subject, every method has been tried—the absence of both, as well. Cinematic montage and cubist collage and action painting, aleatory music and blues and mantras; brutalism's severed limbs, irony's least finesse, the dream's furthest lair—all are in place. Along with every arrangement and derangement of line, rhythm, metric, texture, tone, voice, narrative, and lyric address. With an archaeological curiosity, each past-mastered style has been retrieved, imitated, ruffled, or parodied. Experiment has been the standard. That first generation restrung the lyre with raw nerve. Since then, the mind has played curator, hipster, traitor; the heart is now a rag-and-bone shop, now a moving toyshop, a knot garden, or grenade. Those worry beads named Authenticity, Originality, Sincerity, Spontaneity, Naturalness, Expressivity, and Grandeur clicked by. The rallying cries went up: radiant node, still point, gyre, variable foot, memorable speech, open field, deep image, dream song, *Om*. . . . Ideogram and orality, typography and graphics have been imprinted on the young. Every conceivable—or rather, inconceivable—obscurity has been dealt the scholars as fast as they could explicate. Poetry's feet have been fixed in concrete, transistorized into tankas, wired up into cross-cultural turbines. The new automatic writing has drugs and tape recorders and the novel's monotone as parts of its high technology. There is no street corner, guerrilla outpost, soapbox, or congress without its bard. Every ideology has found its voice, every cause its dialect. Translation's conglomerate enterprise has made its own global village, and no sooner had its little red schoolhouse grudgingly accepted Frost into the curriculum than its graduate programs were eagerly offering seminars on Sylvia Plath. Canons gave way, too. Eliot was the first Censor. His preference for the impacted, polyphonic, allusive, and disjunctive held sway until the late 1950s, when the yawp replaced the urn, and Whitman ousted Donne. New energies and a new license were released on the land, but not for long. Within ten years the "New American Poetry" had itself been impatiently disrupted. The suddenness of contemporary traditions set in, and a host of originators—each a parable of sensibility to his disciples—was granted iconic status, from Robert Lowell and Yvor Winters and Pablo Neruda, to James Wright, W. S. Merwin, Frank O'Hara, Anne Sexton, Mark Strand. And meanwhile, the sociology of poetry, its goods and services, was overtaken with consumerism: more poets and more readers, more outlets and readings and workshops, more eye-stabbing, more puffery, more boodle.

And yet, *had* very much changed after all? Or is "change" merely the factor of a short memory? Surely those who believe, say, that Allen Ginsberg's popularity was unprecedented have never heard of Edna St. Vincent Millay. Whoever is awed by Gopher Prairie surrealism cannot have read much Rimbaud or Lorca. After *Un Coup de Dés* can Charles Olson's fieldwork still seem so remarkable? Can John Ashbery be more confusing than Gertrude Stein? Can those who hail the latest poetoid's breakthrough or breakdown have read much at all?

Part of this dilemma is that, so much having "happened" and so noisily, one forgets how little *can* happen. Poetry is the most conservative of the arts. When one thinks of the difference between Bach and Cage, or of the range of styles available to the visual artist, from the now hieratic easel to performance (nailing yourself to the roof of a Volkswagen is old hat), then poetry's resources seem limited indeed, and its very possibili-

5

ties for change narrowed to them. A poem—any poem—written yesterday will seem closer to Homer and Sappho than the buildings in which those poems were conceived would resemble each other. Why? I don't know. Perhaps the nature of language itself, perhaps the channels of imagination, perhaps an abiding response to a few themes and stresses. The advantage to the true poet is that he or she is kept close to the origins and traditional tasks of his art. The disadvantage for the state of the art today is that so few poets know what those are. Certainly the apprentice poet knows less about verse than the young painter knows about drawing, or the young composer about harmony. We live in a time of universal suffrage. Poetry is anything, or anything but itself—therapy, self-expression, performance, what-you-will. But here—anticipating Pound—is Hazlitt's warning, in his 1812 essay called "Why the Arts Are Not Progressive":

> The diffusion of taste is not the same thing as the improvement of taste; but it is only the former of these objects that is promoted by public institutions and other artificial means. The number of candidates for fame, and of pretenders to criticism, is thus increased beyond all proportion, while the quantity of genius and feeling remains the same; with this difference, that the man of genius is lost in the crowd of competitors, who would never have become such but from encouragement and example; and that the opinion of those few persons whom nature intended for judges, is drowned in the noisy suffrages of shallow smatterers in taste.

If anything has truly changed since Pound's complaint, it has been the deteriorating quality of reading (and thereby of writing), and the crowd of competitors. The balance of poetic power during this century tipped decisively toward America. That, in turn, reinforced our native regionalism, the clamor of clans. Social fashions, followed by educational policies in the

1960s and after, by enfranchizing "creativity" promoted a general flattening, but also a general and confusing fluency. That will always be a difficulty in this country where there is no national standard, no single voice with which our poets aspire to speak. "American" poetry continues to be a federation, a patchwork of regionalisms, a country of one-eyed kings. New York, Boston, West Coast, Northwest—each has a distinctive tone, a set of demands and passions. Far from splintering poetry, this diversity adds grain to the texture. In fact, even more than the congeries of individual geniuses, it has been the very absence of a "national" style—a program of expectations and their easy fulfillment, such as prevails in England—that has kept our poetry (or, I should say, our *poetries*) vigorous during the past quarter century. And regionalism is not limited to noting the Agrarians, or the New York School, or the Stanford Wintersians, though certain places and strong figures continue to be centers of attraction. It would be fair to describe many other literary movements—black, feminist, gay, pop—as "regional" as well. Two such regions over which a great deal of ink has been shed are the avant-garde and the academic. As redskin and paleface, they have been pitted against one another from the start. Yet our sense of these terms, or any sense beyond mere jargon, is by now bleared by the smoke screen of habit. What does "academic"—the very word is a leaden echo —mean? A poem that can be taught, or one written by someone who teaches? But surely that covers everything and everyone these days. Does it mean a poem that mistakes itself for a text? One that scans? Or paints itself an inch thick? One that asks to be read twice? Or is decorous, or difficult? Clearly, the term is handed out, like a pink slip, to whatever needs to be dismissed—because carefully written, or thematically challenging, or strict and exact and literate. "Academic" is no paleface, but a straw man, a public convenience. And "avant-garde"? Has there been a more automatic term of praise in our century than this? And in a country whose "traditions" are by definition always gullibly new, and whose lust is for celebrity, it has been a gushing mainstream: from Maxwell Bodenheim to E. E. Cummings to Kenneth Patchen, from José Garcia Villa to the Beats. In anyone's quick retrospective, of course, they are yesterdays's headlines: nothing fades faster.

In truth, though regularly invoked, neither term means much anymore. Few such evaluative terms do, especially in a country with so motley and lenient an aesthetic as ours has become in the last thirty years. What *could* shock or muster these days? Anything goes—as often as not in one ear and out the other. Some poems please. Most do not. But very few provoke. As the numbers increased, the energy waned—the energy to read, to imagine, to care. Why should this be the case? For one thing, yesterday's headlines are today's variorum editions. Every redskin has his university reservation. The old originals and mugwumps and third-estate bards have not only barely survived their admirers (what literary conference does not call for more papers on semiotic contractions in Pound, or fricatives in Olson's postscripts, or clitoral subterfuges in Mina Loy's early work), but have prevailed. Applauded and appealed to, they have become the shaggy, genial, respectable classics: the Longfellows of our day. And the poets who have followed their lead—smoothing the edges and incorporating the novelty—soon stocked the workshop faculties, hustled the trade routes, have dominated the quarterly pages (giving second wind to the phrase "magazine verse"), and created the current crop of Writing Students whose unversed minds became the measure of all things. The inevitable result was a class of poet: the new bourgeoisie, with its suburban outlooks, soft at the center, complacent about its prerogatives. Once established, mediocrities were endlessly recapped, and with a hearty self-flattery. First the magnanimity of Whitman and Dickinson, then the distinctions of high modernism, of Yeats' *gravitas*, of Stevens' boreal splendor, of Auden's probing intelligence—all of these were sacrificed to the bland new household gods: the everyday life of psychopathology, the penny dreadfuls of domesticity, the software of sensibility, surrealism with a heart, Zen advertising copy, urban chanties, epiphanies around the backyard barbecue, work songs for the twice-divorced kitchen brigade, political simplism, the folkways of the New Journalism, minimalism on a gigantic scale, the thumbed-smooth small coin of the realm (in denominations of Soul, Pain, Stone, Wind, and You). Everyone is "good"; whatever is not lost, and nothing is, is "blessed"; platitude stares down like . . . like the cold moon. If by little else, most contemporary poetry is marked by a formalism of content.

This situation has been abetted by every kind of technical failure—including that of most critics to notice it. The charities of free verse, of course, cover a multitude, and underneath lurk rhythmical slackness, syntactic vacuity, a poverty of images, absurdities of composition and tone, emotional banality. Voice is the most obvious victim. The dry rot of simple, present-tense declaratives has eaten away at the foundations of subtlety and dramatic invention. It is part of a larger tyranny of the demotic. The insistence on "natural speech" for poetry is not new, but has never been more commonplace. Wordsworth's man speaking to men, Coleridge wrote, was actually "a person of elevated rank and of superior refinement, in a happy *imitation* of the rude unpolished manners and discourse of his inferiors." Wordsworth's rustics are today's mad housewives, Detroit factory workers, and Vietnam veterans. But the unrelieved tedium of speechliness affects more: subject matter, tone, diction, all walk in that deep American fear of "artifice." That is as misplaced a fear as it was when Whitman let loose his gaudy French words; though there are some signs of change, the last few decades have witnessed the debasement of *style*. The demotic, of course, is as contrived as any court language, and a deliberately "antipoetic" rhetoric turns into the formulaic slogans of reportage. The latest theory is a neat metaphor: speech and discourse depend on the brain's left hemisphere; song—and all intuitive binding patterns, including poetry—on the right. The language of the poet should be the speech of his or her community, but that community should never be confused with society at large, or with the dictionary. I like what Hopkins had to say, in a letter to Robert Bridges: "It seems to me that the poetical language of an age should be the current language, *heightened*, to any degree heightened and unlike itself, but not (I mean normally: passing freaks and graces are another thing) an obsolete one." Not only is the language of most contemporary poems—as distinct from their animating emotions—not *heightened*, but its very flatness is a symptom of unplanned obsolescence.

That last phrase brings me to the crowd of competitors. Eighty years ago, or even half that number, what did the fledgling poet face? A few lions, the long shelf, the solitary charge. And today? A babble and an industry. Workshop sharecroppers, taught to write like their teachers (it isn't hard, after all), drift from program to program, then complete the short circuit by teaching in a similar place, in a similar way. The ranks swell, indentured to the system. They are not encouraged to pursue other disciplines, to train their critical skills, or even to read with a broad, discerning sympathy (today's automatic writing is fostered by so much automatic reading). Advanced degrees are awarded for thin sheafs; later, government pensions, the gravy train of group encounters, a preen-for-pay slot at the local State U. The managers having made poetry over into a commodity—one that, in Allen Grossman's words, "pleases by immediate recognitions, but does not instruct by the setting of hard tasks"—the petitioners made it mere enfranchisement. These latest technocrats had been offered fluency, backslapping peers, upward mobility on Parnassus, and quotas of publicity. And they set out—still do—to stew an All Natural product, no preservatives added. The price was real authority and permanence. The resources of greatness were exchanged for the means for promotion. To legitimize personal experience or to qualify for the aura of Creativity—these count for more than the "hard tasks." And no wonder. Gratification is subsidized.

I was not surprised a few years ago to read the conclusions of the National Assessment of Educational Progress, a federal study group meant to monitor the musical and artistic knowledge of elementary and secondary school students during the 1970s. According to *The New York Times*, "students of all ages tended to respond to art on the basis of subject matter, showing little appreciation of color, form, and sensory aspects. Moreover, large numbers of students judged the merits of works of art on how 'true-to-reality' they were, considering them 'good' if they were representational and 'bad' if they were abstract. 'Students' responses to works of art are much more narrow, shallow and uniformed than seems desirable,' the report said of the findings, calling most students 'artistic literalists.' 'Indeed, students' unwillingness to engage works openly and to explore a wide range of their features probably means that paintings, sculpture, prints and drawings are not able to convey their important meanings and realities, nor their pleasures, to many young Americans,' the report said." I wonder if one of those students grew up to be Lydia Lunch, the "no wave" rock singer and poet. According to a recent interview with her in *The Times*, she boasts: "If what I write is literature, I guess you'd better emphasize the 'litter.' . . . I'm anti-art and anti-poetry. As much as possible I want to inflict my personal pain on the rest of society. . . . At the typewriter it just spills out, and I don't edit or alter anything. The next step is to insult the public with it."

But let's look to the teachers of such students. In their case the literalism is more practiced but no less deadening, no less *unwilling*. It springs from a compulsion to copy faddish and speedily exhausted modes, with less and less accuracy or flair, so that the results are invariably mechanical. Literalism darkens and levels. The colors of a Stevens poem blaze and shift as you turn it in the light of a larger idea or of a later image. The perplexities of a Frost monologue, so much more intimate than the confessionalist's diary and more dense than any Black Mountain scholia, continue to haunt. But not the new literalists. They take everything literally, even fame, which for them comes with a pair of stick-on wings made from Pinhead Press deluxe editions, and the gold star of another prize or grant given by those they voted for. Theirs is, literally, a negative capability, a solution without a problem. Literalism consists of satisfying rather than creating expectations, of trimming rather than extending the art. "Poems," continues Grossman, "should have an empowering strangeness about them which summons its audience rather than receives its audience." Would it be fair to describe most poetry written today as enfeebled and too familiar? Is it not time again to recognize, as Pound did before, that certain ideas have waned, that there are limits to respectable failure?

There are more poets and readers today than ever, but the proportion of good poets and right readers is probably the same as it was a hundred years ago. During the so-called golden age, Longfellow's *Hiawatha* was bought and read as a national epic, while Whitman's *Leaves of Grass* (published the same year, 1855) was ignored. It is not that we have no great poets among us now, or at least poets of empowering strangeness. I have written about some of them in this book, though anyone's short list, even mine, would include a few more names—in England, Ireland, and the Caribbean, and a few younger poets as well. Their names comprise no hegemony of style or sensibility. Together, their aims—discursive, witty, political, auto-

biographical, visionary, or meditative, by turns and at once—
are a summary of poetry's service, but each poet's voice has its
own inflection, and emphasis, and strength. Not his, or hers,
but *its—our* voice. At the end of his lectures on Shakespeare,
despairing of any more precise definition of his genius, Cole-
ridge says, "Shakespeare is a poet insofar as, for a time, he
makes you one." I take Coleridge to have meant two things by
that. First, that the great poet helps us—as Wallace Stevens
said all poets must—live our lives. That is the work of knowl-
edge and of power, and it results not from the beneficence of
craft but from the arguments of myth making. Our best poets
continue to see the grain of sand alight with eternity, continue
to attend to the grit of the first things and to the magnitude of
the last, and to how both crisscross and constitute the daily life.
If they argue with history, it is the better to provide the
moralities of vision. In Auden's phrase, their poetry is "the
wholly human instrument," whose purpose is to add meaning
to the world; not to recount experience, but create it. Poets do
this by making myths (I use the old term with new urgency),
first of themselves, and so of us. Greek or Christian, Navajo
or Freudian, myths, like math, are figurative narratives about
the relationships and exchanges of power. The point today is
not to copy the old myths, or to pretend that the prosaic
anecdotes of "real life" are myths. Our important poets use
the fictions of autobiography or the logic of dreams, the gram-
mar of history or the hermetic codes of memory—any and all
of these, images and ideas, to make poems that both matter and
enspirit, challenge and console. Here is James Merrill:

> What at this late date
> Can be done with the quaint idiom that slips
> From nowhere to my tongue—or from the parchment
> Of some old scribe of the apocalypse—
> But render *it* as the long rendering to

Light of this very light stored in our cells
These past five million years, these past five minutes
Here by the window, taking in through panes
Still bleary from the hurricane a gull's
Ascending aureole of decibels,
As numberless four-pointed brilliancies
Upon the Sound's mild silver grid come, go?
The message hardly needs decoding, so
Sheer the text, so innocent and fleet
These overlapping pandemonia:
Birdlife, leafplay, rockface, waterglow
Lending us their being, till the given
Moment comes to render what we owe.

And here is Adrienne Rich:

Vision begins to happen in such a life
as if a woman quietly walked away
from the argument and jargon in a room
and sitting down in the kitchen, began turning in her lap
bits of yarn, calico and velvet scraps. . . .
Such a composition has nothing to do with eternity,
the striving for greatness, brilliance—
only with the musing of a mind
one with her body, experienced fingers quietly pushing
dark against bright, silk against roughness,
pulling the tenets of a life together
with no mere will to mastery,
only care for the many-lived, unending
forms in which she finds herself,
becoming now the sherd of broken glass
slicing light in a corner, dangerous
to flesh, now the plentiful, soft leaf
that wrapped round the throbbing finger, soothes the wound;

and now the stone foundation, rockshelf further
forming underneath everything that grows.

Though never reluctant to learn, innovate, undo, these poets
have not been intimidated into pious reverence for the ortho-
doxies of modernism or for the flatulant heresies of post-mod-
ernism. Not "make it new," but "make it last" is their motto.
So they know that the poet's morality is verbal, that his or her
most crucial responsibility is to language and its shaping possi-
bilities. Octavio Paz calls poetry a fate and a faith, the latter a
poet's loyalty to the word: "The word is the lover and the
friend of the poet; his father and mother, his hammer and his
pillow. It is his enemy, too; his mirror." This touches on
Coleridge's second and deeper meaning. Poetry's work of
knowledge and its access to power lie in the poet's instinct, as
well as in the reader's capacity, to take *poesis* itself—its reper-
tory of song, choice, play, pattern, logic, trope—and see it as a
model of experience, and use it as the means to fathom those
same sources of authority and transformation in our lives.

A few weeks before his death in 1977, Robert Lowell was in
Moscow, on a State Department tour to urge on the officials
there a freer exchange of poets. The Soviet bureaucrats balked,
mumbling about ideological necessities. "Art does not make
peace," said Lowell. "That is not its business. Art *is* peace."
That is a familiar and tempting assertion, but to some a deeply
suspect one. It has, after all, been used to sanction every ex-
treme of subjectivity, every inward turning, every denial of the
commonweal, every excess of originality, defiance, and obscu-
rity. If one man's art, or one man's peace, is not everyman's,
then what value is there in art? What, indeed, do words like
"value" and "art" come to mean? There is an answer, a hard
answer, that sweeps aside such worries. More eloquently than
any other advocate, Harold Bloom has argued that poetry is

precisely that sanction: the defense of the self against *every-thing*—ideology, history, nature, time, others, even against the self, and especially against "cultural force"—that might destroy it. If the best poetry today seems more demanding or eccentric than it did when Longfellow, or even Whitman, was writing, so are the conspiracies against the self.

The best poets in our tradition have been outsiders, excluded by temperament or sex or fashion: Whitman, Dickinson, Hart Crane, Wallace Stevens. (Robert Frost can be added to the list because he was so long mistaken for a banner when all along he was a burr.) And of course the list can be, must be, extended to the poets at work among us. With the giants, hindsight is insight. But with our contemporaries? The late James Wright once wrote to a friend: "What makes our bad poetry so bad, so ironically bad, has nothing to do with its sweet technique. By this time, God help us, everybody in college knows how to write like Pound. What makes the new poetry so bad is its failure to realize that there is no sound poetry without intelligence. There is no poetry without its own criticism. You can take your minor elegance and throb around it. I have nothing against the minor elegance, because I have nothing against the failure to think. But if the young friends who live and write after the generation of Pound are going to matter in the United States, they are going to have to develop a criticism of their own." Wright's barb is well aimed, and his indictment of poets for failing is think is sound. What he means is not just that they have not read and absorbed the poetry of their tradition, but also that they have largely failed to see that tradition as (this phrase is Lincoln Kirstein's) "the expression of a sensibility present as a continuum, to be seized upon by important possibilities."

Let me offer an example—one from the dozens possible—of a poet engaged to making myths for our time. Adrienne Rich, who was born in 1929, wrote poems as a child, read Keats and Rossetti in her father's library, was a musical prodigy. The year she graduated from Radcliffe, her first book of poems was chosen by W. H. Auden for the Yale Younger Poets series. Auden introduced the book by saying that Rich's poems "are neatly and modestly dressed, speak quietly but do not mumble, respect their elders but are not cowed by them, and do not tell fibs: That, for a first volume, is a good deal." But for a career, it is not enough. The title of two of her later books describe her courage and her project: *The Will to Change* and *Diving into the Wreck*. "We're living through a time," she wrote in one poem, "that needs to be lived through us." During the 1960s and 1970s, she abandoned the comfortable gestures and rhetoric of her early work—but never its artful force—and at the same time turned, with an often startling intensity, on herself: her marriage and her children, the nature of emotional and social relationships, the stresses on them and the oppression they make, the civil turmoil and warring blindness in America then. Rich's poems remain a mirror of that time in our national life, and a reminder that our lives in the world are determined by a balance within. The conflict between the energies of creation and the energies of relation played itself out in poem after poem—each one meant by the poet to be an instrument of discovery and analysis:

> of a woman trying to translate pulsations
> into images   for the relief of the body
> and the reconstruction of the mind.

Since the early 1970s, her radical feminism has been an abiding passion; it is both an argument with the self and the effort—as much poetic as personal—to recover a power prior to patriarchy. And that passion has since been subsumed by Rich's lesbianism, which she sees as an emotional component, not a sexual characteristic; it is a quality shared by all, and "the primary intensity between women." (I hear the accent of

Whitman in that, of his *Democratic Vistas,* our national manifesto for a democracy of ideal eroticism.) Rich has been extremely polemical—but in her essays. Her poems are never (good poems never are) two-dimensional demands. Here is a poem from 1974, entitled "Power," from her collection *The Dream of a Common Language:*

Living in the earth-deposits of our history

Today a backhoe divulged   out of a crumbling flank of earth
one bottle   amber   perfect   a hundred-year-old
cure for fever   or melancholy   a tonic
for living on this earth   in the winters of this climate

Today I was reading about Marie Curie:
she must have known she suffered   from radiation sickness
her body bombarded for years by the element
she had purified
It seems she denied to the end
the source of the cataracts on her eyes
the cracked and suppurating skin of her finger-ends
till she could no longer hold a test-tube or a pencil

She died a famous woman   denying
her wounds
denying
her wounds   came   from the same source as her power

The poem's argument is direct: if you don't ask about the causes and uses of power, but merely lay hands on it, you will be burned. The relationship between knowledge and power, like this poem's problematic heroine, is a difficult one. Even the words of the poem float free in a sort of moral solution, freed of habitual associations, free for the poet's new charging of them. It is a poem about a woman that combines several women in its meditation. There is the "famous woman," Marie

Curie. And there is the poet herself, watching, reading. (The scientist with her pencil, the poet with her bottle—they are subtly merged.) Then, too, there are the anonymous women whose fever (melancholy? repressed desire?) sought relief in a Lydia Pinkham opiated tonic instead of in science or poetry— the lost women buried by time. How we *all* live in history, and with ourselves, is Rich's subject. Where is our power? she asks. In the earth, in the elements. But what sort of power is it that can both purify and destroy, exalt and erase? The power of delusion and denial is here too. Rich has a revisionary imagination. She wants to restore the past by bringing the present to bear on it. She isolates Curie as her ambivalent example of an incautious woman, but joins her to a line of timid, faded women—and Rich puts herself between them. It is a "political" poem, yes. It is a poem about history. But it is more than that.

In a speech she gave a few years ago, Rich recalled Yeats' early hold on her: "the dialogue between art and politics excited me in his work, along with the sound of his language . . . lines rang in my head for years." Perhaps it is no accident, then, that the final lines of "Power"—and then, in retrospect, the whole poem—recall Yeats' "Leda and the Swan," and that where Yeats wrote of *knowledge* ("Did she put on his knowledge with his power?"), Rich revises it to *wounds*. Where Yeats had written of Leda's destructive accession to divinity, Rich writes of Curie's more terrifying denial: of her humanity. Rich has made here what I call a contemporary myth. Made it first with language: "The energy of language," she once told an interviewer, "comes somewhat from the pressure and need and unbearableness of what's being done to you." And from necessities beyond language: "There seems to be a connection between an oppressed condition and having access to certain kinds of energy, vitality, and subjectivity." Rich is that rare artist who can combine both, to fashion those myths that allow us to rethink our lives and correct our feelings. "Did you think

I was talking about my life," she has written in a poem. "I was trying to drive a tradition against the wall."

After more than three decades, there are signs of a recovery from poetry's boom, of a turn back to those hard tasks that poets like Rich and Merrill, Lowell and Ashbery have set for themselves. A number of books in the past several years have been distinguished by the tilth of their language, their respect for charged conventions, a generous and nervy thematic range, a clear-eyed love for the world's appearances, along with a sense of beauty, an amplitude of vision, and even the rigor of the sublime. For the arts generally, this appears to be a time of recuperation. Long absent disciplines—figural, tonal, schematic—are again the artist's properties. The language of the old masters resounds. "I composed *Tristan*," Wagner reminds the artist of any age, "under the stress of a great passion, and after several months of theoretical meditation." In the beginning, perhaps, is a passion, not a word. The poem fuses them. It does so by refining the fire, yielding to a sensible vertigo. This is what a few of our poets have known. There is hope now that our younger poets may revive the quickening connections between poetry and philosophy, between "the high hum of mind" and the speech of earthliness, between criticism and vision, and that by a delighted instruction of the spirit they may make those myths in which men and women recognize themselves as the truth to be faced, the figure to be followed.

II
READING

THAT DAY is gone when the reader, taking up a new poem for the first time, can comfortably dismiss it as too "difficult." Our professional readers—critics and teachers, and of course the poets themselves—have accustomed us to respect the authority of difficulty, and no longer as a mere problem, but as a necessary condition of true poetry, and of our theories about it. How "life" is interpreted through texts, or a text as life, by both poets and their interpreters is not just an academic industry; it is an article of faith. But having granted that, it remains to be said there is a stubborn difference between the business of critical interpretation and the practice of reading a contemporary poem—of opening any new volume of poetry and trying to make sense of it. Even the most experienced reader may panic, suddenly transformed back into the teenager first encountering *The Waste Land,* or the college student called on in class to explain "The Emperor of Ice Cream."

This difference was never more sharply, even shockingly, apparent to me than at a faculty meeting several years ago. Down a long table, the English Department was discussing committee assignments and duties, and the question arose—at first it seemed a minor procedural matter—of what to do with student poets. They were entitled to a credited tutorial, but with whom? Should they be directed by the three staff poets, or by any of the professors? For predictable reasons, the poets argued for help. For less obvious reasons, they met stiff resistance. Finally the chairman stood up, both to propose a decision and to offer himself as an example of his reasoning. "How can *we* advise these students?" he shrugged. "I wouldn't know what to say about a poem written last week. I wouldn't even know how to *read* it." I sat hunched in my chair. The man who had said that, with a rippling tremor in his voice that disturbed the surface of his grin, is one of this country's leading literary theorists, the author of a dozen critical books, even one about the first generation of modern poets. If *he* was scared of a contemporary poem, then what of the less specialized and knowledgeable reader? If this was the attitude among the English faculty, what of the rest of the university? If a new poem was not welcome where poetry is studied, then where? I am neither proud enough as a poet, nor naive enough as a reader, to think there are no reasons—*perceived* reasons, *wrong* reasons—for this impasse. But the problem is the reader's, not the poet's.

Or the problem may be that the criticism of the last half-century has helped us to read poems, but not to listen to them. Yet that is how poets write, by hearing almost inaudible resonances, the glide of a phrase, the cadence of a line, the course of the lines through a stanza. We don't often now use the word "voice" literally; it has become a weak synonym for "style," or a shorthand term for a poet's sensibility. But *voice* is our most immediate, and may be our most lasting, source of pleasure in a poem. Our first impressions of verse, in nursery and counting rhymes, were made by repeating them aloud, by *voicing* them. And those poets whom we most passionately and privately love—for some it may be Keats and Frost, for others it may be Browning and Dickinson—we love for their manner of speaking. If, as Frost said, poetry is what gets lost in translation, then he was referring to the poem's voice, which is its moral presence, its emotional texture, its veritable voiceprint (diction, rhythms, enjambments—all of them an idiom as personal as the sound of birdcalls or Ella Fitzgerald). We speak excitedly of a distinctive "new voice" only when it can be distinguished from all the others. Whole movements in poetry are matters of voice, whether two hundred years ago when "poetic diction" was the operative term, or right now when the Language poets or the New Formalists are speaking up for themselves. And in each strong line written, each sentence advancing the narrative or proposing an idea, there is something prior. "Give me a sentence," said Thoreau, "which no intelligence can understand. There must be a kind of life and palpitation to it, and under its words a kind of blood must circulate forever." Translation, Frost might have said, is a sort of bloodshed. It cuts a poem's throat. It's a little like merely "reading" a poem, but not listening to it.

In order to speak, the poet, too, listens. Small wonder that the stock portrait of the poet should show him with elbow on the table, head palmed and gazing off, listening to his Muse. Many poets have said that a poem starts not from an idea but from a recurrent rhythm, or a set of phrases that need a context. They "hear voices," and they consult them. James Merrill, for instance, like Auden before him, has imagined a gallery of readers in his head. "Is this diction crisp enough for Herbert?" he'll ask. "Is this stanza's tessitura too high for Maggie Teyte?" Each poet has his or her own preferences, turns, or quirks of phrase: Lowell's jamming of consonants and syllables, say, or Merrill's puns, or Bishop's adverbs and hesitations. Line-length as a measure of voice is a peculiarly American phenomenon. The parents of our poetry, Whitman and Dickinson, each wrote such a different line (Whitman's long-breathed, expansive yawp, Dickinson's lilting or jolting phrases) that the range available to us is broad enough for anyone to find a suitable perch, and pitch. Aware they are speaking a poem—and indeed, the speaking voice has become a standard for the prevalent style in American writing—poets are also aware that they are speaking *against* other voices. Behind them is the chorale of past poets to harmonize with, and sometimes the poet will speak over or under certain themes, avoid or parody them in order to do more than double the voice line. How a poet listens to the past—to the tradition of other poems, and to his or her own earlier poems—is important to our understanding. How the poet speaks to the future, addresses the reader in such a way to attract new meanings, is also decisive. But these are often what is hardest to hear in a contemporary poem, unaccustomed as we are to its new accent. What I want to do in this chapter is listen closely to poems by three exemplary poets: Elizabeth Bishop, John Ashbery, and Charles Wright, one from each of three generations, and each a very different kind of poet. My intention is not only to come to a better understanding of their methods, but to provide a model for reading other contemporary poems, a model based on listening to the voice in a poem.

I WANT to listen first to Charles Wright's "The Southern Cross," the title poem of his fifth collection, published in 1981. It is a long poem, in twenty-five sections of unequal length. In all his mature books, Wright has tended to cluster his short poems into sequences, lending each poem more weight by its collaboration with others. But "The Southern Cross" is a single, sustained poem. Its very title points to its effective origins: on the one hand, to the Southern heritage he bears; and on the other, to Dante's *quattro stelle*, the sign over his purgatorial ascent. This helix of native and acquired resources—what the poet himself would probably call, after the titles of the two books that preceded *The Southern Cross*, his "bloodlines" and his "traces"—has been a crucial emphasis in Wright's poetry from the start, as often as not embodied in a diction that swerves from slang to grandiloquence.

The epigraph to *The Southern Cross* is also from Dante, the last seven lines of Canto xxi of the *Purgatorio*, where Statius kneels to embrace his teacher Virgil's feet, having just wished Dante that *his* great labor may come to good (*"Se tanto labore in bene assommi"*). Dante then startles the old poet by revealing that Virgil, the strength of both their poems, stands before him. The episode is a touching encounter, and a literal community of poets, master and pilgrim, across time. That same sense of community is one of Wright's burdens in "The Southern Cross," a poem that is above all the reconciliation of his two inheritances, of the natural and the poetic, of Fate and Power. Wright has acknowledged the strong accents of others in his way of speaking, but he has singled out two masters: Ezra Pound and Eugenio Montale. Pound, I suspect it is proper to say, was Wright's instructor; Montale was an influence.

"I discovered poems in Verona," Wright once told an interviewer. (He was stationed there in the Army, at age twenty-three.) "I was given a book, *The Selected Poems of Ezra Pound*, and told to go out to Sirmione, on Lake Garda, where the Latin poet Catullus supposedly had a villa. . . . I read a poem that Pound had written about the place, about Sirmione being more beautiful than Paradise, and my life was changed forever."

The poem was Pound's gaslit "Blandula, Tenulla, Vagula," and its first line set Wright the question his subsequent career has sought to answer: "What hast thou, O my soul, with paradise?" That quest for the sublime, not only in "the impalpable / Mirrors unstill of the eternal change," but in an earthly paradise "wherein the sun / Lets drift in on us through the olive leaves / A liquid glory," has since been Wright's own. It has allowed him to gaze on both the gold leaf of his beloved Venice and the foliage of his native East Tennessee with equal wonder. Pound no doubt initiated Wright into modernism's "broken bundle of mirrors," taught him how to read a poem (for its rhythm and logopoeia) and where to find one ("only emotion endures"), prompted him perhaps with a syllabus in cultural cross-referencing, and fixed his attention on the image. Wright was not alone in turning to Pound's work as the pattern for the image as that "instant when an outward and objective thing is transformed to a thing inward and subjective." Over the course of modernism and beyond, the image has been elevated from trope to genre. Every new dispensation from imagism itself to surrealism to the Writers' Workshop, has encouraged imagery to do the work of reason and music, physical description and emotional narration. Wright is one of the new contemporary poets with a sure command of the technique of images, whereby he can both epitomize and depart from a point in his poem.

Pound's example led to the identification of the image with the fragment, or series of phrasal units, and to that technique of dealing them out that Wright calls "jump-cutting." Pound taught Wright how to move through a poem by association rather than by narrative. I'd prefer to call this *linkage*. "It's linkage I'm talking about," he says in the title poem of *The Other Side of the River*, "and harmonies and structures / And all the various things that lock our wrists to the past." Linked images, then, are not just a means to structure a poem or harmonize its conflicting pressures; they are—as they were for Proust—the work of memory itself, and the way of spiritual enlightenment. These images are conceptual rather than exclusively visual, and from the beginning—it is important to remember—have been a way of listening. "Pound came to me aurally," he's said. "I really didn't know any of the background of the *Cantos,* so all I heard was the sound as I read it. . . . It just became a part of the way I hear things." (He also says he dreams this way—in vivid but dissociated fragments.) What this finally means is that Pound taught him to listen not to words, but to language; and less to language than to the *movement* of language, to those harmonies of sound that underlie the meanings of words.

He began writing, then, having read Pound. And having begun to write, he started translating Montale. "At such a formative time in my own development," Wright has said, it "was a real gift—I was able to see the grooves and dovetailings, the suspensions and stresses and, in general, most of the physical ways he put poems together." Translation has always been this kind of classroom for a poet, where poems can be dismantled and reassembled. And few poets in this century put poems together better than Montale. The polyphony of his twenty-part *Motetti* is echoed in Wright's various sequences. In many other ways too Wright has seen to it that his work— everywhere his method, and sometimes his material—stands together with Montale's. What would have first attracted him? Certainly the interplay in Montale's lines between sound and silence; his complex analogies, especially between landscape and heartscape, and the austere luxuriance of his language; his *eretismo,* a privatism at once intimate and enigmatic, like a music heard at a great distance.

Of course there is other music to be heard in and behind Wright's lines. Country music, for instance. That phrase itself is now the title of the edition of his selected early poems. What Italian opera was for Whitman, so for Wright are the rhythms and blues of Earl Scruggs, Lester Flatt, the Carter Family, Roy Acuff, and Merle Travis. Sometimes the echo is intentional. Here are the last two lines from each of the three stanzas of "Laguna Blues":

Something's off-key in my mind.
Whatever it is, it bothers me all the time.

. . .

I'm singing a little song.
Whatever it is, it bothers me all the time.

. . .

Something's off-key and unkind.
Whatever it is, it bothers me all the time.

The lines, especially taken out of context, are as flat as the refrains in the standard villanelle. But put two guitars and a fiddle behind them. . . . The influence, of course, is usually more subtle, and the subject matter of country music—adultery, divorce, heartbreak, revenge, the soap opera of love—is precisely what is *not* in Wright's work. What he has caught instead are both the broader "lifey/deathy/afterlifey" themes of the songs, and their sense of phrasing—the long, swelling strophes, the punched-out refrains. He has listened for this music in poetry too, and hears it—maybe he alone can hear this—in Emily Dickinson, whose work he wittily calls "White Soul." Mention of her poems also brings to the mind's ear the hymns he heard in church and on the radio during his childhood, the rhythms of the catechism, the Bible, and the Book of Common Prayer. Once asked to define his poetic voice, Wright said "it's some kind of speech on the outside of the stained glass looking in." Often in his work you hear the cadences of prayer. Here is a section of "Holy Thursday" (a poem that also owes something to Blake's two poems of that same title):

There's always a time for rust,
For looking down at the earth and its lateral chains.

> There's always a time for the grass, teeming
> Its little four-cornered purple flowers,
>
>   tricked out in an oozy shine.
> There's always a time for the dirt.
> Reprieve, reprieve, the flies drone, their wings
> Increasingly incandescent above the corn silk.

At other times, his lines may sound like the ejaculations of private prayer, or the steady catalogue of a litany or holy office. But more often, this measured, balanced tone can be heard. Much more than blank verse, these steady ecclesiastical rhythms are his contact with the rhetorical tradition. They are rhythms that invoke and celebrate a communal striving, and when they sound in a "personal" poem they give it greater dimensions. The high priests of modernism had a role too. The "freed" verse of T. S. Eliot and the pentameter of Wallace Stevens or Hart Crane (whose own "Southern Cross" is a register of Wright's) are undoubtedly part of it, but when Wright talks about his disdain for flat language and his love for a richly rhetorical art, it can be no accident that his metaphor comes from church: "I always like the organ in the background of a poem. I like those *profundo* notes, that swell." And it is his rhetoric, enriched and heightened, that distinguishes his work from that of poets he is usually associated with—Mark Strand, Charles Simic, and James Tate, the sound of whose work is more dead-pan or sardonic, more anecdotal and ordinary.

Wright dedicated *The Southern Cross* to H. W. Wilkinson —who is not anyone the poet knows. It just happens to be the name stenciled onto an old metal footlocker that Wright keeps near his desk, and in which he stores old family letters and documents and heirlooms, even a lock of Robert E. Lee's hair. Appropriately then, this book is dedicated to a voice box. The rhythms of family and region, so early imprinted, are a part of any poet's voice. This century's Southern poets, from Allen Tate and Robert Penn Warren to James Dickey and Dave Smith, have favored the orotund periods of preaching and the tale, and Wright too loves what he calls "the sound and weight and rub and glint of words," and likes stacking them. The Southern landscape that prompts these words is itself a kind of text. "When I write to myself," he told an interviewer, "I'm writing to the landscape, and the landscape is a personification of the people on the other side." It is, in other words, a map of memories and a route to the dead, his mother in particular. And, it is important to remember, he listens to their voices through the other texts he hears. The ritual of symbolism is one, and its repertory of charged images: stars, mirrors, crystals, wings, and silence itself. Other voices come to him in the bunched accents he has heard in Gerard Manley Hopkins, and in the speeded-up leaps of association of Rimbaud.

Even in his early poems, the hallmarks of Wright's style can be heard. Here is a brief description of the Arno in moonlight, a three-line stanza from the middle of "Nocturne":

> The Arno, glittering snake, touches
> The white cloister of flame, easing
> Its burden, the chill of its scales.

The perspective is as from a great distance. The tone is mysterious. Phrases interrupt, overlap, qualify. An internal network of sounds trembles with connections, whereby "glittering" and "chill," or "snake" and "flame" pull the lines together and bind the images. The bel canto of long, open vowels tend to slow down the line—"The *white cloi*ster of *flame, ea*sing"— and short consonantal bursts give it a snap. The pauses in the lines are variously distributed, twice near the end of the line to emphasize the action ("touches" and "easing"), and then earlier in the final line so that the image, which brings together the cold moonlight and the cold-blooded snake, the backlit ripples and the monastic plainchant, is allowed its full resonance.

Or, to study the "movement" of a complete poem, here is "Snow," from *China Trace* (1979):

> If we, as we are, are dust, and dust, as it will, rises,
> Then we will rise, and recongregate
> In the wind, in the cloud, and be their issue,
>
> Things in a fall in a world of fall, and slip
> Through the spiked branches and snapped joints of the
>   evergreens,
> White ants, white ants and the little ribs.

The poem is a single sentence, in two tercets. If the meter is unsteady, that is because the poem's rhetoric is its true binding agent. Its opening conditional sentence proposes a syllogism, and its rationalist logic is used to set up an improbable situation. In many poems, Wright alludes to the language of argument, or scatters bits of narrative, in order to invoke the energies of those kinds of discourse without lapsing into their rigors. The first stanza glides easily from legal to biblical terms —a "cold" diction—the better to prepare us for the surprises in the second stanza. Where before was resurrection, now is a miniature wasteland, the fallen world, threatening and disjointed. The first stanza ended with a birth, the second ends with a death. The snow we may have expected to cover or disguise the "world of fall" in fact reveals it, strips it to the bare bone. The snowflakes swarm and devour. Yet the tone seems one of acceptance; ours is "a world of fall," of process, of becoming and unbecoming. (The poem is preceded by one called "Childhood," and followed by one called "Self-Portrait in 2035.") And I think that tone is achieved by Wright's masterful control of pace and image. Each line of this second stanza has three blocks of sound and reference, three lapping waves. Their even distribution adds its own equanimity. The terms are strange, but the rhetorical pattern is familiar, nearly lulling. Wright's is a poetry of nouns and adjectives, of phenomena and qualifications, of metaphor—not of action and definition—and this lets his linked images create a marvelously fluent texture. The voice is depersonalized—literally drained of "personality," quirks, and traits. Its rhythms are musical and insistent; "most of my poems," he says, start "with a rhythm rather than a structure." And his rhythms tend to be primal—rising and falling—or formulaic. A good deal of ordinary material—exposition, transitions, explanation—has been deleted in the interests of a taut line, and the line itself is given an independence and prominence. It is as if each line bore the weight of the whole poem. As it is, the line for Wright is "the linchpin of the poem." "It is as though the lines," he says, "were each sections of the poem attached by invisible strings to the title, the way the various parts of a marionette are attached by strings to the control board." So in "Snow" we are directed back to and on by the control board, the dominant image.

But let me resume this discussion by turning now to "The Southern Cross" itself. Here is the opening section:

> Things that divine us we never touch:
>
> The black sounds of the night music,
> The Southern Cross, like a kite at the end of its string,
>
> And now this sunrise, and empty sleeve of a day,
> The rain just starting to fall, and then not fall,
>
> No trace of a story line.

The poem starts under the sign of the Cross. We begin with a premise, which the setting is then supposed to confirm; and we end with an observation which doubles back to the first line, and instructs us how to read the poem that follows. "Things that divine us"—and we then know what those "things" are, the sounds and sights and symbols of night turning into day. "Divine" means both to *understand* and to *foretell*; it can also mean to *make gods of*. "We never touch," on the other hand, means "We never contact" or "never violate." The poem opens, then, with a troubled transcendence. What knows us is unknown to us. What makes us more than human—that is, less ourselves—is something we can never wholly approach, a note we can't clearly strike. The aphoristic language seems affirmative, but its message is one of denial, reversal, absences.

When Wright says there is "no trace of a story line" to be found here, he is using an image that is linked with the earlier image of the constellation as a kite: there is no "line" that connects observer and heaven, poet and sublime. But he is also talking about his method in the whole poem—in all his work, really. His poems do not develop by a "story line," linearly or horizontally. They develop, let us say, vertically, lines and phrases overlaid on one another. Helen Vendler's description is apt: "They cluster, aggregate, radiate; they add layers, like pearls." This technique, central to other latter-day imagists like James Wright or Galway Kinnell, is part of their surrender of voice. The effort is to have the poem write the poet. Its wise passivity represents the pure ascendancy of the poet's material, of spiritual analogies rather than intellectual analysis. This is the heritage of *epiphany*, whereby the familiar is revealed with new force; and it is our contemporary agency of *the sublime*, whereby the poet may be imbued with otherness, may transcend the self by erasing or expanding it. The next section of "The Southern Cross" drifts on its images, and treats the self as an object, insubstantial and evanescent:

All day I've remembered a lake and a sudsy shoreline,
  Gauze curtains blowing in and out the open windows all
    over the South

It's 1936, in Tennessee. I'm one
And spraying the dead grass with a hose.
The curtains blow in and out.

And then it's not. And I'm not and they're not.

Or it's 1941 in a brown suit, or '53 in its white shoes,
Overlay after overlay tumbled and brought back,
As meaningless as the sea would be
               if the sea could remember its waves . . .

Nothing is sustained here; things come into focus only to fade again. The brief sections, with their one, two, or three line stanzas see to that. The lines pulse; their strong caesuras divide the line into two or three phrases; each phrase is a pair of terms, often a noun and adjective that may be both joined and contrasted. The poem is conjured rather than displayed. What is true for each section is true for the whole. "My poetic structures," Wright says in his notebook, "tend toward the condition of spider webs—tight in their parts but loose in the wholes." He prefers structure to form. That is to say, he works with a set of abstract ambitions and designs for the poem that evade many traditional formal assumptions and prescriptions.

Two sections later, we are given some classic Wright description:

All day the ocean was like regret,
               clearing its throat, brooding and self-
               absorbed.

Now the wisteria tendrils extend themselves like swan's
    necks under Orion.

Now the small stars in the orange trees.

Water is the entire poem's dominant image. It is above all "the blank / Unruffled waters of memory"—amniotic fluid and developing solution. It washes through the poem, through the canals of Venice and into Lake Garda and the Adige and the California ocean. And throughout, as in the first line here, it is identified with the poet's own voice. It is a voice that seems to include its own echo. The dropped hemistich in the first line— and it is used all through the poem—functions antiphonally, as a sort of choral response to the first half of the line. One might even call it a sort of stichomythia. This is another of Wright's experiments with the line. At different times, he has stated his intentions differently. Sometimes he speaks of wanting to "relax" the line, to slacken the pentameter. Elsewhere he has spoken of wanting to lengthen the line "to see just how long I could make it and still have it be an imagistically oriented line and not a discursive, or narrative-based line: the extended, image-freighted line that doesn't implode or break under its own weight." Having cleared its throat, this sea-voice then speaks of the wisteria in such a way that its natural beauty is extended toward the sublime. I could imagine Whitman writing such a line. And he might also, like Wright, have then brought those same stars down to earth, as orange blossoms. The danger Wright runs is that he may miniaturize or aestheticize the sublime. He may do so to avoid the pressures of moralism or of history, but by "purifying" or essentializing his quest he sometimes falls short, underestimates its demands, refuses its power. This is a danger Wright largely avoids, however, and besides, it is his drive toward rather than his prolonged engagement with the sublime that matters, because it helps determine the underlying rhythms of his imagination. This upward urging of the beautiful toward the sublime counterbalances the lure back and downward of the elegiac note sounded everywhere in the poem as well. These shifts of tone and perspective give the poem its "sweet" but restless ambition, its weight and authority. Like the ebb and flow of water and wind, of memory itself, the voice of this poem moves through its "ghostly litany."

Away on waters, we move to Italy, where the clouds are "dragging the sky for the dead / Bodies of those who refuse to rise." This is another kind of divining: trying to raise the dead. As he searches the "river of sighs and forgetfulness" he realizes that "Dante and Can Grande once stood here," and before that Catullus, and "before that, God spoke in the rocks . . . / And now it's my turn to stand / Watching a different light do the same things on a different water." Boldly, Wright links himself with the great voices, the *original* voices. History is domesticated, and the self is aggrandized by its chosen company. His true parents then join these artistic parents. Valéry once remarked that one keeps in memory only what one has not understood. That is what is haunting about Wright's poem, and about his method of linkage.

> They're both ghosts now, haunting the chairs and the sugar
>   chest.
>
> From time to time I hear their voices drifting like smoke
>   through the living room,
> Touching the various things they owned once.
> Now they own nothing
>   and drift like smoke through the living room.

But in the poem's ebb and flow of the domestic and the sublime, these ghosts bring back Dante's, and at once another kind of divining occurs. To remember is, figuratively, to embody again: "Thinking of Dante, I start to feel / What I think are wings beginning to push out from my shoulder blades, / And the firm pull of water under my feet." As if become a soul in Dante's poem, he envisions "the great flower of Paradise, /

And the thin stem of Purgatory rooted in Hell." But as the *Commedia* implies, the vision of Paradise returns us to earth.

> Thinking of Dante is thinking about the other side,
> And the other side of the other side.
> It's thinking about the noon noise and the daily light.

Then follows, as the eleventh section, a long evocation of Venice, the most virtuosic in the poem. It is the Venice of cold pearl skies and mirror-of-steel canals. The only human figure is the aged Ezra Pound:

> I remember the way that Pound walked
> > across San Marco
>
> At *passegiata*, as though with no one,
> > his eyes on the long ago.

It is worth pausing here to note how few people are present in Wright's poems. The epigraph to *Country Music* is from Hemingway: "The country was always better than the people." But it would be a mistake to think of Wright as merely a descriptive poet. People, he says, "become landscapes that I have loved in my life. Landscapes that have nourished me, landscapes that I have walked through, landscapes that have remained with me. Their works are landscapes." That is to say, landscape is a personification of both the dead (like his parents) and the poets. Places are either shrines or texts to "read," as well as a means to see and recover the self. For Wright, landscape is opposed to nature, but not entirely opposed to eternity. The landscape *speaks* to this poet. But the voices always trail off; are overlaid with others, or with silence:

> As always, silence will have the last word,
> And Venice will lie like silk
> > at the edge of the sea and the night sky,
> Albescent under the moon.

> Everyone's life is the same life
> > if you live long enough.

Venice *lies* because it does not have the last word. What does is the blank page on which the poem rests and shifts its weight. "The white space is really white sound," he explains, "sound the ear doesn't always pick up but which is always there, humming, backgrounding, like silences. It's what pulls the lines through the poem, gauging their weights and durations, even their distances. It is the larger sound out of which the more measured and interruptable sounds of the line are cut." So the last word is also the first music, the ground note from which melodies briefly arise. The poet's task is how and when to break silence. As we look at the *mise-en-page* of a poem by Charles Wright, we must realize that the "white space" connects as it divides the lines. His is a poetry of pauses and feints, as if his very reluctance to speak forced his extreme concision and elegance. Silence too is a voice in the poem.

At its midpoint, the fourteenth section, after the long Venetian cadenza, the poem starts again, with a paraphrase of the opening:

> There is an otherness inside us
> We never touch,
> > no matter how far down our hands reach.
> It is the past,
> > with its good looks and *Anytime*,
> > > *Anywhere* . . .
> Our prayers go out to it, our arms go out to it
> Year after year,
> But who can ever remember enough?

One could link this with a later passage that speaks (like Cocteau) of imagining "a mouth / Starting to open its blue lips / Inside me." *On me dit.* The otherness within is not alien; it is both the past and the voice that would speak of the past. But are memories enough to propitiate this otherness? " It's what we forget that defines us" is Wright's answer.

"The Southern Cross" is a very American poem because it worries about an old world and a new. But this is not the venerable polarity of Europe and America. California and Montana, where the poem is being written, constitute a present, while the Tennessee of his boyhood is the past. Venice, Verona, and Rome have both an antiquity and a past (when Wright lived there, a dozen years before the poem was written), and they have a presence in his reading. The poem next casts a wide net over his *Italienischereise*. This is not so much a man remembering as a man observing his memories. It is another way to efface himself, to let things speak for themselves. His long catalogue of sense-memories, though, is an odd erasure, denying what it includes, as here:

> I can't remember the colors I said I'd never forget
> On Via Giulia at sundown,
> The ochres and glazes and bright hennas of each house.

"Time is the villain," he concludes; it takes these details away, not just from us but from the things themselves. And if we recall that "villain" originally meant "one who lives in a city," then it's an appropriate term for the process. The poem now leaves the city for the pastoral fields of longer memory. Time itself is the landscape of this poem, and "its landscape is the resurrection of the word." As the poem moves toward its conclusion, there is a literal race against time. It begins with a note of Keatsian plenitude: "I can't remember enough."

> How the hills, for instance, at dawn in Kingsport
> In late December in 1962 were black
>   against a sky
> The color of pale fish blood and water that ran to white

As I got ready to leave home for the 100th time,
My mother and father asleep,
                              my sister asleep,
Carter's Valley as dark as the inside of a bone
Below the ridge,
                         the 1st knobs of the Great Smokies
Beginning to stick through the sunrise,
The hard pull of a semi making the grade up US 11W,
The cold with its metal teeth ticking against the window,
The long sigh of the screen door stop,
My headlights starting to disappear
                              in the day's new turning . . .

I'll never be able to.

The finale is his resignation. Sitting on his step—as if it were a rung on the mount of the *Purgatorio*—the poet watches "a brute bumblebee working the clover tops." This Dickinsonian bee is Wright's thrush or nightingale. It goes about its sweet business; so do the lupin and bog lilies, and the wind signs a *Let-us-pray* and "the golden vestments of morning / Lift for a moment." We are back at the morning the poem opened with, but with the poet's realization that "everything has its work, everything written down." All the voices choir in harmony. And again, it subsides to a silence—the sound of the wind, of breath itself:

The life of this world is wind.
Wind-blown we come, and wind-blown we go away.
All that we look on is windfall.
All we remember is wind.

The liturgical cadences here can't disguise the puns. The tone is somber—as if we were meant to hear "dust and ashes" instead of wind—but the larger sense of process, and of the poet's resignation to it, gains by our participation in the moment: *we* look, *we* remember. A windfall is a sudden stroke of good fortune; and memory becomes inspiration itself. So the wind is destroyer and preserver both. Can we link it with Shelley's West Wind? "Be thou me," Shelley implores the wind, surrendering himself, his voice, "lift me as a wave, a leaf, a cloud . . . make me thy lyre."

"Pickwick was never the wind. . . ." So the last section begins, naming his birthplace. In a poem woven out of Proustian *intermittences du coeur,* it is only right that we return to his earliest memory now at the end. But this memory is not of a place, but of the idea of a place—and so Pickwick merges with Pound's paradisal city in *The Cantos,* and perhaps with Dante's Rose of Light as well. Again the poet alternates a memory and the scene of remembering, the past and a visionary future, activity and entropy, the human and the natural worlds—and above all, speech and silence. For this poet, who wants to make the world speak through him, whose lines are like beads for us to tell and to praise that world, to fall silent is to have accomplished his task.

> It's what we forget that defines us, and stays in the same place,
> And waits to be rediscovered.
> Somewhere in all that network of rivers and roads and silt hills,
> A city I'll never remember,
>   its walls the color of pure light,
> Lies in the August heat of 1935,
> In Tennessee, the bottom land slowly becoming a lake.
> It lies in a landscape that keeps my imprint
> Forever,
>   and stays unchanged, and waits to be filled back in.

Someday I'll find it out
And enter my old outline as though for the 1st time,
And lie down, and tell no one.

W. H. AUDEN can be credited with helping to launch John
Ashbery as a poet. To begin with, he provided Ashbery with a
model to imitate; "he was the first big influence on my work,"
says Ashbery, who particularly admired Auden's combination
of colloquial speech and romantic tone. Then, in 1956, Auden
chose Ashbery's first book, *Some Trees,* for the Yale Younger
Poets series. But it was also Auden who, later in his life, told a
friend that he had never understood a word Ashbery had writ-
ten. I wonder if that isn't also a dilemma other readers find
themselves in—praising *and* puzzling over Ashbery's poems?
He has, from the start, seemed always to be a figure out of the
recent future: unpredictable, innovative. Like Auden, he has
explored the byways of formal possibilities in verse, and has
also looked under more rocks of contemporary life than most
any other poet in his generation, continually discovering fresh-
ened channels and sources of poetic energy. But strong pockets
of resistance to his work remain here and there, along with a
more widespread uneasiness about its intentions and status.
For many readers, his poems seem to have a purpose, but no
meaning. Theories have sprung up to account for this impres-
sion. Some of the more impassioned plead for chaos: the point
is, there *is* no meaning. And, in the words of one recent critic,
"each moment, each line of a poem, establishes its autonomy
by a swerving away from its antecedents." But of course that
is not a description of anything worth being called "poetry,"
and Ashbery's lines have everything to do with each other—
with *antecedents* in both the poem itself and in the literary
culture his poems have enriched.

If we held to Schiller's distinction between the naive and

the sentimental artist, then we might call Charles Wright—at least by comparison with Ashbery—the naive poet. That is to say, a self-effacing one, a lapidary force of calm and natural order rather than a disruptive, exhibitionist intelligence. By contrast, Ashbery is Schiller's sentimental poet: ironic, self-interrogating, delighting in irregular forms, with a quizzical wit and sly manners. There is a remarkable range of idiom and tone in his poems, and we have grown used to an account of them as a transcript of consciousness itself, the experience of experience. "I think that any one of my poems," he remarks, "might be considered to be a snapshot of whatever is going on in my mind at the time—first of all the desire to write a poem, after that wondering if I've left the oven on or thinking about where I must be in the next hour." If this were all they are, his poems would be merely the most naturalistic written—Hume's bundle of sensations. But they are less distracted, and more random than that.

I prefer another of Ashbery's phrases about his own poems—that they are "paradigms of common experience." For anyone, but especially for a New Yorker, that implies eccentric sources. "I look out my window," he says of living in New York City, "and see what seems to be a Gothic church tower and a big building that says ABIE'S BABY on it right next door." One hears likewise in his work the accents of traditional verse alongside the clichés and banality of everyday speech. The poet himself says he depends on overheard bits of street-talk, on advertisements and snatches of radio announcements, on newspaper features and old movies on TV—the whole apparatus, in short, of popular culture, "a kind of confused but insistent impression of the culture going on around us." Ashbery uses the analogy of music—specifically, of John Cage's practice of "environmental" music: notated accident. But music also provides a larger analogy: "What I like about music is its ability of being convincing, of carrying an argument through successfully to the finish, though the terms of this argument remain unknown quantities." *Ideas, meaning, subject matter*—these seem to concern him less than a poem's texture, its dynamics, its effect. "I write with experiences in mind," he says, "but I don't write about them, I write out of them." An Ashbery poem, then, with its hybrid form and unemphasized tonality, seeks to become a context for meanings rather than a repository of meanings. William James once said that truth *happens* to an idea, and in much the same way meanings *happen* to Ashbery's poems. Different readers at different times in different ways will read into these poems what they find there— their own thought process reflected back at them. And to achieve this, the poet counts on what he calls "a choir or cluster of voices" in a poem. "I think I am trying to reproduce the polyphony that goes on inside me."

This is a demanding method—not least because it seems merely method and no moral inquiry or unfolding of the emotions, like music without a melody—and in hands less skillful than Ashbery's can be self-indulgent. Early on in his career, despairing of a large readership, he determined to write only for himself. It worked. "Very often people don't listen to you when you speak to them," he wryly observes. "It's only when you talk to yourself that they prick up their ears." But this is not merely a question of talking to himself. It is a matter of *listening* primarily to himself, even while he cannot help but hear what sounds off around him. And he has said that what he listens to is another self; that he thinks of himself as John, and of the person who writes his poems as Ashbery. "Of course, my reason tells me that my poems are not dictated, that I am not a voyant. I suppose they come from a part of me that I am not in touch with very much except when I am writing." Who or what is this other self? How, in other words, can we listen to an Ashbery poem the way he first hears them? If we can do that, we will not pluck the heart out of his mystery, but we can approach the deeper mystery of his work. "In our art," he once wrote about some American originals, "we want to get beyond 'mysteries of construction,' to quote Miss Moore's useful phrase, into mysteries of being which, it turns out, have their own laws of construction."

Many years ago, in a review he wrote of Gertrude Stein's *Stanzas in Meditation*, Ashbery compared her work to Henry James', and noted that the bewildering luxuriance of both "seems to obey some rhythmic impulse at the heart of all happening." And rather than merely applaud his poems or dismiss them as digressive, disjunctive, obscure, or evasive, I think it more practical to figure out the underlying "rhythmic impulse." As I have described Ashbery's method so far, it might seem to resemble Charles Wright's passive layerings, his imagistic linkages. But to my mind's ear, Ashbery is the more dramatic poet, and his method essentially dialectical. What I hear are two voices in urgent dialogue, as if the text of the poem or eclogue were a casual glade and their voices a pastoral pair. Their dialogue gives both shape and momentum to a poem, and when they are braided and streaming across one's consciousness the effect is very heady indeed.

I sometimes wish there might one day be a red-letter edition of Ashbery's poems, to distinguish between these two voices. Of course, a single poem may be entirely in one voice or the other; sometimes poems slip through such categories altogether; but in his best poems, both voices can be heard. How to characterize them? "Trefoil," a poem from *A Wave*, speaks of "trees / Of two minds half-caught in their buzz and luster." Buzz and luster. Let us call the first voice *buzz*. It is the voice —the voices—he hears around him. It brings into a poem an *environment* of (so one poem catalogues them) "scenes from movies, plays, operas, television; decisive or little-known episodes from history; prenatal and other early memories from our solitary, separate pasts; events yet to come from life or art;

calamities or moments of relaxation; universal or personal tragedies; or vignettes from daily life that you just had to stop and laugh at, they were so funny, like the dog chasing its tail on the living-room rug." In his own person, this voice of Ashbery's (or perhaps we should call it John's) is that of the citizen and ironist; it can be abstract and colloquial, rational or journalistic, bitter and witty and silly. The other voice is all *luster*; it is the voice he listens for in himself; it is "Ashbery." This is the deep call of memory, desire, impulse, art. It can sound romantic, fantastic, disjunctive. Wallace Stevens called it imagination: "Sometimes," wrote Stevens, "I believe most in the imagination for a long time and then, without reasoning about it, turn to reality and believe in that and that alone. But both those things project themselves endlessly and I want them to do just that." So too in Ashbery's work do both voices project themselves endlessly, in a repressive dialectic of attention and reverie:

> Something
> Ought to be written about how this affects
> You when you write poetry:
> The extreme austerity of an almost empty mind
> Colliding with the lush, Rousseau-like foliage of its desire to
>   communicate
> Something between breaths, if only for the sake
> Of others and their desire to understand you and desert you
> For other centers of communication, so that understanding
> May begin, and in doing so be undone.

Wallace Stevens had a wilier set of terms; asserting that "interaction is the source of poetry," he used the milkman and moonlight, or the missal found in the mud as his examples. However the terms may be defined or defended or skewered, it is their interaction that matters. As I've said, Ashbery's best poems are powered by alternating currents; they combine the two voices, set up collusions and collisions between them. One voice longs to yield to the other, but, feeling guilty, merely tries to analyze or accommodate or overwhelm it. While we read the poems, this is both the psychological drama that shapes them, and a rhetorical play that gives them their theatrical panache. Again, Stevens in his essay "Imagination as Value": "What, then, is it to live in the mind with the imagination yet not too near to the fountains of its rhetoric, so that one does not have a consciousness only of grandeurs, of incessant departures from the idiom and of inherent altitudes?" To live *in* the mind *with* the imagination. Ashbery's phrase for this is "fence-sitting / Raised to the level of an aesthetic ideal." The condition is most familiar from Stevens' poems, which bear brightly the little beyond themselves, and bear too the exquisite or ludicrous errors of time. His endlessly elaborating poem—like Ashbery's—displays a theory of poetry as the life of poetry and theory of life.

Let me give a few examples. Here is the middle stanza of "More Pleasant Adventures," a poem from *A Wave*. You can hear the first voice—the blithe, rambling buzz—in the first three lines give way to the lustrous dream-interlude in the second voice, which in the last two lines here drifts back to the homely demotic:

> Heck, it's anybody's story,
> A sentimental journey—"gonna take a sentimental journey,"
> And we do, but you wake up under the table of a dream:
> You are that dream, and it is the seventh layer of you.
> We haven't moved an inch, and everything has changed.
> We are somewhere near a tennis court at night.
> We get lost in life, but life knows where we are.
> We can always be found with our associates.
> Haven't you always wanted to curl up like a dog and go to
>   sleep like a dog?

Elsewhere, the voices are sharply juxtaposed. Here is the opening of "The Wrong Kind of Insurance":

> I teach in a high school
> And see the nurses in some of the hospitals,
> And if all teachers are like that
> Maybe I can give you a buzz some day,
> Maybe we can get together for lunch or coffee or something.
>
> The white marble statues in the auditorium
> Are colder to the touch than the rain that falls
> Past the post-office inscription about rain or snow
> Or gloom of night. I think
> About what these archaic meanings mean,
> That unfurl like a rope ladder down through history,
> To fall at our feet like crocuses.

The second voice is so richly rhetorical that one might be tempted to call it the primary voice, but that would be a miscalculation. The poems depend on both for their emotional resources. A small passage from *Three Poems* is relevant: "But that is the wonder of it: that you have returned not to the supernatural glow of heaven but to the ordinary daylight you knew so well before it passed from your view, and which continues to enrich you as it steeps you and your ageless chattels of mind, imagination, timid first love and quiet acceptance of experience in its revitalizing tide."

Ashbery himself once said of his poems that their "methodology occasionally coincides with the subject." Here is a part of "Ditto, Kiddo," where the interruption of one voice by the other is overtly the topic:

> What if you do listen to it over and over, until
>
> It becomes part of your soul, foreign matter that belongs
>   there?

I ask you so many times to think about this rupture you are
Proceeding with, this revolution. And still time
Is draped over your shoulders. The weather report
Didn't mention rain, and you are ass-deep in it, so?
Find other predictions. These are good for throwing away,
Yesterday's newspapers, and those of the weeks before that
     spreading
Backward, away, almost in perfect order. It's all there
To interrupt your speaking.

Interrupted speaking is the method of Ashbery's major books
—*Three Poems* (1972), *Self-Portrait in a Convex Mirror* (1975),
Houseboat Days (1977), and *A Wave* (1984). But he had found
his way to this manner of speaking as early as *The Double
Dream of Spring* (1970), and I want to turn now to one of the
strongest—and by now best known—poems in that volume,
"Soonest Mended." Its title, of course, is the second half of the
aphorism, "Least said, soonest mended," and itself points to
the problem of speaking. The poem is both "autobiographical"
and fabular. Its opening section makes heroic allusions and
parodies them at the same time:

Barely tolerated, living on the margin
In our technological society, we were always having to be
     rescued
On the brink of destruction, like heroines in *Orlando Furioso*
Before it was time to start all over again.
There would be thunder in the bushes, a rustling of coils,
And Angelica, in the Ingres painting, was considering
The colorful but small monster near her toe, as though
     wondering whether forgetting
The whole thing might not, in the end, be the only solution.
And then there always came a time when
Happy Hooligan in his rusted green automobile

Came plowing down the course, just to make sure everything
    was O.K.,
Only by that time we were in another chapter and confused
About how to receive this latest piece of information.
Was it information?

How to receive information, or make meaning, is the question
the poem poses, and with a good humor that shades into wistful
resignation, the poet entertains suggestions from both voices.
Worried by "our daily quandary about food and the rent and
bills to be paid" (the small monsters near *our* toes), the second
voice transforms the poem momentarily:

To reduce all this to a small variant,
To step free at last, minuscule on the gigantic plateau—
This was our ambition: to be small and clear and free.
Alas, the summer's energy wanes quickly,
A moment and it is gone.

The question now is "holding on to the hard earth so as not to
get thrown off, / With an occasional dream, a vision." I'm
reminded of the concluding lines of "The Man with the Blue
Guitar":

That generation's dream, aviled
In the mud, in Monday's dirty light,

That's it, the only dream they knew,
Time in its final block, not time

To come, a wrangling of two dreams.
Here is the bread of time to come,

Here is its actual stone. The bread
Will be our bread, the stone will be

Our bed and we shall sleep by night.
We shall forget by day, except

> The moments when we choose to play
> The imagined pine, the imagined jay.

In Ashbery's poem too the disparity that troubles both the speaker and the poem's own texture is one between vision and irony, between desire and "talk":

> This is what you wanted to hear, so why
> Did you think of listening to something else? We are all
>   talkers
> It is true, but underneath the talk lies
> The moving and not wanting to be moved, the loose
> Meaning, untidy and simple like a threshing floor.

The second half of the poem resumes the "hazards of the course," switching between "roles" and "rules"—"the being of our sentences." The romantic heroes of our books and our dreams—*ourselves* in our desires—turn out to be players, voices in the drama. The lines that brood on this keep flipping over on themselves as they move from one contrasting conjunction to another, across a series of thoughts mined with puns ("past truth"), misleading similes, and epigrams. But if one listens to the tone of voice shift, the lines can be—exuberantly—followed:

> Night after night this message returns, repeated
> In the flickering bulbs of the sky, raised past us, taken away
>   from us,
> Yet ours over and over until the end that is past truth,
> The being of our sentences, in the climate that fostered
>   them,
> Not ours to own, like a book, but to be with, and sometimes
> To be without, alone and desperate.
> But the fantasy makes it ours, a kind of fence-sitting
> Raised to the level of an aesthetic ideal. These were moments,
>   years,

Solid with reality, faces, nameable events, kisses, heroic acts,
But like the friendly beginning of a geometrical progression
Not too reassuring, as though meaning could be cast aside
    some day
When it had been outgrown.

The poem's final section, then, concerns "learning." It begins casually, trying to formulate agreeable conclusions. The affirming syntax is undercut by the qualifying rhetoric, until the second lustrous voice—however stylized, it would be fair to call it an involuntary memory—overtakes the end. We are returned to the poem's beginning, and to the poem's economy of forgetting and "always coming back." Whether this note Ashbery strikes is one of consolation or of futility depends on the mood a reader brings to the poem:

And you see, both of us were right, though nothing
Has somehow come to nothing; the avatars
Of our conforming to the rules and living
Around the home have made—well, in a sense, "good
    citizens" of us,
Brushing the teeth and all that, and learning to accept
The charity of the hard moments as they are doled out,
For this is action, this not being sure, this careless
Preparing, sowing the seeds crooked in the furrow,
Making ready to forget, and always coming back
To the morning of starting out, that day so long ago.

These two voices in Ashbery's poems may be called many things, active and passive, waking and dreamlike, dialectical or pastoral, but they are the very pulse of the Romantic heart of his work: the randomness of experience countered by the imperatives of subjectivity. Ashbery's poems reach for themselves and for their readers "through vagrant sympathy and a kind of immediate contact." They wander back to their sources of power, then sidle up to us. We recognize their accents as our own, but hear too "the finer accommodation of speech to that vision within." That phrase, and the one just before, are Walter Pater's. And there is no better description of Ashbery's genius or of his poems than these lines by Pater, written in 1868:

> At first sight experience seems to bury us under a flood of external objects, pressing upon us with a sharp and importunate reality, calling us out of ourselves in a thousand forms of action. But when reflection begins to act upon those objects they are dissipated under its influence; the cohesive force seems suspended like a trick of magic; each object is loosed into a group of impressions . . . in the mind of the observer. And if we continue to dwell in thought of this world . . . of impressions unstable, flickering, inconsistent, which burn and are extinguished with our consciousness of them, it contracts still further; the whole scope of observation is dwarfed to the narrow chamber of the individual mind. Experience, already reduced to a swarm of impressions, is ringed round for each one of us by that thick wall of personality through which no real voice has ever pierced on its way to us, or from us to that which we can only conjecture to be without. Every one of those impressions is the impression of the individual in his isolation, each mind keeping as a solitary prisoner its own dream of a world. . . . To such a tremulous wisp constantly reforming itself down. It is with this movement, with the passage and dissolution of impressions, images, sensations, that analysis leaves off —that continual vanishing away, that strange, perpetual weaving and unweaving of ourselves.

IN 1966, with great reluctance, Elizabeth Bishop agreed to teach a poetry workshop for the first time, at the University of

Washington. She was homesick, it rained constantly, and she was dismayed by her students. They didn't *know* anything but the urge to "discover" or "express" themselves. So she set them difficult metrical exercises, and—one ex-student later recalled—hectored them: "You should have your head filled with poems all the time, until they almost get in your way." Bishop's own head certainly was filled with poems, all the time. As a girl, she read constantly in the Victorian poets, and somehow also made her way to Emily Dickinson and Walt Whitman. Later came Hopkins, George Herbert and the other Metaphysicals, and Auden. Certainly her two most faithful readers, Marianne Moore and Robert Lowell, were in her mind. But when she began writing, in the 1930s, her head was filled with another figure: "Wallace Stevens was the contemporary who most affected my writing then," she once told an interviewer. It was an influence that lasted through her life as a poet, and has a crucial bearing on one of her best poems, "The End of March," published in *Geography III* in 1976. I want now to read through the poem, and listen for allusions that add to the sense of it. The apparently natural, conversational tone of Bishop's work can mislead a reader into thinking her artless. But she was a cannily allusive writer—and not least to her own previous work. Charles Wright seems to be what Montale called Pound, "a composite poet," his own voice subsumed by a style that allows things to speak for themselves. John Ashbery's poems have reduced this crowd of voices to just two, both aspects of the self, and set them in dramatic contrast with each other. Bishop seems to speak in her own voice—and in an original, entirely characteristic manner.

Like Frost's, her tone tended to dominate the material in a poem. Shy of ideas and scornful of pretense, her poems don't seem to make rhetorical demands on the reader; their modesty seems to guarantee the sincerity of, say, a friendly conversation. The reader is discouraged from probing for hidden meanings. Sometimes hesitant or uncertain, the poems move steadily forward through their contained narratives or descriptive interludes to make their charmed, provisional conclusions. At the start of Bishop's career, Marianne Moore singled out the "rational considering quality" of her lines, and ever since then critics have hovered over the limpid, agreeable surfaces of the poems. She has been praised for her clarity and poise, her wry whimsy, her ironic control, her informing reticence, her mastery of tonal modulations, her regard for natural detail and for adroit images. Occasionally, the critics extended their descriptions into thematic speculations. If the poems are more perceptual than conceptual, then their subject is the motives and maneuvers of consciousness itself, the shifting play of the mind around static objects or conceits. Or, under the pressures of moralism, they may have ascribed to Bishop an unflappable stoicism. The reserve and obliquity of most of Bishop's poetry indeed encourage such modest "appreciations." Her sense of narrative is largely anecdotal: pointed and even elliptical rather than extensive or complex. She tended to center her attention on the incident—a word implying both transience and typicality—and often seemed self-consciously to be defending her poems against any impulse toward analysis or proposal. Clearly, for whatever more instinctive motives, she wanted to use language referentially, to seem to be recording rather than creating experience, and evolved an ingenuous style without the least aggression or strain—like her own speaking voice, flat and unemphatic. Perhaps, then, it is because her poems seem so "easy" that they are so difficult. If we can't hear the allusions she is subtly making—and her early readers did not— then we can't estimate the true power of the poems—their thematic ambitions, their autobiographical bearings, the rightful place they should assume in the traditions of American poetry.

Let me read through the poem twice, once by itself and in

the context of Bishop's other poems, and then again with an ear cocked for its further sources and extensions. First, then, the title itself, "The End of March." It seems only to designate the poem's setting, or season. But "end" also means both "purpose" and "goal." And if we take "march" to stand in for "walk," then the title directs us to look, from the very start, to the meaning of the anecdote—indeed, makes the account into an allegory. There is even an (unintentional but apposite) allusion to a phrase from one of her earliest poems, "The Imaginary Iceberg," where she speaks of "the end of travel." And this late poem, like several other poems in *Geography III*, is shot through with troubled feelings about the end of a life, and an art, spent traveling in search of home. The title also sets up a series of important references. Bishop was always interested in folklore and superstitions, in customs and hymns and old saws. One adage must be kept in mind for this poem: *March comes in like a lion, but goes out like a lamb.* The lion in that saying, of course, comes to dominate Bishop's poem. But it lies down here with the lamb too. On her beach walk, the poet's eye, as it looks out on and creates the horizon, divides the elements into sky and sea. The sky comes to be the lion's element. The sea, which is said to be "the color of mutton-fat jade," is the lamb's. We might further construe the season as Eastertide, and so the paschal lamb is its sign. This is, after all, a poem with a "dead man" (the sodden ghost of string), a kind of tomb, and then at its conclusion an extraordinary, "majestic" resurrection—a risen Son who destroys death, or bats down a kite with its cross-shaped frame. These symbols (or perhaps, because she was not a believer, it would be better to call them motifs) wait in the wings of the poem, but never, I think, make enough of an appearance to merit much notice. Bishop is telling another kind of story.

We begin with the scene, a cold, windy shoreline:

It was cold and windy, scarcely the day
to take a walk on that long beach.
Everything was withdrawn as far as possible,
indrawn: the tide far out, the ocean shrunken,
seabirds in ones or twos.
The rackety, icy, offshore wind
numbed our faces on one side;
disrupted the formation
of a lone flight of Canada geese;
and blew back the low, inaudible rollers
in upright, steely mist.

This is a sort of zero-point. Her use of "our" indicates she is
not alone on her walk. (Her companions evidently are the
poem's dedicatees, the poet John Malcolm Brinnin and his
friend Bill Read, the editors of a famous anthology, *The Mod-
ern Poets*—a point with some resonance later in the poem.)
But the feeling in these lines is hardly companionable; it is,
rather, like some purgatorial climb out of Dante: in these
conditions company only increases one's sense of isolation. The
wind is the most prominent feature here, and Bishop's details
are carefully placed to heighten the odd perspectives and ex-
tremes that make this a literally chilling scene. What else is
meant to be noticed here? Perhaps the mention of Canada geese
recalls to the alert reader Bishop's childhood in Nova Scotia—
an obsessive subject in her work—and that in this search her
beginnings are connected with her "end." Perhaps. But at least
we can recognize the scene as one we've encountered before in
other of her poems, starting in the very book this poem was
collected in, *Geography III*. The island in "Crusoe in England,"
the dentist's outer office in "In the Waiting Room," the distant
lighted surfaces in "Night City"—all of these are mysterious,
rather forbidding landscapes that are subsequently contrasted

with enclosed or interior spaces (hut, cabin, inner office, plane, or bus), which promise shelter but can be deceptive. This shoreline recalls earlier poems too: in "The Monument," "The Bight," "The Sandpiper" (whose emblematic "preoccupied" bird, "looking for something, something, something," is a version of the speaker here), and most famously in "At the Fishhouses."

The first stanza having set the scene, the next introduces a complication. Appropriate to the mystery, the tone takes on a vaguely Agatha Christie-ish manner, carefully factual and then —as we move into a participial present tense and the anaphora builds tension—downright melodramatic:

> The sky was darker than the water
> —*it* was the color of mutton-fat jade.
> Along the wet sand, in rubber boots, we followed
> a track of big dog-prints (so big
> they were more like lion-prints). Then we came on
> lengths and lengths, endless, of wet white string,
> looping up to the tide-line, down to the water,
> over and over. Finally, they did end:
> a thick white snarl, mansize, awash,
> rising on every wave, a sodden ghost,
> falling back, sodden, giving up the ghost . . .
> A kite string?—But no kite.

Here is the first problem in the poem. An apparently random detail is gradually, by the length of the poet's attention to it, made more conspicuous. And to what end? We don't return to this "ghost." And *is* it string at all, or is it simply sea-foam, a trail of spume her eye follows to a floating patch of it offshore? The line between detail and image is blurred here, and this is because the poem is moving into a new register. We are directed here to look less at the scene and more at the observer.

The ghost may thereby be a projection of her own despondency. If the ghost she raises now is herself, it is certainly lurking in the next stanza. But there is another possibility—not a competing one so much as a complementary one. There is a ghost in the very phrase "a sodden ghost." The opening of Wallace Stevens' "The Comedian as the Letter C" has this striking phrase: "Nota: man is the intelligence of his soil, / The sovereign ghost." I take this to be a phrase for the imagination itself, and if we read that sense back into Bishop's echoing phrase "a sodden ghost," then we are prepared for much that occurs later in the poem. What she sees, a ghost giving up the ghost, may be her poethood itself, her own name writ in water.

The very next stanza should be the poem's climax, which the final stanza might then gracefully round off. It describes, after all, the *end* of her walk, an imagined ideal. But as Penelope Laurans has noted, "everything in the diction and movement of the verse here—its ordinariness, its prosy, conversational sound and flow, as if Bishop were simply talking to the reader—works to diminish the excitement of the ideal she is imagining." Its very first words—"I wanted"—announce a new intimacy; until now the narrative voice had been "we." The poem's pace quickens; both her doubts and her desires mount. But the stanza is in three continuous sections; here is the first:

> I wanted to get as far as my proto-dream-house,
> my crypto-dream-house, that crooked box
> set up on pilings, shingled green,
> a sort of artichoke of a house, but greener
> (boiled with bicarbonate of soda?),
> protected from spring tides by a palisade
> of—are they railroad ties?
> (Many things about this place are dubious.)

As Laurans says, the movement here is misleading. At first, Bishop seems to be riffling through terms for the shack, and then to joke about its color. This is the sort of casual tone and comic relief she uses—the hymn-loving seal in "At the Fishhouse" is another example—whenever a poem approaches its most serious concerns, as if to guard against any easy thematic formulation or to withdraw (indraw?) any boldly lyrical mode. Even so, this passage is fraught. Her palisade of railroad ties seems a humorous incongruity, but why a *palisade?* A poet so warily precise in her choice of words as Bishop must be asking us—if we are listening to her—to understand something more than she is saying. The first meaning of "palisade" is a fortification, a spiked barricade defending against enemy assault. It is not the only defense mechanism in the poem. There's her dream-house. The more she describes it, the more it resembles a coffin's crooked box, a crypt, perhaps a cell. In any case, we are invited by that conjunction of prefixes, "dream-" and "crypto-," to interpret this house psychologically. I wonder, for instance, if it mightn't be, in her imagination, the room her mother occupied in the sanatorium, after she was taken away (when Bishop was nine) never to be seen again. In some sense, Bishop then imagines herself *as* her own mother. The association of *the house* and *mother* is an ancient and still powerful one.

Many things about this stanza are dubious. But though her mother's "ghost" hovers, I don't think the poem can be reduced to such a reading. We should first keep in mind the other houses in her poems—"Songs for the Rainy Season," for instance, or the perishable "fairy palace" that is "Jerónimo's House," In both poems, the house is, in Jerónimo's phrase, "my shelter from / the hurricane." These are not the domestic hearths and parlors of her family poems, or even of the delightful "Filling Station." There is only—uncannily—room for one. The stanza (the very word is one for "room") continues:

I'd like to retire there and do *nothing,*
or nothing much, forever, in two bare rooms:
look through binoculars, read boring books,
old, long, long books, and write down useless notes,
talk to myself, and, foggy days,
watch the droplets slipping, heavy with light.
At night, a *grog à l'américaine.*
I'd blaze it with a kitchen match
and lovely diaphanous blue flame
would waver, doubled in the window.

An astonishing passage, and the poem at its most "indrawn."
Yes, there's a drizzly, fogbound coziness to it, born of a child-
hood in Nova Scotia and summers in Maine. Yes, there's an
appealing torpor. I sometimes think those long boring books
she'll read are by Coleridge (a favorite author of hers)—say,
his *Aids to Reflection.* How slowly the raindrop slips down the
glass, as if into the flamed spirits which reflect it back again
onto the pane. But there's something uncanny here as well.
I'm put in mind of an eerie little poem by Emily Dickinson:

> I was the slightest in the House—
> I took the smallest Room—
> At night, my little Lamp, and Book—
> And one Geranium—[. . .]
>
> I never spoke—unless addressed—
> And then, 'twas brief and low—
> I could not bear to live—aloud—
> The Racket shamed me so—
>
> And if it had not been so far—
> And any one I knew
> Were going—I had often thought
> How noteless—I could die—

But one needn't look so far for this same room. In an essay on Bishop that discusses the polarity of travel and imprisonment, Alfred Corn has perceptively drawn our attention to connections between "The End of March" and Bishop's early story, "In Prison," written forty years before *Geography III*. "I can scarcely wait for the day of my imprisonment," the story starts. "It is then that my life, my real life, will begin." The narrator, we gather, feels liberated by his isolation (that is also the burden of "Crusoe in England") and by the confinement. "One must be *in*," he says, "that is the primary condition." And while in his ideal prison, "my one desire is to be given one very dull book to read, the duller the better. A book, moreover, on a subject completely foreign to me; perhaps the second volume, if the first would familiarize me too well with the terms and purpose of the work." Like this protagonist, the speaker in "The End of March" seems to want to escape from *purpose* and *terms*, to secure a relief from the trials of self-consciousness, to deaden the pain of being in the world. (If we let Bishop's mentally disturbed mother's ghost haunt this passage, it can strike us as an affecting gesture of identification and sympathy.)

Another early story, "The Sea & Its Shore" (1937), then lets us see the house in this poem not as a cell but as an idea. The story's protagonist is named Edward Boomer; the initials are Bishop's own, and "Boomer" is a version of Bishop's mother's maiden name, Bulmer. He lives "the life of letters"—that is, he picks up papers from the beach all day (like Wordsworth's Old Leech-Gatherer) and ponders them all night (like Henry James' nun of art). His house is a wooden shack, "with a pitched roof, about four by four by six feet, set on pegs stuck in the sand. There was no window, no door set in the door frame, and nothing at all inside. . . . As a house, it was more like an idea of a house than a real one. . . . It was a shelter, but not for living in, for thinking in." *For thinking in.* This seems the opposite sort of shelter from those offered by the prison cell. But it is not, for "In Prison" goes on to describe the effect of reading that dull book: "From my detached rock-like book I shall be able to draw vast generalizations, abstractions of the grandest, most illuminating sort, like allegories or poems, and by posing fragments of it against the surroundings and conversations of my prison, I shall be able to form my own examples of surrealist art." She will be inspired to write on the walls—though she uses the grander term "inscribe." She will write poems there, "brief, suggestive, anguished, but full of the lights of revelation," not at all unlike the poems that came to be Bishop's *Collected Poems.*

But is it fair to read all this into "The End of March"? I think so. Other Bishop poems make similar connections. In "The Bight," for instance, a gas flame—like the flamed shot-glass here—reminds the poet of Baudelaire. In "The Monument," what one viewer considers a heap of piled-up boxes, cracked and unpainted, another sees as a commemorative and sheltering object "the beginning of a painting, / a piece of sculpture, or poem," and "each day the light goes around it / like a prowling animal." And in "Jerónimo's House," we are invited to "Come closer" and inspect his "gray wasps' nest / of chewed-up paper / glued with spit." At night one can see "the writing-paper / lines of light" on its walls. This cluster of images recurs in all her work: a withdrawn, dreamy state as the matrix of creation; the house as artwork, and art as a homemade shelter; a cell of light, stone to inscribe, paper to catch fire. These are connections to be made with "The End of March," but they don't seem to be *in* the poem—or at least not in this part of the poem. Instead, the delicate questioning continues until the daydream is slapped by a cold, realistic wind:

There must be a stove; there *is* a chimney,
askew, but braced with wires,
and electricity, possibly
—at least, at the back another wire
limply leashes the whole affair
to something off behind the dunes.
A light to read by—perfect! But—impossible.
And that day the wind was much too cold
even to get that far,
and of course the house was boarded up.

Again, the exposition is so offhanded; she is speaking in what
Emerson called "the language of facts." But the passage is
carefully worked. The word "leashes" links with the dog-prints
and with the kite. Mightn't the house even somehow *be* the
kite to which she has been led? The reading light is positioned
between the droplet of light on the window and the sun, about
to show itself. And the heart-catching phrase that may be the
poem's motto: "perfect! But—impossible." It is so oddly but
fastidiously punctuated that we pronounce it with just the right
initial enthusiasm and subsequent deflation. What is even od-
der is that the phrase—indeed, the realization—is followed by
"and," not "because." Her ideal is impossible not because it is
unattainable right now, but because it is forever out of reach,
perhaps even because it is "perfect." If this is a poem, finally,
about the imagination, then so far it has been a Dejection Ode,
a meditation on her failing powers. From the opening emphasis
on the icy wind—or frozen inspiration—to this dream-house
of a shelter within art that eludes her, she has been thwarted
in her quest. Here is a diction of denial, strung out in cata-
logues that sum up a fallen world slipping away from her.
What Randall Jarrell once wrote of Frost—a poet whose tem-
perament Bishop shares—is apt: "The limits which existence

approaches and falls back from have seldom been stated with such bare composure."

It is now, only when she turns away from her ideal, her stated goal, that the poem sets at large its astonishing power. I'm reminded of the letter Bishop once wrote to Anne Stevenson describing Darwin: "But reading Darwin one admires the beautiful solid case being built up out of his endless, heroic observations, almost unconscious or automatic—and then comes a sudden relaxation, a forgetful phrase, and one feels that strangeness of his undertaking, sees the lonely young man, his eye fixed on facts and minute details, sinking or sliding giddily off into the unknown." The final stanza of "The End of March" is a kind of giddy sliding off as well. The tone dramatically shifts to one more rich and strange. As Penelope Laurans says, "Bishop releases her poem lyrically only at a moment which is not explicitly its thematic high point. Of course this moment becomes its high point, but that is another matter. The important fact is that Bishop seems reluctant to allow metrical intensity and plain-spokenness to correspond, as if she were afraid that the one might spoil or cheapen the other." But it is equally true that the one is used to heighten the other. As in "At the Fishhouses," the long declarative foreground has suppressed the lyrical outburst so that it surprises both poet and reader with a sudden force that nearly unsettles the poem but finally secures it. In both poems, the poet is overwhelmed by elemental forces—the sea or the sun—that teach at the same time as they exalt. Here is the final stanza of "The End of March":

> On the way back our faces froze on the other side.
> The sun came out for just a minute.
> For just a minute, set in their bezels of sand,
> the drab, damp, scattered stones
> were multi-colored,

and all those high enough threw out long shadows,
individual shadows, then pulled them in again.
They could have been teasing the lion sun,
except that now he was behind them
—a sun who'd walked the beach the last low tide,
making those big, majestic paw-prints,
who perhaps had batted a kite out of the sky to play with.

As always in Bishop's poems, details are matched without ever
being insisted on. The "long shadows" here reach back to the
"long, long books" and to the "lengths and lengths" of kite
string. That string, those paw-prints—the trail she's been fol-
lowing—all lead her to the sun. We can feel the decided con-
trast here, the sudden, dazzling emergence of the sun, a daylit
world of consciousness that is the opposite of everything in her
dark dream-house. Or we can sense the continuity, the sun
having been present all along in drops of daylight or in the
lovely diaphanous blue flame. It is a kind of magic fire, at once
alluringly beautiful and destructive. It can be found elsewhere
in Bishop's work—in the volcano spilling over in rivulets of
fire in "In the Waiting Room," for instance, or in Nate's
blacksmith shop in "In the Village."

Here in the austere grandeur of its conclusion, "The End of
March" becomes a poem very different from the one we had
been reading, a poem situated in absences and inabilities for
which she compensates by an unnerving solipsism. Now the
tone of voice grows elevated, and fanciful. The imagined ghost
on the water gives way to a personification. How are we to read
this parable (for that is how the poem urges us to read it now)?
Is it an exuberant tribute to the imagination that can conjure a
lion out of the sun, or can dream of an alternative life, or can
write the poem we are reading? Or do we have a rather grim
image of the poet imprisoned within herself, the pitting of a

scrappy human existence against the cold giant realities of nature? Perhaps the poem is deeply and darkly ironic, actually mocking, with a sad sympathy, the necessity for and inadequacy of our compensatory imaginings?

To answer such questions it is necessary to read the poem again, this time listening for its allusions to other poems which will complete or interpret it. Bishop was always a "literary" poet, building her poems out of her reading—a reading so thoroughly absorbed that it was indistinguishable from memory itself. At key moments in some poems she will quote directly from the Bible or George Herbert or Tennyson or Felicia Hemans or whomever. Elsewhere, she more slyly insinuates an older text, or echoes another poet's idiom or rhythms —now Keats or Neruda, now Donne or Yeats—so that the attentive reader will bring those other texts as a light to illuminate her poem. And it seems to me that in "The End of March" she had Wallace Stevens so strongly in mind that to read her poem correctly it is necessary to supplement it with several Stevens poems. I have already quoted Bishop asserting that Stevens was the main influence on her early work, and it seems right that in this late poem in some way about her career in poetry she again turns directly to Stevens. The playfully fabular quality of that lion-sun might as well be a trope from Stevens. And on a more serious level, the pathos of Bishop's sense of exile and dislocation, pressing in all her work, she may have learned to articulate from Stevens' example—the Stevens who wrote "From this the poem springs: that we live in a place / That is not our own and, much more, not ourselves, / And hard it is in spite of blazoned days."

But she may be making a more systematic series of allusions to Stevens. I want first to consider his short poem from 1930, "The Sun This March"—an important poem in the Stevens canon because it was the first he wrote to break a six-year silence that followed the publication of *Harmonium*. It is a poem about that silence, and about the voice of the imagination finally breaking through his dark nature:

> The exceeding brightness of this early sun
> Makes me conceive how dark I have become,
>
> And re-illumines things that used to turn
> To gold in broadest blue, and be a part
>
> Of a turning spirit in an earlier self.
> That, too, returns from out the winter's air,
>
> Like an hallucination come to daze
> The corner of the eye. Our element,
>
> Cold is our element and winter's air
> Brings voices as of lions coming down.
>
> Oh! Rabbi, rabbi, fend my soul for me
> And true savant of this dark nature be.

The network of images here—March, cold, sun, lion—is too obviously like that in Bishop's poem for me to comment. One may note a resemblance without invoking an influence, but here the resemblance is too close. And we can look still closer. In a letter, Stevens once explained his use of "rabbi" as referring to "the figure of a man devoted in the extreme to scholarship and at the same time to making some use of it for human purposes." The figure of Bishop hunched over her old books springs at once to mind. Harold Bloom has compared Stevens' "rabbi" to Emerson's "scholar"—in both instances a term for "poet." "In 'The Sun This March,' " writes Bloom, "the rabbi, like the poet, is always in the sun, and his function is both to defend and to shift Stevens, to reilluminate the poet's dark nature so that he can write poems again."

Let me pursue some of these images in other Stevens poems.

March was a symbolic season for him. The final poem in his *Collected Poems,* "Not Ideas About the Thing But the Thing Itself," is set in this "earliest ending of winter"—that is, the moment we may first turn from the mind of winter, the reductive and essential First Idea, and begin reimagining that First Idea as something more human, more fictive. The "scrawny cry" of March seems "like a sound in his mind":

> It was part of the colossal sun,
>
> Surrounded by its choral rings,
> Still far away. It was like
> A new knowledge of reality.

Or consider "Vacancy in the Park," and substitute sand for snow:

> March . . . Someone has walked across the snow,
> Someone looking for he knows not what. [. . .]
>
> It is like the feeling of a man
> Come back to see a certain house.

The certain house in "The End of March" may also be found in Stevens. I look to the second section of "The Auroras of Autumn":

> Farewell to an idea . . . A cabin stands,
> Deserted, on a beach. It is white,
> As by a custom or according to
>
> An ancestral theme or as a consequence
> Of an infinite course. The flowers against the wall
> Are white, a little dried, a kind of mark
>
> Reminding, trying to remind, of a white
> That was different, something else, last year
> Or before, not the white of an aging afternoon,

Whether fresher or duller, whether of winter cloud
Or of winter sky, from horizon to horizon.
The wind is blowing the sand across the floor.

Here, being visible is being white,
Is being of the solid of white, the accomplishment
Of an extremist in an exercise . . .

The season changes. A cold wind chills the beach.
The long lines of it grow longer, emptier,
A darkness gathers though it does not fall

And the whiteness grows less vivid on the wall.
The man who is walking turns blankly on the sand.
He observes how the north is always enlarging the change,

With its frigid brilliances, its blue-red sweeps
And gusts of great enkindlings, its polar green,
The color of ice and fire and solitude.

The auroras he observes are an image of his own imagination, "as grim as it is benevolent," a glorious violence without that challenges the violence within:

He opens the door of his house

On flames. The scholar of one candle sees
An Arctic effulgence flaring on the frame
Of everything he is. And he feels afraid.

The sun in Bishop's poem is her aurora, in sharp contrast to the small blue flame in her dream-house, where she is the scholar (or poet) of one candle. We could leave our reading of the poem here: two modes of imagination held against one another. But Bishop is rarely so stark. And if we follow Stevens a little farther, we can better gauge the ambivalence in Bishop's poem. This room we are in now is what Stevens elsewhere calls "a foyer of the spirit." And further, "Suppose these houses are composed of ourselves," Stevens asks in "An Ordinary Evening in New Haven," "Impalpable habitations that seem to move / In the movement of the colors of the mind. . . . colors whether of the sun / Or mind." He says this because he finally identifies the house with the sun, and so the sun with the self, and the self with the imagination: "what is this house composed of if not the sun, / These houses, these difficult objects, dilapidate / Appearances of what appearances, / Words, lines, not meanings, not communications, / Dark things without a double, after all."

At the end of Bishop's poem the sun is said to have "walked the beach the last low tide," exactly as the poet herself had been doing, encouraging us to make the identification. And this is the moment when Bishop is celebrating her powers by embodying them. Stevens had often used this same image. It is, notes Bloom, "an emblem of the power and menace of poetry." "The lion sleeps in the sun," writes Stevens in "Poetry is a Destructive Force," "It can kill a man." In its Transcendentalist representation, it presides over section XI of "An Ordinary Evening in New Haven":

> In the metaphysical streets of the physical town
> We remember the lion of Juda and we save
> The phrase . . . Say of each lion of the spirit
>
> It is a cat of a sleek transparency
> That shines with a nocturnal shine alone.
> The great cat must stand potent in the sun.

Bishop's lion is no killer; he merely bats kites. But if we have Stevens' use of the image in our mind's ear then we can calculate what mixed feelings Bishop is controlling by miniaturizing them, and what her true intentions are. The final word, unspoken in Bishop's poem, is also from Stevens. What happens (to ask a disallowed question) *after* her visionary moment? If we can further imagine the poet's walk back on that Duxbury beach, and then a fade-out, I wonder if the conclusion to "A Postcard from the Volcano," where Stevens broods on a poetry that outlives its saying, might not be a last flickering reflection on Bishop's poem:

> Children,
> Still weaving budded aureoles,
> Will speak our speech and never know,
>
> Will say of the mansion that it seems
> As if he that lived there left behind
> A spirit storming in blank walls,
>
> A dirty house in a gutted world,
> A tatter of shadows peaked to white,
> Smeared with the gold of the opulent sun.

It is hard to escape the conclusion that these are deliberate allusions, and that Bishop is asking us to read them into her poem. Stevens' grander version of these themes is both the context of Bishop's poem and its "meaning." Allusion is the lifeblood of poetry, coursing from poet to poet. Both Bishop and Stevens, of course, are part of a larger tradition of Romantic poetry whose images and themes they draw into their own work. Stevens once characterized tradition as "the frame of a repeated effect." If we just think of Bishop's proto-dream-house by the shore, or of Stevens' cabin on the beach, we can see them as poems in an American tradition of "shore odes" that stretches from Whitman to Ammons. It is a quintessential American mode: the poet alone on the margin, confronting the elements. But these same images are part of an older Romantic tradition as well. One thinks of Coleridge's Xanadu or Yeats' Byzantium, symbolic structures of eternity—"the dome of

Thought, the palace of the Soul" is Byron's phrase—placed on a shore, the rushing of time's mortal waters. Poets live between them, eternity and time, structures and space. The poetry of the past is itself a structure in which to shelter: a sun, a lion, a dream, a life.

III
WRITERS AND READERS

ROBERT PENN WARREN

RARE PROSPERITIES

ROBERT PENN WARREN's *New and Selected Poems 1923–1985* was published on the poet's eightieth birthday, not so much a tribute as a further installment. This was the fourth time Warren had made a selection of his poems. His first was in 1943, just before he embarked on his renowned series of novels that began with *All the King's Men*. His third selection was made in 1975, and in some ways it remains the best. Each time, of course, new work is favored at the editorial expense of earlier work, and his 1985 *New and Selected Poems*, because its opening section, "Altitudes and Extensions 1980–1984," is weaker than what follows it, makes a less forceful impression than the *Selected Poems* of a decade before.

The poems of Warren's old age find their directions by compass points that have guided him from the start: *near, far, now, then*. But there is a gravity at work called "downwardness" so that the poems, almost compulsively, explore

> The most secret channel a root drills in its personal reason.
> Here gravity is the only god, what knows no more
>
> Than the list for downwardness, and the deepest coil.

A characteristic opening for these late poems is "even as I begin I / Remember." And long memories prevail, from childhood and young manhood, or later encounters with the isolate self or with nature. The reasons are not only nostalgic, but enabling and emblematic. Warren's imagination has always been historical. He thinks in terms of history. Rather than an escape from or dominion over the constraints of history, language for Warren, and poetic language especially, is a product of history:

> If there is no history, there is no story.
> And no Time, no word.
> For then there is nothing for a word to be about, a word
>
> Being frozen Time only. . . .

The long poems of his career, from *Brother to Dragons* (1953; revised 1979) on through *Chief Joseph of the Nez Perce* (1983), are his most evident attempt to confront American history, and "frozen Time" may account for a certain stiffness—a hint of the *tableau vivant*—that pushes all of them but *Audubon: A Vision* to the side of one's main interest in Warren's work. What is compelling in these long poems is not their costume drama but their relentless moral inquiry, the true mode of the historical imagination. At their best, their motive is to unravel "the world's tangled and hieroglyphic beauty," to solicit its abiding mysteries, and to press charges against its failures and perversions. But this is a temperament that puts Warren at odds with the Emersonian strain of American literary culture —as it runs from Whitman to Stevens—that would recognize no beginnings but the present, no otherness but the self's own terms. This has been a literary argument that has not blotted Warren's imagination but enriched it. This questing and questioning temperament also puts him at odds with the lyrical and sublime instincts of his verse, and helps explain the abrupt shifts and peculiar harmonics in many of his shorter poems.

Any moral inquiry is discursive by its nature; it needs categories and conclusions, which have an emblematic function in Warren's poems. This, and the high rhetorical tradition he has worked in, combine to produce a manner of speaking that some readers object to. It is true that his late poems trade too easily, or at least too readily, in words like *doom, existence, vision, God, truth* (or worse, *Truth*). Because he had long since raised the important questions, he is inclined in these late poems merely to reiterate them. I prefer somewhat earlier versions.

These gatherings—and again, the 1975 edition makes this point more emphatically than the 1985 can—are valuable as a comprehensive survey of Warren's character and achievement as a poet. Certainly it is his poetry on which rests his claim to greatness, although two decades ago few would have predicted that with real confidence. After all, so much else about this artist was distracting. During the half-century of his career, his contributions to nearly every aspect of the literary art have been recognized, but his novels now seem more sturdy than significant, and his essays more feisty than definitive. But the poetry he has produced in the past twenty years has altered our sense of his career and its consequence. Given Warren's odd habit of arranging his *Selected*s in reverse chronological order, his newer work allows us to see his earlier verse as both an anticipation and an echo, the effect of which is to throw his recent poetry into an even higher relief and so to dramatize a remarkable event in the literature of our time by suddenly revealing to us a poet of unexpected and extraordinary power. Instances are rare of poets discovering such absolute strength so late in life, but a phrase from John Ashbery's *Three Poems* almost describes the phenomenon: "The great careers are like that: a slow burst that narrows to a final release." That is not exactly the right term for Warren, since his grand late release is not a narrowing but an expansion—of language into a heightened virtuosity and intensity, and of theme into his special version of the visionary mode. Still, one is eager to say, the great careers are like that. In fact, Warren's most recent and distinctive advocate, Harold Bloom, is now arguing in print that alone among living writers Warren deserves to be counted with the best American poets of our century. The risks of both hyperbole and prophecy are well known, and I am less interested here in ranking Warren than in responding to the obvious excellence of his work.

There are three conspicuous phases to Warren's poetic career, and I often ask myself why I cannot read the first of those phases—the poems written before 1954—with much excitement or pleasure. Clearly "Bearded Oaks" or "Picnic Remembered" have long ago earned a place on the shortlist of permanent poems. But I suspect that is less because they are worthy in themselves than because they are good poems of a certain kind. The kind of poem, that is, written by the group of Fugitives who were Warren's first peers and in whose company his work has since been discussed, compared, equated. John Crowe Ransom's wry (and overrated) elegies, and Allen Tate's severe odes and indictments are the products of true neoclassical sensibilities. But the rough-hewn narratives and abstracted metaphysics of Warren's work from this period seem awkwardly restrained by their dry formalism and uncertain diction, as if to check the indulgence of his essentially American-Romantic imagination. The effect is like a bust carved in burl oak. Like so many other poets of that era, he was under the spell of Eliot, though less the lure of Eliot's techniques (which were superior) than of his tastes and attitudes. And so, in doctrine disguised as paradox, Warren lamented over "the inherited defect," and brooded on unredeemed human nature, on the violence and despair of a time "born to no adequate definition of terror." I am left unconvinced by such poses.

Once he abandoned cultural mythologies and confronted history more immediately, his verse strengthened measurably, and the volumes from *Promises* (1957) through *Incarnations* (1968) give ample evidence of that. There are four long central poems that anchor this second period of his career, two celebrations and two elegies: "To a Little Girl, One Year Old, In a Ruined Fortress," for his daughter; "Promises," for his son; "Mortmain," for his father; and "Tale of Time," for his mother. Each of these moving familial poems is a part of Warren's effort during this time to explore "how cause flows backward from effect"—effects of either gain or loss, birth or death. His emphasis shifts now from guilt to grace; and even as grace, the reverse of guilt which gives form to experience, gives freedom, so too Warren's verse grows more supple and expressive, favoring sprawling forms whose dimensions and dynamics were determined by the life they record. It was during this period, too, that several characteristics of his work emerged more distinctly—among them his juxtaposition or conflation of the narrative and the meditational, modes that most nearly parallel his instincts and notions. As a Southerner raised in a tradition of tale-telling, and as a gifted novelist, narratives seem a natural choice for Warren's poems, but behind the method is his deeper conviction that experience transpires in time. This idea extends even to Warren's obsession with book titles that include the dates of composition, and with arranging his poems into sequences that stress dramatic interplay and cumulative force. And on the other hand, there is his penchant for discursive meditation, always inflected by his personal accent. As if experience and history were not fully self-sufficient, Warren often epitomizes them into conceptual dialectics. "To have truth," he says in one poem, "Something must be believed, / And repetition and congruence, / To say the least, are necessary." Truth, then, lies somewhere between the instance and eternity, the fact and the form. Poem by poem, Warren explores both sides of that border.

Incarnations was a traditional book, and an uneven one;

indeed, all along Warren seems to have had trouble recognizing his own most successful work—a question of taste, not talent. But I remember being astonished by several poems when that volume first appeared. They are still superb: "Natural History," "Myth on Mediterranean Beach: Aphrodite as Logos," "Masts at Dawn." The poet here begins to unfold the world's parable with the bold intellectual and sensuous command that has marked his poetry since that time. What might seem a surrender—"The world means only itself," concludes "Riddle in the Garden"—is actually his more complex project to find beauty in "the fume-track of necessity." "Masts at Dawn" offers the injunction another way: "We must try / To love so well the world that we may believe, in the end, in God." This necessity is urged in tones increasingly sharp, spare, eccentric, and often oracular. All of the work in this later phase of his career is spoken by his new voice. What before had struck the ear as stiff now sounds nearly scriptural. (In fact, I suspect that the Old Testament cadences are the strongest influence on Warren's new line.) The verse is now often free, the voice more formal. Again, some readers consider it fustian or old-fashioned, but they miss the strange, at times unsettling impact his use of inversion and stark enjambments produces. And there is always a marvelous lyrical counterpointing, such as this interlude from *Audubon: A Vision* (1969):

October: and the bear,
Daft in the honey-light, yawns.

The bear's tongue, pink as a baby's, out-crisps to the curled
    tip,
It bleeds the black blood of the blueberry.

The teeth are more importantly white
Than has ever been imagined.

The bear feels his own fat
Sweeten, like a drowse, deep to the bone.

Bemused, above the fume of ruined blackberries,
The last bee hums.

The wings, like mica, glint
In the sunlight.

He leans on his gun. Thinks
How thin is the membrane between himself and the world.

That quiet moment is one of the many superimposed images that make up *Audubon* and its cumulative definition of man, identified now with his passion, now with his fate. It is easy to see why the figure of Audubon—in his own words, "the Man Naked from his hand and yet free from acquired Sorrow"—must have been compelling to Warren, for he is at once artist and adventurer, always on the edge of things, wilderness or legend. The details Warren evokes from Audubon's history center on how "the world declares itself" to such a man, and portray how truth cannot be spoken or even embodied but "can only be enacted, and that in dream." What cannot be understood can be known. "What is love? / One name for it is knowledge." Poised between engagement and comprehension, between violence and awe, Audubon is Warren's most eloquent characterization, and his story has been shaped into one of the best long poems ever written by an American.

Such a poem might have capped the career of any poet less unusual than Warren. Instead, he went on to extend and amplify his mastery in six more full collections, from *Or Else* (1974) to his *New and Selected*. At first glance, they seem a sort of anthology of Warren's tried and true: the down-home ballad, the political prayer, homages to dead writers, the rural narratives and metaphysical lyrics. He returns to all the familiar forms, but with a new emphasis and artistry. Throughout, he is driven by the "compulsion to try to convert what now is *was* / Back into what *is*." The blunt title of *Or Else*, for instance, implies both ultimatum and alternatives. Both are echoed in the staccato delivery of these overlapping attempts to sift lost evidence—his father's death, himself as a boy, a remembered chair or saw—for some sense of the continuity of a life's experiences. It is the noble Wordsworthian ambition to recapture redemptive spots of time: to wake, as Warren says, from "that darkness of sleep which / Is the past, and is / The self," with a question: "Have I learned how to live?" Warren often sounds such a moralistic note, but it can be deceptive since his concern is more existential—the necessarily defeated effort to restore the logic of the original dream, to resolve the innocence since fulfilled in "the realm of contingency."

Since "Time / Is the mirror into which you stare," the discovery of its history is always a self-definition—mirrored in a few controlling images: "Man lives by images. They / Lean at us from the world's wall, and Time's." Like the conjuring process of staring, there are certain images that are obsessive for Warren, that recur continually in his work and are at once its source and surface. The poem "Rattlesnake Country," for instance, ends among the dark roots of his "Indecipherable passion and compulsion":

<blockquote>
I remember
The need to enter the night-lake and swim out toward
The distant moonset. Remember
The blue-tattered flick of white flame at the rock-hole
In the instant before I lifted up
My eyes to the high sky that shivered in its hot whiteness.
And sometimes—usually at dawn—I remember the cry on
    the mountain.

All I can do is to offer my testimony.
</blockquote>

That mountain cry is sometimes a bird hung high in the sky, or a star, as in "Birth of Love," one of the best poems Warren has ever written. On another of these night-swims, a man watches a woman climb ashore ahead of him to dry herself off with what light remains. It is a moment "nonsequential and absolute," a spot between times,

> . . . and in his heart he cries out that, if only
> He had such strength, he would put his hand forth
> And maintain it over her to guard, in all
> Her out-goings and in-comings, from whatever
> Inclemency of sky or slur of the world's weather
> Might ever be. In his heart
> He cries out. Above
>
> Height of the spruce-night and heave of the far mountain,
>   he sees
> The first star pulse into being. It gleams there.
>
> I do not know what promise it makes to him.

An example of how obsessive these images are for the poet is the fact that this poem flashes back to a scene from a book now over forty years old, *All the King's Men*. Jack Burden is remembering a storm-struck picnic with Anne and Adam Stanton when the three of them were teenagers. Jack and Anne are swimming under a dark sky: a gull crosses high over them. He watches her floating profile sharpened against "the far-off black trees."

> That was a picnic I never forgot.
> I suppose that that day I first saw Anne and Adam as separate, individual people, whose ways of acting were special, mysterious, and important. And perhaps, too, that day I first saw myself as a person. But that is not what I am

Robert Penn Warren   87

talking about. What happened was this: I got an image in my head that never got out. We see a great many things and can remember a great many things, but that is different. We get very few of the true images in our heads of the kind I am talking about, the kind which become more and more vivid for us as if the passage of years did not obscure their reality but, year by year, drew off another veil to expose a meaning which we had only dimly surmised at first. Very probably the last veil will not be removed, for there are not enough years, but the brightness of the image increases and our conviction increases that the brightness is meaning, or the legend of meaning, and without the image our lives would be nothing except an old piece of film rolled on a spool and thrown into a desk drawer among the unanswered letters.

The image I got in my head that day was the image of her face lying in the water, very smooth, with the eyes closed, under the dark greenish-purple sky, with the white gull passing over.

That is a crucial gloss on the method and meaning of Warren's poetry. The brightening image which he has been unveiling for as long as his career is the deliberate mystery of identity, of the legends that alone define and sustain identity. His primary scene's most impressive aspect is the bird above—which in his poetry can be a hawk or star or sun, the symbol of power with which Warren has identified his ambitions from the very beginning, in a high Romantic gesture. Several of his most impressive late poems—"Red-Tail Hawk and Pyre of Youth," "Heart of Autumn," "Mortal Limits"—participate in this symbol. The glorious "Evening Hawk" is perhaps its fullest testament:

> His wing
> Scythes down another day, his motion

Is that of the honed steel-edge, we hear
The crashless fall of stalks of Time.

The head of each stalk is heavy with the gold of our error.
Look! look! he is climbing the last light
Who knows neither Time nor error, and under
Whose eye, unforgiving, the world, unforgiven, swings
Into shadow.

      Long now,
The last thrush is still, the last bat
Now cruises in his sharp hieroglyphics. His wisdom
Is ancient, too, and immense. The star
Is steady, like Plato, over the mountain.

If there were no wind we might, we think, hear
The earth grind on its axis, or history
Drip in darkness like a leaking pipe in the cellar.

The rather anti-climactic mention of history at the end of this poem is meant to inhibit Warren's total giving of himself over to his ecstatic vision. But that is a measure of this poet's wisdom, or what he would call the "perfected pain of conscience": to be able to encounter the sublime directly, and yet to temper his visionary impulse with a self-consciousness that includes both conscience and an eye for the incongruent detail. That hawk is, of course, the transcendental poet, but also a terrible divine presence, not unlike the "God" of Warren's late poetry who is an indifferent, unknowable, immanent principle of reality both feared and desired.

In his *Democracy in America*, de Tocqueville predicted that the poetry of the future here would have as its subject not the senses but the inner soul and destinies of mankind, "man himself, taken aloof from his age and his country, and standing in the presence of Nature and of God, with his passions, his doubts, his rare prosperities, and inconceivable wretchedness." I can think of no better description of Robert Penn Warren. Among his contemporaries he is our most truly American poet, working in a large-scale imaginative tradition that continues to be a vital source for poetry.

ROBERT LOWELL

A BACKWARD GLANCE

S OME POETS embody a culture. Others are appropriated by
it—as, in a sentimental way, Robert Frost was—despite
the antagonisms in the poems themselves. Still other poets,
while seemingly poised at the center of things, manage to keep
themselves at a critical distance. Their work is the product of a
sensibility at once aggressive and transformational. They have
a body of knowledge, plus an unusual diagnostic talent. Their
poems are not merely commentaries on the life of men and
women in history, but acts of imagination to restore that life
to its true moral and emotional dimensions. W. H. Auden was
such a poet. His career, with its shifting philosophical alle-
giances and stylistic maneuvers, both followed and guided the
currents of feeling in his lifetime, their public manifestations
and their unconscious motivations. Robert Lowell was also
such a poet. Ours has been called, in fact, the Age of Lowell.
Not only did his poetry, volume by volume, display the char-
acter of his generation, most often revealed in the details of his
own personality, but transcended that character to become its
animating conscience as well. He was, in Richard Poirier's deci-
sive phrase, "our truest historian."

The interpretations brought to Lowell's poetry have been

encouraged by the very traditional ambitions of his career and by the distinctive changes in his work. Insofar as he was both heir to and spokesman for several, often contradictory traditions—from Old Boston to the New Left—his readers have been able to find a key to his career in concerns as different as confessional realism and apocalyptic politicism. What makes his *Selected Poems* so intriguing is that the book provides Lowell's own sense of his career. There are 203 poems in it. At least a third of each collection, except for *Life Studies,* has been deleted, and though any given reader's favorite poem may be missing, we must allow the poet his choices: to each his disown. There are a few minor revisions of little consequence. For instance, in lines from "Beyond the Alps" that we are familiar with as "long-haired Victorian sages accepted the universe, / while breezing on their trust funds through the world," Lowell has altered "accepted" to "bought," and thereby substituted a minor quibble for the appropriate verb. There occurred, as well, yet another rearrangement of those endlessly revised and reordered sonnets that so obsessed the last phase of Lowell's formulation of experience. Poems from *For Lizzie and Harriet* have been moved back into *History,* and that book has been split into two dominant sections of meditation and autobiography. The reasoning behind this ordonnance, and that of the selection generally, is explained by Lowell in his prefatory note as an attempt to marshal from the range of his life's work a cumulative series of integral sequences, in order to clarify the topical preoccupations of any one volume and the thematic interconnections among them all. To that extent, and with a few exceptions, this *Selected Poems* continues to afford us an adjusted vantage on his extraordinary art. His impulse toward existential narrative, his calculated use of surreal imagery, his deployment of historical allusion—all of these emerge with a heightened resonance. Likewise, his confessional method, first announced in *Life Studies* and later reaffirmed in *The Dolphin*, is revealed with new force.

AS IN his career, so too in his *Selected Poems* is *Life Studies* given a centering pride of place. A stark claim by one of his critics has come to seem, after nearly thirty years, less imposing and more inevitable: "It can be said of *Life Studies*, as it can be said of Walt Whitman's *Song of Myself* and of T. S. Eliot's *The Waste Land*, that American poetry could not be the same after Lowell's book was published." Not only has the book been regarded as a profound influence on American poetry generally and as both the origin and sanction of the confessional movement, but it has been represented as the radical, decisive reversal of Lowell's early style and subject, so that the poet discovered significance at once in and for himself. For so momentous a moment, Lowell himself offered an ironically simple explanation: "Well, I remember I started one of these poems ["Commander Lowell"] in Marvell's four-foot couplet and showed it to my wife. And she said 'why not say what really happened?' " What *really* happened was new to *Life Studies*, but Lowell had been trying to say it all along. In a discussion of *Life Studies* that recalled *Lord Weary's Castle*, the poet was not merely being coy when he said: "I don't feel my experience changed very much. It seems to me it's clearer to me now than it was then, but it's very much the same sort of thing that went into the religious poems—the same sort of struggle, light and darkness, the flux of experience. . . . All your poems are in a sense one poem."

The subject of that "one poem" was consistent—what Jay Martin once termed "the fate of selfhood in time"—and its plot, through successive volumes was to articulate the actuality of that fate. His earliest and best critic, Randall Jarrell, quickly perceived the pattern of concern in the poet's development, and his judgment of *Lord Weary's Castle* was prophetic for the career itself: "Anyone who compares Mr. Lowell's earlier and later poems will see this movement from constriction to liberation as his work's ruling principle of growth." "Growth" may seem an odd word to describe a process that involves stylistic decomposition and thematic regression, but since that process also involves Lowell's self-discovery, as poet and man, its progress of risks is the growth into himself. That progress is at once tortuous and simple: a king's through the guts of a beggar. Its literary modes of expression — from the symbolic to the mythological to the historical — reflect his personal deconversion from faith to fiction to fact. In his *Notebook*, there is a line that could be used to graph the intention and effect of all his work: "I am learning to live in history."

In his Introduction to Lowell's first book *Land of Unlikeness* (1944), Allen Tate offered an important observation about the early poems — one that applies equally to *Lord Weary's Castle* (1946) which incorporates the best of *Land of Unlikeness* and so is the convenient focus for a discussion of Lowell's beginnings. There are, Tate noted, two types of poems in the collection, "not yet united." The first are "the explicitly religious poems" with their intellectualized and often satirical Christian symbolism, and the second are those "richer in immediate experience," "more dramatic, the references being personal and historical and the symbolism less willed and explicit." Together, they comprise what Hugh Staples called a "poetry of rebellion," and to that extent it reflects Lowell's own insistent series of rebellions: his departure from Harvard for Kenyon, his conversion to Catholicism, his adoption of the stern disciplines of Tate and Ransom, his conscientious objection to wartime military service and his subsequent jail-term. It was an attitude — a "fanaticism of spirit and form" — which R. P. Blackmur found either mirrored in or affecting Lowell's struggle with his materials: "It is as if he demanded to *know* (to judge, to master) both the substance apart from the form with which he handles it and form apart from the substance handled in order to set them fighting." But rebellion was less the reason for than the result of the informing vision and voice of these poems. The epigraph from St. Bernard affixed to *Land of Unlikeness* offers the cause in a comparison: *Inde anima dissimilis deo inde dissimilis est et sibi* (As the soul is unlike God, so is it unlike itself). This alienation, suspended from "the jerking noose of time," is masked behind a Catholic mysticism that holds the poet apart from both unredeemed nature and the burdens of history. His "New World eschatologies" pose the poet as Moses on the mountain, scornfully watching his contemporaries worshipping a golden calf fattened on three centuries of Puritan hypocrisy that has rendered unto Caesar and Mammon what is God's. "Our ransom is the rubble of his death," our punishment the rubble of ours: "Raise us, Mother, we fell down / Here hugger-mugger in the jellied fire: / Our sacred earth in our day was our curse" ("The Dead in Europe"). This "kingfisher dives on you in fire"; as he said at the time, of Hopkins: "His daring is sober, his obedience is alive."

Lowell's militant faith served him also as a defiance of and defense against the "sewage" that "sickens the rebellious seas" ("Salem")—his own past and that of his family, which emerge only emblematically in *Lord Weary's Castle*. In such poems as "In the Attic" and "In the Cage," or the family sequence, "The Quaker Graveyard in Nantucket," "In Memory of Arthur Winslow," "Winter in Dunbarton," and "Mary Winslow," the personal elements, as Gabriel Pearson has noted, function as pretexts rather than as motives for the poems, whose energies are further drained from their subjects to the foreground of their verse. A description of his dying grandfather, for instance, is refracted in allusions that bully rather than broaden or penetrate the experience:

> This Easter, Arthur Winslow, less than dead,
> Your people set you up in Phillips' House
> To settle off your wrestling with the crab—
> The claws drop flesh upon your yachting blouse
> Until longshoreman Charon came and stab
> Through your adjusted bed
> And crush the crab . . .
>   and the ghost
> Of risen Jesus walks the waves to run
> Arthur upon a trumpeting black swan
> Beyond Charles River to the Acheron
> Where the wide waters and their voyager are one.
>
>   ("In Memory of Arthur Winslow")

The difference between the procedures of *Lord Weary's Castle* and those of *Life Studies* can best be seen by comparing their poems on Lowell's prison experience. "In the Cage" minimizes its details, anxious to reduce them to symbol:

> Canaries beat their bars and scream.
> We come from tunnels where the spade
> Pick-axe and hod for plaster steam
> In mud and insulation. Here
> The Bible-twisting Israelite
> Fasts for his Harlem. It is night,
> And it is vanity, and age
> Blackens the heart of Adam. Fear,
> The yellow chirper, beaks its cage.

What this poems portends, "Memories of West Street and Lepke" portrays—the "truth" of the experience is dramatized rather than extrapolated. The later poem is given a specific human context—first of all, one of retrospection, set by the opening stanzas, which makes past and present analogous rather than symbolic. And secondly, one of temporality: instead of the timeless abstraction "It is night, / and it is vanity," Lowell offers the unique moment: "teaching on Tuesdays," "I have a nine months' daughter," "These are the tranquillized *Fifties*, / and I am forty," "Given a year, / I walked on the roof of the West Street Jail," and the details of life in that jail are opened out towards epiphany rather than closed down in symbol. Even more exemplary is the poem "Rebellion" in *Lord Weary's Castle*, which describes his traumatic striking of his father:

> There was rebellion, father, when the mock
> French windows slammed and you hove backward, rammed
> Into your heirlooms, screens, a glass-cased clock,
> The highboy quaking to its toes. You damned
> My arm that cast your house upon your head
> And broke the chimney flintlock on your skull.

Then at once the incident is cast as a parricidal nightmare and symbolized to stand for a universal pattern of corrupted authority and cruel rebellion:

> Then
> Behemoth and Leviathan
> Devoured our mighty merchants. None could arm
> Or put to sea. O father, on my farm
> I added field to field
> And I have sealed
> An everlasting pact
> With Dives to contract
> The world that spreads in pain;
> But the world spread
> When the clubbed flintlock broke my father's brain.

After the almost ritualistic degradation of his father, from "The Mills of the Kavanaughs" to "91 Revere Street" and "Commander Lowell," the poet returns to this incident in *Notebook*. Here the reworked details yield to statement rather than symbol:

> There was rebellion, Father, when the door slammed . . .
> front doors were glass then . . . and you hove backward
>   rammed
> into the heirlooms, screens, the sun-disk clock,
> the highboy quaking to its toes . . . father,
> I do not know how to unsay I knocked you down.

And added to the incident, in a preceding poem, is its apparent explanation—a bit of collegiate chivalry excusing deeper motives:

> My father's letter to your father, saying
> tersely and much too stiffly that he knew
> you'd been coming to my college rooms alone—. . .
>
> then punctiliously handing the letter from my father.
> I knocked him down. He half-reclined on the carpet;
> Mother called from the top of the carpeted stairs—
> our glass door locking behind me, no cover; you
> idling in your station wagon, no retreat.

There is neither cover nor retreat from the guilt admitted in this new recollection:

> I struck my father; later my apology
> hardly scratched the surface of his invisible
> coronary . . . never to be effaced.

The sense of guilt is extended by further regret in a later reverie, where the two men speak across a dream:

> We are joined in the arts, though old. Then I,
> 'I have never loved you so much in all our lives.'
> And he, 'Doesn't it begin at the beginning?'

In *History's* still later versions of these poems, Lowell even names the girl (Anne Dick) and the year (1936), a specificity

that pressures a revaluation that turns finally towards under-
standing:

> I think, though I didn't believe it, you were my airhole,
> and resigned perhaps from the Navy to be an airhole—
> that Mother not warn me to put my socks on before my
>   shoes.

("To Daddy")

The *Selected Poems* rather self-consciously minimizes the
impacted apocalyptic aspect of *Lord Weary's Castle*, in favor of
those poems Tate referred to as "richer in immediate experi-
ence." Gone are some of the standards by which we are accus-
tomed to evaluate the book: "The Dead in Europe," "Children
of Light," "Salem," and "Concord," just to cite a convenient
quartet. Stripped of its mystical contortions, it is easier now to
see the book's treatment of concentric alienations as the prelude
to Lowell's versions of the theme, under different guises, in
subsequent collections. But what disturbs me is that the same
argument which may have resulted in his decision may also
have occasioned the poet's grievous cuts from his next book,
The Mills of the Kavanaughs (1951). Perhaps Lowell came to
agree with the majority of his critics who, unlike myself, seem
to consider the book an exercise in verbal self-indulgence. As if
to correct that impression, Lowell omitted one of the volume's
seven poems, cut out the second part of "Her Dead Brother,"
lopped 107 lines from the middle of "Thanksgiving's Over,"
and retained only the final five of the title poem's 38 long
stanzas. Not only is the tonal impact of the book's secular
melancholy lost, but by sacrificing the narrative and psycholog-
ical coherence of individual poems, he distorted the crucial
importance the book maintains as his ambitious and pivotal
compromise between his early manner and his later material.
Its series of dramatic monologues, which grows out of such

similar but less accomplished poems in *Lord Weary's Castle* as "Between the Porch and the Altar" and "The Death of the Sheriff," shifts Lowell's objective method from equivalent symbols, which abstracted experience to a point viewed *sub specie aeternitatis*, to organizing myths, both allusive and invented, which express feelings as events rather than as images, in a narrative form which stresses personality and association, contingency and motive. Though these mythic monologues remain dramas of remission and evasion, they indicate that Lowell no longer wished to transform or transcend his personality, but to integrate its conflicting motifs. Poems like "Falling Asleep over the Aeneid" and "Mother Marie Therese" seem self-absorbed in a gorgeous display of the form itself, but generally in this book Lowell, like one of his characters, has "gone underground / Into myself." The voice is subdued to a new control, the scope narrowed from cultural to personal decline, from civilization to the family, from the Church to a marriage. Though myth tends to repress its determining history and restricts identity to fiction's individualized type, it allows access to more intimate human relationships and adjusts its structures to such subjects. Each poem in *The Mills of the Kavanaughs* deals with a present relationship to the past, and as one critic says, the book "shares with *Life Studies* this intensity of memory." Like "The Fat Man in the Mirror," Lowell reflects on the consequences of time: "This I . . . serves / Time before the mirror." But as yet that mirror gives back doubled images—"the bars / Still caged her window— half a foot from mine. / It mirrored mine" ("Thanksgiving's Over")—fictionalized variations of themes from Lowell's own life: fantasies of incest, parricide and suicide, memories of adultery and emotional betrayals. The poems all link thematically into a question anguished over by one of their characters: "Michael, was there warrant / For killing love?" ("Thanksgiving's Over").

From our later perspective, we can see clearly the continuity and the concessions. "Mother Marie Therese" evokes the world of his grandparents, and "Falling Asleep over the Aeneid" that of Mordecai Myers, whom we know from *Life Studies*. More direct, though still reticent, is the title poem, which conflates the stories of two failed marriages: Lowell's parents', and his own to Jean Stafford. The correspondences are sufficiently obvious. To his parents: a decaying aristocracy in a Maine setting: the Kavanaugh family motto ("Cut down we flourish") which is the same as that of Lowell's maternal ancestors, the Winslows; Harry Kavanaugh's naval career and ignominious end. To himself: the famished Catholicism, along with details that recur in a later poem about Jean Stafford, "The Old Flame." The guilt thus introjected and projected—"her gambling with herself / Is love of self"—is maneuvered through Anne Kavanaugh's dreams and memories of her weak husband, ironically interwoven with reference to Pluto's rape of Persephone. Beneath her fantasies lies the need to redo, to undo the reality she finds she has given—and lost—her life to:

> "God knows!" she marvels. "Harry, *Kavanaugh*
> Was lightly given. Soon enough we saw
> Death like the Bourbon after Waterloo,
> Who learning and forgetting nothing, knew
> Nothing but ruin.

It is this same ruined reality which cuts through the mythic resonance of her conclusion: "Love, I gave / Whatever brought me gladness to the grave."

DURING THE eight years that intervened before his next book, *Life Studies* (1959), Lowell's philosophy of composition underwent a radical revaluation. The influences on that process were multiple: some of them personal (the death of his mother in

1954, and his subsequent hospitalizations and private psycho-
therapy), some of them literary. The poet himself began to
think that the style of his early poems was "distant, symbol-
ridden, and willfully difficult," and occluded their sense. His
exposure to the Beats and to the peculiar responsibilities of
communication demanded by reading poetry aloud, interested
him in a more colloquial approach to diction and the dynamics
of narrative, while his simultaneous immersion in prose studies
—especially the subdued, realistic precision of Chekhov and
Flaubert—confirmed him in the need for a more relaxed rhythm
and line, for a syntax responsible to voice and a tone that would
both prompt and project his subject. And aside from his ac-
quaintance at this time with the confessional verse of W. D.
Snodgrass and his student Anne Sexton, the work of two other
poets was also a necessary example. Lowell's praise for them at
the time points to the lessons he learned, when he singled out
the "simplicity and nakedness" of William Carlos Williams'
charged details, and Elizabeth Bishop's "unrhetorical, cool, and
brilliantly thought out poems." The immediate results of this
Nacherziehung are, sadly, not included in the *Selected Poems*.
The first is his "translations" from Continental poets, gathered
as *Imitations* (1961), a project Lowell called "both a continua-
tion of my own bias and a release from myself." Both the
impulse behind and the subject of Lowell's exploration of the
major European tradition is self-consciousness. His cultural
memories, rather than his strictly personal ones, are drawn out
into his characteristic voice and are narrowed to his thematic
concerns. In his Introduction, Lowell insisted that the poems
be read "as a sequence, one voice running through many per-
sonalities, contrasts and repetitions." That "one voice" speaks
of the disgust and longing, despair and endurance, the art and
morality that his own experiences focus in *Life Studies* and the
later confessions. The second result was another sort of imita-
tion from life—the prose of "91 Revere Street," the medium

from which he transposed the initial poems in the "Life Studies" sequence. By means of these experiments, he found a new style, and as with any strong poet dominated the influences on his work, so that the emergent voice was something new for American poetry. Replacing the strictures of imposed form, Lowell's new voice worked with subtle modulations of stanza, varying rhythm, unobtrusive rhyme and sharp detail, to achieve an effect of "heightened conversation." Mark Strand once called this voice "a rhetorical compromise between nostalgia and horror"—that is to say, between memory and interpretation, between emotional response and moral reaction. This is not so much a compromise as a cause, since the technical achievement was subordinated to a larger purpose. Lowell explained it this way: "In *Life Studies* I wanted to see how much of my personal story and memories I could get into poetry. To a large extent, it was a technical problem, as most problems in poetry are. But it was also something of a cause: to extend the poem to include, without compromise, what I felt and knew." So the mystical commitment of the early symbolist verse becomes a moral commitment in the confessional verse; honesty replaces devotion, fact replaces faith, in the poet's shift from ideology to history, from Catholicism to psychoanalysis as a method of self-interpretation, from apocalyptic rebellion to ironic detachment.

The two poems which open and end *Life Studies* (1959)— "Beyond the Alps" and "Skunk Hour"—should be read as complementary. Both recount Lowell's partial recoveries—in the one poem, from his loss of faith in God; in the other, from his loss of belief in life. The first is set at dawn, while the second transpires during "a dark night"; the first involves a new freedom depressed by reality, the second struggles against what Lowell calls a "final darkness where the one free act is suicide." Even details are paired: the Paris pullman becomes a Tudor Ford; the Alps are levelled to "a hill's skull," the Vatican to a Trinitarian church, Minerva to a hermit heiress, skirt-mad Mussolini to a summer millionaire, Pius XII to a "fairy decorator," the "monstrous human crush" to a column of skunks, the Etruscan cup to a cup of sour cream. And both poems converge on the single, dark realization of the volume: "I myself am hell." That ironic, existential affirmation is both suffered and earned in the poems between these two. *Life Studies* begins with a renunciation of the consolations of culture and religion that had previously sustained Lowell's art and life: "Much against my will / I left the City of God where it belongs." Will surrenders to experience, eternity to history, as Lowell sets out to discover where *he* belongs. In this modern, parallaxed *Prelude*, the poet arranges his significant spots of time, pausing at moments of crisis like infernal circles, into the definition of himself that presents a life in which the only innocence is insanity, the only resolution a scavenging survival.

Among the several "objective" poems in the book are four tributes to writers. Two of them—Delmore Schwartz and Hart Crane—are posed as Lowell's ambivalent self-portrait as poet, both stalled and visionary: the vantage his past has afforded. As one possible self, his memory of Schwartz parodies the paralysis of ambition:

> We drank and eyed
> the chicken-hearted shadows of the world.
> Underseas fellows, nobly mad,
> we talked away our friends. . . .
>
> The room was filled
> with cigarette smoke circling the paranoid,
>
> inert gaze of Coleridge, back
> from Malta—his eyes lost in flesh, lips baked and black.
>
> ("To Delmore Schwartz")

The "Words for Hart Crane," on the other hand, count the cost of achievement: "Who asks for me, the Shelley of my age, / must lay his heart out for my bed and board." The other two, older writers—Ford Madox Ford and George Santayana—are recalled by Lowell less as eventual versions of himself than as father-figures. In both there is the natural nobility of the artist—as in his description of Santayana dying at Santo Stefano:

> Old Trooper, I see your child's red crayon pass,
> bleeding deletions on the galleys you hold
> under your throbbing magnifying glass,
> that worn arena, where the whirling sand
> and broken-hearted lions lick your hand
> refined by bile as yellow as a lump of gold.

("For George Santayana")

The groping ineptness he mildly mocks in Ford is redeemed by simple affection: "Ford / you were a kind man and you died in want" ("Ford Madox Ford"). Lowell's gentle tolerance and genuine sympathy for Ford are in sharp contrast to the relentless severity in the portrait of his own father in "91 Revere Street," the long prose reminiscence which precedes and grounds the "Life Studies" sequence, and which establishes the model of failed relationships which the poems further explore. By eliminating the prose, the "Life Studies" sequence in *Selected Poems* is a less effective foreshortening of the elaborate family romance Lowell was dramatizing. In the original, it functioned as an incisive study of exhaustion and compensation, and the leisure that prose allows extended the perspective of time and the perceptions of memory, as the adult's art reconstructs the child's experiences from which that art derives: "The things and their owners come back urgent with life and meaning— because finished, they are endurable and perfect." Unlike the poet when he writes, his past is *une nature morte*, a life to be studied for what it may yield to the unfinished, endured present. The resulting poems—the only real sequence completely preserved in the *Selected Poems*—are thus restored photographs, still moments of present time, "open and single-surfaced." The first three deal with the child's desperate hold on the static but secure, masculine world of his grandfather. Like Proust, Lowell reverts in his research to the primary sensations of our instinctual origins: "One of my hands was cool on a pile / of black earth, the other warm / on a pile of lime." From such details his grandfather's home and way of life are narrated: "Like my Grandfather, the décor / was manly, comfortable, / overbearing, disproportioned." The child is another ornament in this décor—"I was a stuffed toucan"—a part of the same refuge he sought from his parents:

> "I won't go with you. I want to stay with Grandpa!"
> That's how I threw cold water
> on my Mother and Father's
> watery martini pipe dreams at Sunday dinner.
> . . . Fontainebleau, Mattapoisett, Puget Sound. . . .
> Nowhere was anywhere after a summer
> at my Grandfather's farm.

But Lowell slowly undercuts this indulgent Edwardian world, as in the description of his "Great Aunt Sarah" who would sit all day at her dummy piano, a parody of her life forty years earlier when

> Each morning she practiced
> on the grand piano at Symphony Hall,
> deathlike in the off-season summer—
> its naked Greek statues draped with purple
> like the saints in Holy Week. . . .
> On recital day, she failed to appear.

And a world, a time, narrows to "My Last Afternoon with Uncle Devereux" who he learns is dying of cancer at 29, a realization which cancels childhood by turning sensations into consciousness:

> He was dying of the incurable Hodgkin's disease. . . .
> My hands were warm, then cool, on the piles
> of earth and lime,
> a black pile and a white pile. . . .
> Uncle Devereux would blend to the one color.

"Dunbarton" continues the transference to his grandfather in order to invoke an attenuated identity, and the next poem, "Grandparents," suddenly shifts to the present with an allusion to Henry Vaughan: "the nineteenth century, tired of children, is gone. / They're all gone into a world of light; the farm's my own." This complex poem, one of the book's strongest, maintains its doubled perspectives, adult and adolescent, until they blend in a conclusion which rescues its own sentimentality by balancing the necessary nostalgia for a secure love with the pattern of rebellion familiar from Lowell's earlier poetry:

> Grandpa! Have me, hold me, cherish me!
> Tears smut my fingers. There
> half my life-lease later,
> I hold an *Illustrated London News*—;
> disloyal still,
> I doodle handlebar
> mustaches on the last Russian Czar.

The following six poems move from that impossible relationship on to the failed lives and marriage of Lowell's parents, as if they were the overdetermining factor in his own. The tone of "Commander Lowell" is, at best, one of condescension— "Poor Father"—and at worst, one of scorn—"[I] cringed because Mother, new / caps on all her teeth, was born anew / at forty." Their empty life, together and alone, is carefully detailed, Lowell falling back on quoted phrases and understatement to document and dead-pan his revelations until the narrative is overtaken by a sort of resigned sympathy:

> Ready, afraid
> of living alone till eighty,
> Mother mooned in a window,
> as if she had stayed on a train
> one stop past her destination.

("For Sale")

And the harsh realism of "Sailing Home from Rapallo" allows its irony to discover the kinship in sonship:

> In the grandiloquent lettering on Mother's coffin,
> *Lowell* had been misspelled LOVEL.
> The corpse
> was wrapped like *panetone* in Italian tinfoil.

The next group of three poems—"Waking in the Blue," "Home After Three Months Away," and "Memories of West Street and Lepke"—turn to his hospitalizations and imprisonment, analogous versions of the entrapping past: the poet's failed relationships with himself and his society. "A sheepish calm" falls over this section: "Cured, I am frizzled, stale and small." (That adjective "sheepish" reminds me of how often Lowell used animals as emblems both of the natural order and of a sacrificial victimization—victims along with the children, parents, and prisoners in his poems. For a man so fascinated by power, he also knew its cost.) Cured of the past's illusions and sterilities, Lowell's sense of his release back to himself is of anxious, reduced capacity, which he projects into a parable of observation:

Recuperating, I neither spin nor toil.
Three stories down below,
a choreman tends our coffin's length of soil,
and seven horizontal tulips blow.
Just twelve months ago,
these flowers were pedigreed
imported Dutchmen; now no one need
distinguish them from weed.
Bushed by the late spring snow,
they cannot meet
another year's snowballing enervation.

This enervation turns his earlier scorn and outraged stoicism into the guilty self-hatred of the final poems of his own marriage. The opening phrase of his most famous poem ("Man and Wife")—"Tamed by *Miltown*, we lie on Mother's bed"— returns both poet and reader fatalistically back past his childhood security to his parents's own desperate marriage. Driven darkly down and back, Lowell returns from the New York City of his marriage to the Maine of his childhood for what he calls the "Existential night" and staccato stanzas of "Skunk Hour." To overcome suicide, the impossibility of grace gives way to the minimal evidence of a skunk's stubborn concern for her kittens. The garbage of a decayed and careless society provides, provides.

THE SINS of the fathers revisited in *Life Studies* revealed a helpless and ironic repetition in his life that Lowell was determined to avoid in his art. In a letter to M. L. Rosenthal, he looked back on his breakthrough as something unique: "Something not to be said again was said. I feel drained, and know nothing except that the next out-pouring will have to be unimaginably different—an altered style, more impersonal matter, a new main artery of emphasis and inspiration." *For the Union Dead* (1964), with the grand public manner of its title poem, is the "more impersonal matter," the retreat from self to sensibility: "I am tired. Everyone's tired of my turmoil" ("Eye and Tooth"). Gabriel Pearson's misguided judgment of *Life Studies* is more nearly applicable to the "Patersonizing" Lowell manages in *For the Union Dead*: "in explicitly treating his life as materials, he was not making his poetry more personal but depersonalising his own life." His guilts become figures in an "unforgivable landscape," his neuroses change the studied confessions into impulsive, lyrical meditations. The therapeutic and critical success of *Life Studies*'s revelations seems to have occasioned a self-consciousness that demanded both release and restraint. The *paysage moralisé* of this book is rocky seacoasts, deserted lots, single rooms and beds which isolate the poet with himself. From such settings his "disturbed eyes rise, / furtive, foiled, dissatisfied / from meditation on the true / and insignificant" ("Hawthorne"). Lowell himself has said the subject of these meditations is "witheredness," inspired by the Tenth Muse, "my heartfelt Sloth"—"all those settings out / that never left the ground" ("Tenth Muse"). The energies of memory have evaporated, and by making its inability its subject—"my lowest depth of possibility"—the book risks an insubstantiality which Lowell seeks to avoid by turning the blank in his own eye towards society's "savage servility." But that rhetoric refocuses the real quarrel with himself, which Irvin Ehrenpreis rightly suggests is "the hold that history has on the present, the powerlessness of the self to resist the determination of open or hidden memories." *For the Union Dead*, in other words, is the effect of *Life Studies*, what Lowell calls "suffering without purgation, / the back-track of the screw" ("Going to and fro"). Another poem precisely defines the book's anesthetic effort, and details the ennui and the fatal terms of escape, desertion or suicide:

The man is killing time—there's nothing else. . . .

The cheese wilts in the rat-trap,
the milk turns to junket in the cornflakes bowl,
car keys and razor blades
shine in an ashtray.

("The Drinker")

Poems like "Water," "The Old Flame," and "Middle Age"
reduce the expansive evocation of *Life Studies* to the constricted
anguish of spare lines:

At forty-five,
what next, what next?
At every corner,
I meet my Father,
my age, still alive.

The privacy of despair encodes his account again in assertion or
symbol, and the rich detail that accumulates in *Life Studies* is
pared away to discontinuous and obscure remnants:

My eyes throb.
Nothing can dislodge
the house with my first tooth
noosed in a knot to the doorknob.

Nothing can dislodge
the triangular blotch
of rot on the red roof,
a cedar hedge, or the shade of a hedge.

("Eye and Tooth")

In so self-conscious a collection, a reader might expect, and
indeed is given, one poem about the others. "Night Sweat" is
Lowell's apology for his "stalled equipment" that "cannot clear
/ the surface of these troubled waters here":

my life's fever is soaking in night sweat—
one life, one writing! But the downward glide
and bias of existing wrings us dry—
always inside me is the child who died,
always inside me is his will to die—
one universe, one body . . . in this urn
the animal night sweats of the spirit burn.

The political poems that are the positive achievement of *For the Union Dead* are the reason for Lowell's subsequent book, *Near the Ocean* (1967), which draws on his previous talents for elegy and imitation to complete—along with his staged poems *The Old Glory* (1965) and *Prometheus Bound* (1967)—his Juvenalian indictment of mid-century American political and spiritual failure. Written during the period of Lowell's own most active political involvement, the book sheds a good deal of personal malaise coincident with the national. For instance, "Waking Early Sunday Morning," which resumes Yeats' tone and reverses Stevens' tactic, is his bitter lament for America's influence on the earth now "a ghost / orbiting forever lost / in our monotonous sublime." But between its original magazine appearance and its publication in the title sequence, this poem, like those accompanying it, was revised away from private document toward public declaration, and the further changes in the *Selected Poems* version underscore the tense, tight-lipped anguish at the vacuity he is indicting—the exhaustion of energies, private and public, aesthetic and moral. But I must agree with those critics who were disappointed by *Near the Ocean*—except for its interesting reversion to a strict prosody, presumably to emphasize the severe moral tone these poems adopt. After *Life Studies*, Lowell seems to have experienced a difficulty—or possibly a diffidence—in combining the confessional and political modes. The large experiment he next undertook to overcome that difficulty—*Notebook 1967–68* (1969)—created difficulties of its own, as evidenced by the constant recycling of its format and contents, first as *Notebook* (1970) and then as *History* (1973), the version from which he draws on in his *Selected Poems*. The very immediacy of the project, its insistent present tense, with its accommodating sprawl and improvisational flexibility, obviously encouraged those difficulties. The poet here resumes history by recording it, not by narrowing it to the slant of private vision but by opening his vision to the rush of outer accidents, tempered only by the seasonal cycle that underlies it and the involuntary memories that intrude upon it. It is his effort to accommodate a life in history and the life of history—though many of its first readers found it merely one damn poem after another.

What Lowell once said of Philip Larkin is equally true of his own effort: it "is particularly good at finding words for the instants of action, a person in his instant of time and place, colors that come only once." The rambling sequence of blank verse sonnets the poet chose to structure his episodic account risks not only tediousness but a distortion of the described experiences or reflections, which may require more or fewer than the 14 lines of a sonnet's narrow cell. Lowell probably took Berryman's *Dream Songs* as his organizational model, with its random chronicle formalized by an established pattern that controls the dynamics of fact and tone. And Lowell's poetic strength has always been the integrity of his line—its accuracy and finality like that of graven metal—and it is the line and the book itself that are essential: its sonnets are not discrete poems but forwarding stanzas.

History's final unifying rearrangement—which the *Selected Poems* reproduces in miniature—converts the original diaristic round into a more vast historical chronology, in which his own revisited autobiography is finally caught up—the family history preceded by and combined with the outsized figures of history-as-family. The intention, then, of such an incremental ordering, with its convergence of type and time, is ultimately exemplary, with the figure of the poet (both within and behind his work) as victim and exponent of his conspiracy with forces beyond him. The insufficiency of truth apart from the ambivalent human experience of it is the understanding of this collection, whose cohesion depends on a sensibility which seeks to define the self by rediscovering it among the "horrifying mortmain of / ephemera." It is an unfortunate necessity that the present book cannot reproduce *History*'s convulsive particularity and sacrifices its scope to a fine sample from his catalogue of tyrants and saints, artists and criminals, each a variation on the type of the monster, so that his meditations are really personalizing studies of the themes of will, authority, breakdown, and recrimination in his own history. And when he comes to review that, in a selection now subtitled "Nineteen Thirties," the emotional pressures on his *temps perdu* have been reduced by previous release, so that these matters-of-fact lend their more casual tone and plangent understandings to the sonnets—often in the exchange between aphorism and obscurity, both memorial instincts, which register these associative reminiscences.

I take it that Lowell has here intentionally abandoned the lengthy political considerations that absorb so much of *History*'s attention. By themselves, they stood as a discursive disclosure of the wary relativism and conservative analysis of radical feelings that dictated his interpretations of recent American political events. His portrayal of a discontented civilization derives from the late Freudian model, whose sense of instinctive aggression is finally suicidal—itself an illuminating comparison with Lowell's confrontations with both himself and his society. Instead, these *Selected Poems* close on an intensely personal note, with sonnets from *For Lizzie and Harriet* (1973) and *The Dolphin* (1973), both of them sequences with the private, overheard quality shared by Meredith's *Modern Love* and Lawrence's *Look! We Have Come Through!* It is a coda, strikingly situated, that confirms Lowell's search for poetic origins within his own experience, and again stresses the importance and example of his confessional concerns, returning his art to its sister, life. If Martin Buber was right to claim that "genuine responsibility exists only where there is real responding," then these poems reassert a mortal authority for Lowell's confessional poetry with their unsparing response, their genuine responsibility for choice and honesty. The 27 domestic poems to his second wife Elizabeth Hardwick and their daughter Harriet celebrate small joys and lament love's mortality, even as Harriet's growth discovers her parents' graceless aging and necessary alienation, most poignantly expressed in the haunted, elegiac realization of "Obit":

> Our love will not come back on fortune's wheel—. . .
>
> I'm for and with myself in my otherness,
> in the eternal return of earth's fairer children,
> the lily, the rose, the sun on brick at dusk,
> the loved, the lover, and their fear of life,
> their unconquered flux, insensate oneness, painful
> "It was. . . ."
> After loving you so much, can I forget
> you for eternity, and have no other choice?

The subject of *For Lizzie and Harriet* is, in the end, a fulfilled enclosure of human experience: "Before the final coming to rest, comes the rest / of all transcendence in a mode of being, hushing / all becoming." Such a stifling perspective has in the past been inimical to the purposes of Lowell's restless art, and the more congenial if painful struggles of "becoming" are the subject of his most intimate and controversial book, *The Dolphin*, an account of his divorce from Hardwick, his remarriage to Caroline Blackwood and the birth of their son Sheridan. With less than a third of its original length intact here, the carefully antiphonal structure of its narrative—the forward flow of events and the backward pull of memory, psychic deterioration and emotional rescue, regret and relief, New York and London, the two families, the two women—is blurred. But in another sense, its story now reads less like "the common novel plot" Lowell calls it: one man and two women, the triangle familiar from Freud and French novels, of the stricken husband confronting the dilemma between respect and passion, moral authority and sensual liberation, Elizabeth's "black silhouette" and Caroline's "bright trouvailles." With the melodrama diluted, we are now offered glimpses of the wrenching affair, which leaves it with an appropriate immediacy yet lends it a retrospective quality of accomplishment. In this abbreviated memoir, Lowell seems less like what Erving Goffman calls "a performed character" in his own story, with the diminished moral agency that implies. The reason for this, I suspect, is that Lowell's selection from the poems preferred those in which his role as creator is prominent, so that while the human drama is distanced, the parable of artistic rebirth is more pronounced. Lowell's own "dolphin"—a traditional symbol of love, swiftness and diligence, associated with Apollo—restores too "the man of craft, / drawn through his maze of iron composition," as the verse itself (among Lowell's strongest) becomes evidence of the rescue and the tribute to its own achievement.

SOME YEARS ago, in an *Encounter* review of Philip Larkin's new edition of *The Oxford Book of Twentieth Century English Verse*, Lowell engaged in some fascinating shoptalk. Not surprisingly, he agreed with the indexed consensus—Hardy, Yeats, Auden, Eliot and the others are justly and predictably sanctioned. But occasionally, when epitomizing another poet's art, he might well be implicating his own—as when of Auden he remarks that "his many styles are renewed by new thoughts always in the browning shadow. He journeys through time and himself, not space, journeys with much moralizing chat, then a sudden slow moment, the miraculous." Or when he says that Eliot's *Four Quartets* "make his other work different and better, each line in place and earned—finally, a mysterious relenting of his fate." More interesting still is his digression on the sometimes puzzling progress of American poetry, from Whitman ("our best and the wind of the great dream let loose") to Frost. And when he comes, vigorously, to defend our major modernist tradition from a sour British view that might dismiss it as "a sequence of demolitions, the bravado of perpetual revolution, break-through as the stereotype with nothing preserved," he singles out his own acknowledged precursors—Pound, Eliot, Williams, and Hart Crane among them—for having written in "styles closer to the difficulties of art and the mind's unreason." There is no better descriptive praise for Lowell's own work than that, and his *Selected Poems* is both the abstract and particulars of the successful risks he took to bring the mind's unreason to the orders of art, to bring the difficulties of art to the history of human experience.

ROBERT LOWELL

SOME LAST PHOTOGRAPHS

HIS DEATH at sixty, in 1977, caught everyone off guard—
except perhaps himself, who is said to have wanted it to
be that way: sudden, fierce, ordinary. Like everyone who cared
for the man and his work, for poetry and culture, I was shocked
and saddened by the news. And I suppose I felt more deeply
hurt by Lowell's loss than by the then recent deaths of, say,
Nabokov or Auden, not only because it seemed arbitrarily to
have stopped a vital, still evolving career, but also because I had
met the man not long before his death, listened to him speak
about poetry, absorbed his almost frightening intensity, felt
the daunting force of his intelligence, energy, openness, skep-
ticism, and compassion. It was literally shocking to contemplate
their absence from our lives, disheartening not to be able to
anticipate the publication of another of his books, each of which
had before confounded the expectations of his admirers and
critics, and had changed or defined the American poetic ambi-
tion.

When I wrote about his *Selected Poems,* it prompted a
worried letter from the poet: "Still I feel I have written too
much. I can't help it, and can't stop. If I had ground down as

perhaps I should have, I would only have perhaps three books, themselves defective and not altogether my best." But he liked what I had written about his work, and suggested we meet. When I was next in Boston, we did—at a reception and reading for *Canto* magazine, held at a Harvard club.

At first sight, from a distance, his appearance was disarming. A huge presence that seemed stooped, nearly frail (uncannily recalling photographs of T. S. Eliot as the Elder Statesman), mussed, oddly and shabbily dressed. This was from across the room at a cocktail party by which both of us were bored. So after muffled introductions we retired to a corner and began a conversation that continued uninterrupted through a cold supper and a nightcap. As he spoke, in that bemused drawl of his, his real power emerged, an almost physical force of concentration and calculated phrasing. When he first met Emily Dickinson, Col. Higginson wrote to his wife, "I never was with anyone who drained my nerve power so much. Without touching her, she drew from me." Lowell had the same effect. He was omnivorously curious, and a relentless questioner. Did I prefer Dante or Goethe? What did I think of my Yale colleagues? Which poems by X did I think most of? Which least? What languages did I read? He listened closely, nodded or disagreed, enjoyed objections. The conversation was fiercely, almost obsessively, literary, whether it centered on Greek tragedy or the latest gossip. His answers to my questions—that is, when what he had to say was an answer to the question posed; there was some of the great man's indifferent self-absorption in his manner—were frank or guarded, depending on the subject. He could be as brutal in his dismissals as he was open in his enthusiasms. Of his old teachers Tate and Warren, he'd always find the best to say. But, as if threatened, he was coy about his own generation of poets; as if embattled, he hedged his opinions about the generation immediately ahead of and behind his own. He was not modest about his gifts, but was uncertain of his achievements, and disconcertingly sought reassurance about his work and decisions.

A month later, in New York, at the annual meeting of the American Academy of Arts and Letters, Lowell was awarded its Gold Medal for Poetry. (He was happier about the check that went with it; in fact, he liked to boast about money, but that was probably a shy man's way to describe another sort of success.) He began his brief, gentle speech by slyly poking fun at some subtly self-aggrandizing remarks made by his fellow medalist Saul Bellow just beforehand. At the thronged reception afterwards, I spoke with him only long enough for us to set a dinner date. Beads of sweat stood out on his forehead. His tall figure, now a target, was jostled by a crowd of gawking or pushy congratulators. He seemed abstracted, even confused. As I left, I watched his arm grabbed by a beautiful but tipsy Russian woman poet. She spun him around, began hugging and mugging, then signaled her photographer to snap them together. Lowell did not seem to mind—it had happened too quickly for anyone to mind—but I wondered how the picture would be captioned in Moscow.

In a couple of weeks, again in Boston, along with poets Alfred Corn and Frank Bidart, we met at Jake's, the nondescript Cambridge restaurant he frequented, perhaps because he was recognized there but left to himself. By now he was more comfortable, intimate and expansive, speaking with sometimes startling candor about his marriages and family (his son would be a historian, he proudly predicted), his past career and future plans, his upcoming trip to Russia and his tennis game (he was only fit for doubles those days). The four of us swapped anecdotes and opinions. He seemed to have read everything and could quote at will; I was surprised when he said he was unfamiliar with Rossetti's extraordinary poem "Antwerp to Ghent" and I promised to send him a copy. He would tick off the "ten best poems" by Moore, Jarrell, Roethke, Bishop. Dinner done, he was unwilling to end the evening, anxious always to talk and listen, argue and persuade, always testing and judging. So we drove to Bidart's apartment on Sparks Street while the conversation ran on from Flaubert to Montale to Henry James to Robert Schumann. Not allowed liquor, and there not being any white wine in the house, he settled for Frank's Möet & Chandon (with ice!), and settled back to reminisce about his friends and his art. At one point, looking across the room at a Tiffany lamp and the breeze-blown curtain behind it—which had, I think, a pattern of swans on it—he began to improvise lines of verse, all with that decisive Lowell ring, as if to show how easy it was to make up. Then he suddenly stopped. See, he said, that's just style, it's not a poem because it's not connected to anything that has happened or is true. Then he showed us a few poems from the page proofs of *Day by Day* to amplify his distinction. The proofs were heavily scored, and he explained he was still revising.

Lowell was out of cigarettes; the rest of us were exhilarated but exhausted. We decided to call it a night, and I drove him to his rooms at Harvard. Walking into the dark through a tangle of bicycles, he stopped and turned, saluted with a spread hand and weak smile. The image, in the street-light's monochrome, took on the quality of a photograph.

The next time I visited Boston was for his funeral, a strangely orthodox and impersonal affair, except for Elizabeth Hardwick and Caroline Blackwood and their children coming up the aisle together in a noble grief, and a haggard Peter Taylor reading "Where the Rainbow Ends": "the scythers, Time and Death, / Helmed locusts, move upon the tree of breath." After the service, on the street outside, his two families were preparing to drive to Dunbarton. A swarm of photographers was pestering them, and one of Blackwood's daughters, harried and overwrought, burst into panicked tears which a camera moved in to capture. Hardwick put her arms around the girl, glared at the photographers and with a contemptuous wave of her hand said "Oh *please.*" They shied back, ashamed. The women got into their limousine, behind the one with Lowell's coffin in it, and the two cars edged down the crowded street. There was a sudden eerie silence. Every head turned to follow the body on its way to the graveyard in New Hampshire. I doubt anyone watching had words in mind.

THE COINCIDENCE of Lowell's death and the publication of *Day by Day* was unfortunate. The book was read as if its title had been taken from that line in Act V of *The Tempest,* when Prospero reveals himself to the conspirators and says of his years in exile, " 'tis a chronicle of day by day." Most reviewers took unfair advantage of the temptation to see *Day by Day* as fatalistic or valedictory, as Lowell's breaking his staff and drowning his book. Or, by taking it as Lowell's last word, some attacked the book as enervated and banal, but did so less to comment on the poems themselves than to disparage Lowell's entire career or to cluck over what they took to be its steady decline. One such attack was by Donald Hall—describing Lowell himself as "corrupted" and *Day by Day* as "slack and meretricious." To support his point he cited such authorities as Bennett Cerf and Edwin Newman, and went on to play that cheapest of games: isolate a phrase out of context and then either exclaim over its fatuity or deliberately misconstrue it. Surely there are other ways to discuss this book, and even its weaknesses, with more precision and intelligence. Ways—Helen Vendler's was one—which can accommodate both sympathy with the poet's aim and methods, and an alert perspective on traditions (the poet's and poetry's) which his book is invoking, modifying, parodying, or failing to sustain. I still think, years after the remark was made, that Randall Jarrell was right about

Lowell: "You feel before reading any new poem of his the uneasy expectation of perhaps encountering a masterpiece." There are few masterpieces in *Day by Day*, and the collection as a whole is very uneven. Too many of its poems are incomplete or repetitious or soft. Some, like the terrible "St. Mark's, 1933," are too sterilely self-obsessed. Attitudes too casually struck seem merely silly—as when, at the end of a poem addressed to his old friend Frank Parker, he wonders "What is won by surviving, / if two glasses of red wine are poison?" But though there are many such failures (nearly inevitable, however inexcusable, for a poet of such precarious maneuvers), they are exceptions to the ruling strengths of the book.

IT WAS widely noted (usually with relief) that Lowell had in *Day by Day* broken rank with the lockstep of unrhymed sonnets he had used for a decade. There is a deliberate reversion to the rather loose style, the muted free verse of *For the Union Dead*. Why? There is a case to be made, I think, for *Day by Day* being a transitional book that demanded his abandoning the sonnet form as a preliminary necessity before cutting some new stylistic figure. There are certainly precedents in his earlier work for such an argument, and I detect a measure of casting about in *Day by Day* for an appropriate form and tone—a darting, tentative quality that may account for both his hits and misses. But I suspect a more reasoned motive. The long project culminating in *History* was his attempt, carried out with neurotic heroism, to search out and arrange his *place* in time, the *type* of man he was. The epic scope and stylized format attest to the nearly impersonal character of that ambition; and then, at a time of personal turmoil for him, he continued in *For Lizzie and Harriet* and *The Dolphin*, to shape his experiences, reflections, and doubts into overdetermined sequences of sonnets as a means of both controlling the onrushing present tense of life and of accommodating it into the past record of his own history. That accomplished, at least to his own satisfaction, he issued *Selected Poems* to testify not to his sense of self but to the idea of his career. *Day by Day*, then, is a wholly new venture, but is still essentially a retrospect, old accounts resumed and settled, a version of making peace. As one poem has it, "The past changes more than the present," and so, ironically, makes harsher, more urgent demands. It is those changes and demands that are this book's concern.

They occupy the last two of the volume's three sections. The first section is a series of five poems—among his best ever —that invoke the poet's muse. She is portrayed as both Circe and Penelope, as his waking wife and suicidal succubus. The poet characterizes himself here, but his attention is not on himself as victim or hero but as agent, as a power but not a force. His perplexed relationship with the source of his life as a poet, as dramatized in these refractory, angular self-portrayals, indicate to me that he meant *tone* to be his subject throughout the book. The pretext for such a self-reflexive design is introduced at once, when he says of his Ulysses: "Young, / he made strategic choices; / in middle age he accepts / his unlikely life to come." Age, as a condition rather than an event, as fate rather than history, gives *Day by Day* its worried, nostalgic impetus, and prompts his later soliloquies on generation, and a detached amusement that verges at times on black humor.

Like the later books of Auden, or like the best of Coleridge (the poet Lowell most fittingly recalls in this book), the bulk of *Day By Day* is occupied with domestic poems. They center on friends and family, his health and daily rounds, the view from his window, sleeping alone. Often, these are, in turn, settings or occasions for longer memories of the "changing past"; and the most recurrent image in the book—the photograph—takes on an emblematic quality. Snapshots, actual or figurative, as

spots of time to be revisited, recalculated, revalued. Sometimes
Lowell is looking at himself, or rather at images of himself—
"50 years of snapshots, / the ladder of ripening likeness"—
seeking not their evidence of flux but their intimations of
fulfillment, and comparing "the awful instantness of retrospect"
with the prolonged blur of "my huddle of flesh and dismay."
Sometimes he takes out the family album familiar from *Life
Studies* on: "How quickly I run through my little set / of
favored pictures . . . pictures starved to words." Stricken with
"the infection of things gone," he runs through his "set" of
friends to count the losses. The best of these poems is a haunt-
ing elegy for John Berryman, but the most sustained and dis-
turbed are the two dejected odes to his parents, with whom he
reconciles himself not with affection or forgiveness, not even
with sympathy. In "To Mother," he poses the situation as
existential rather than merely emotional: "It has taken me the
time since you died / to discover you are as human as I am
. . . / if I am." He does not say *were* human, because the
poem seeks to effect an unsettling identification:

> Your exaggerating humor,
> the opposite of deadpan,
> the opposite of funny to a son,
> is mine now—
> your bolting blood, your lifewanting face,
> the unwilled ruffle of drama in your voice.

His parents, in other words, have died into him. "How uneas-
ily I am myself," he comments in another poem, with the
realization of how much of his life had been led or allowed by
others, how much he is just a part of what preceded him. The
poem to his father, "Robert T. S. Lowell," is an intriguing
dialogue between the two men, as well as between the poem
itself and the one it revises, "Middle Age" in *For the Union
Dead*. It is a dialogue, too, between memory and imagination,

those two "iconoclastic masks," and by projecting his father as himself, himself as his father, he achieves a second and primary identity, and explores the common fate of fatherhood.

Such identifications are made possible—indeed, are forced —by what he elsewhere terms his "realistic memory":

> In the realistic memory
> the memorable must be forgone;
> it never matters,
> except in front of our eyes.
>
> I made it a warning,
> a cure, that stabilized nothing.
> We cannot recast the faulty drama,
> play the child. . . .

To recast is the romantic's sinful privilege, and one that Lowell rightfully refuses himself, though the other alternative—"description without significance, / transcribed verbatim by my eye"—he finds equally unsuitable to the purposes of art. The book's epilogue resumes this dilemma:

> But sometimes everything I write
> with the threadbare art of my eye
> seems a snapshot,
> lurid, rapid, garish, grouped,
> heightened from life,
> yet paralyzed by fact.

His conclusion is that the facts of life are a poem's domain by "grace of accuracy":

> We are poor passing facts,
> warned by that to give
> each figure in the photograph
> his living name.

"Grace," even with its religious overtones, is not the word one might readily choose to describe Lowell's art; his style has always seemed steely, ferocious, driven, demonic. But he is speaking, in this very moving poem, less about the style than about the conscience of his art. He is *warned* by mortality to *give*, by his own insignificance to restore the world's significance. To the mere inventory of facts he gives back the unique life to each. To read *Day by Day*, especially the majority of its poems in which Lowell is speaking from or into or against or for his profound isolation, is to be touched again by that lonely, accurate grace, which had and gave the names we are and live by.

ROBERT LOWELL

HISTORY AND EPIC

THE SAYING goes that great men die twice, once as men, then again as great men. There are those who think that, in Lowell's case, it was the reverse; that, a dozen or more years before his death, the great poet had passed away—back into his reputation as a symbolist prodigy, as a master of the plain style, as public elegist. I do not share those mixed feelings, but it is not hard to account for them in others. And it is no accident that the erosion of Lowell's reputation largely began with the publication of *Notebook 1967–68*. It was a time when every reputation was squinted at; that was the temper of those times, and it is, in fact, what drew Lowell to write his troubled poem. The hallucinatory state of siege was abroad in the land, its violence (war, riots, assassinations, uprisings, marches, occupations) the external manifestation of convulsive psychic currents. Such an economy of upheaval and momentous instability must have seemed to the poet both to match and to wrench the febrile style he had by then perfected. But it was clear from the beginning, even before the nearly neurotic series of revisions, expansions, divisions, reordering and republications, that Lowell himself was dissatisfied with his poem—an unease that gradually affected its readers. The "Afterthought" to *Notebook 1967–68* is diffident to a fault. It backs away from defining the poem by insisting on what it is *not:* "not a conglomeration or sequence . . . not a chronicle or almanac . . . not my diary, my confession." "Opportunist and inspired by impulse," the poem is accused by its "half-balmy and over-accoutered" author of being vitiated by surrealism, plagiarisms, solecisms, even erudition. All too aware, as he puts it at the head of a reference list of crucial events, that "dates fade faster than we do," he also knew that, as he once wrote of Gascoigne, "the flux of life is not poetry."

It took Lowell until 1973 to stabilize the flux, but the book that resulted from all his hammering (the figure in the stone is the poet's own metaphor), *History*, is Lowell's unacknowledged masterpiece; the one book, finally the one *poem*, by which his career can best be characterized and most accurately appraised. By the time *History* appeared, Lowell seemed to have retired from the American literary stage, and the book did not receive the attention it deserved. Nor has it yet. But those critics who have written about it are, fortunately, among our best. I would cite, first, Alan Williamson's pioneering work on *Notebook;* then, Stephen Yenser and David Kalstone. After their commentary, we are in a position to see the poem's shape and interpret its motives; to understand it as, simultaneously, a systematic metaphor, a historical meditation, and an autobiography in colossal cipher. That is to say, first, that the psychosexual helix on which the poem is carried forward is part of what might be called Lowell's expansive-contractile vision, whereby manic-depressive discontents are projected onto civilization itself while the poet explores its cycles of order and violence. The past, in other words, is appropriated by an eerily intimate tone. Second, what David Kalstone calls *History's* "more rigorous and removed context for feelings," a model at once diachronic in format and synchronic in theme, provides a compelling example of personal consciousness as a register of the common past, and stay against historical contingency. And third, these critics have demonstrated how *History* is, in Stephen Yenser's phrase, literally the epitome of and "a synecdoche for the career . . . because this volume *is* a collected poems," cannibalizing its predecessors for material even as those books had fed on Lowell's life and on his reading.

But the question remains not how are we to interpret the poem but how are we to read it? The critics I have mentioned, and others, all refer in a preliminary or summary way to *History*'s epic status, but then hasten by this thorny generic question in order to explore more specific and often more perplexing matters. And this poem's mode—the way it expects to be read—perplexes me all the more when we reflect that, among those long poems of the last three decades with the ambition and scope and complexity to merit the term "epic" (and advocates would put forward poets from Ammons to Zukofsky), Lowell's *History* stands near the top.

No one can doubt that Lowell was preoccupied with the epic —with its demands and capacities, with its cultural centrality, with the kind of poet it makes of its author. In fact, epics bracketed his career. The earliest essay now in his *Collected Prose* is one on the divine and the heroic in the *Iliad*, written at age eighteen and published in the St. Mark's school magazine in his senior year there. Also as a student, he had worked for some years on an epic poem about the First Crusade. When, as a freshman at Harvard, he showed it to Robert Frost, the older poet read a page of it and told young Lowell it was too long, too wooden. However accurate the historical pastiche, there was no voice alive with history—or so Lowell remembered Frost chiding. At the time of his death, forty-two years later, he was working on an essay titled "Epics"—still a fragment, but a revealing one. The texts he broods on—the *Iliad*, *Paradise Lost*, the *Commedia*, the *Aeneid*, and *Moby-Dick*—are canonical choices, but Lowell's interests in them are sometimes surprising. Having so recently completed his own epic, he was no doubt clearing a trail backwards—reading the earlier, enabling poems in light of his own. And if we take his observations as implicit prescriptions, we can get much closer to his thinking about his own achievement. Let me paraphrase. The epic poet is not the conscience, but the soul of his culture, and his "sober intuition into the character of a nation" is less an archive than the dream of that culture's most profound fears and desires. The epic poem should be radial, not dialectical; should be peopled with heroically enlarged but still life-sized human beings ("a human proportion," Lowell says). Again, it is not verifiable history, but a hermetic fiction, working its way by prophecy and hindsight over certain contradictions at the heart of its characters and their culture—prime among them the will to freedom and that will's cruel self-destructiveness.

Small wonder that when he comes to discuss *Moby-Dick*, he says "It is our best book . . . it's our epic, a New England epic." And then he adds: "unless we feel the enchanted discontinuity of Pound's *Cantos* qualifies." Lowell's temperamental affinity with Melville has long since been noted, but he would have other important reasons to choose Melville's novel as our epic. Even when he writes of the European poets, and especially when he writes of Melville, Lowell's sense of the epic is that it is self-contained, tragic, and dramatic. Now, those are decidedly *not* Lowell's own strengths, which tend toward the ironic, the melancholy, the provisional, the lyric. Stephen Yenser proposes that, throughout his career and nowhere more than in *History* itself, Lowell "sought to fulfill an epic ambition with essentially lyric means." I would agree—but add that with the native strain of American epics (I am thinking of Whitman and Crane and Williams) such categories don't exclude each other, even though they don't suit one another. "In the best long American poems—*Leaves of Grass, The Cantos, The Waste Land, Four Quartets, The Bridge*, and *Paterson*—," Lowell once wrote, "no characters take on sufficient form to arrive at a crisis. The people melt into voices."

But Lowell's qualifying mention of Pound, for whom he had a deeply ambivalent respect, is more to my point. If any poet's example is behind *History*, it is surely Pound's, and not least in the latter's description of the epic as "a poem containing history"—that is, both absorbing history and transcending it. There are other parallels to be drawn.

The first is negative. Near the beginning of *History*, in a poem subtitled "the Sacrificial Killing," Lowell makes an admonitory reference to "Pound's Cantos lost in the rockslide of history." Like cantos, sonnets are lyric episodes, contained glimpses. They accumulate rather than narrate, and will always be at odds with epic's traditional dramatic storytelling. The risk is that they are accumulated fragments and won't cohere. But there are advantages. The reined-in effect of Lowell's sonnet sequence, with its crisp modulations and pulsing momentum, is (one can't help feeling) an instructed response to his sense, as a reader, of the documentary sprawl and imploded chaos that derange and finally smother Pound's masterpiece. The sonnet's foreshortened lyric tone also works to inhibit the dogmatic hectoring that wags at the reader from *The Cantos*. But Lowell had some positive lessons to learn as well. For example, though never so stark or demanding as Pound's ideogrammatic method, Lowell's deliberate splicings of private memories with public myths owes something to Pound's collage method. His modern dress redaction of the Clytemnestra story is an instance:

> "After my marriage, I found myself in constant
> companionship with this almost stranger I found
> neither agreeable, interesting, nor admirable,
> though he was always kind and irresponsible.
> The first years after our child was born,
> his daddy was out at sea; that helped, I could bask

on the couch of inspiration and my dreams.
Our courtship was rough, his disembarkation
unwisely abrupt. I was animal,
healthy, easily tired; I adored luxury,
and should have been an extrovert; I usually
managed to make myself pretty comfortable. . . .
Well," she laughed, "we both were glad to dazzle.
A genius temperament should be handled with care."

The poem that is titled "Clytemnestra" in *History* is grouped
with poems of the 1930s in the later *Selected Poems,* and with
good reason. The lines Lowell gives the murderous, bored
queen are his mother's. The reader will remember them from
the portrait in "91 Revere Street." Charlotte Lowell is con-
fronted by Mrs. Billy Harkness, who "hid her intelligence
behind a nervous twitter of vulgarity and toadyism. 'Char-
lotte,' she would almost scream at Mother, 'is this mirAGE,
this MIRacle your *own* dining room!'

"Then Mother might smile and answer in a distant, though
cosy and amused, voice, 'I usually manage to make myself
pretty comfortable.' " The preening bourgeois self-satisfaction
has been transformed, in "Clytemnestra," into a tone alto-
gether more menacing and indulgent; the ellipsis stands in for
a lover. The poem's irony cuts both ways: Lowell's own mother
is seen in terms of the clarifying archetype, and the mythic
figure has added to its history a new overtone—of *bovarysme*
—that quickens its force. *History* is filled with chromatic jux-
tapositions (as with Orpheus in "Genesis," or Adam in a Har-
vard blazer), and sometimes startling correspondences (as when
Caligula recites Baudelaire—another ironic "imitation").

And then there is Lowell's use of heroes in his poem. I am
told by Frank Bidart that when he visited Lowell in England in
January 1972, the poet was preparing a book of about fifty
sonnets, most culled and revised from *Notebook.* The book was

to be titled *Heroes*—and presumably this is the part of his old work that most intrigued him, the part, in fact, that comes to focus *History*. Pound's Sigismundo and Confucius and John Adams find their counterparts in Lowell's roll call of historical figures. And by "figures" I mean to imply metaphors as well, since Lowell was less interested in individuals than in types. Most of them are his fabled "killer kings," whether emperors or criminals, generals or poets, saints or grand failures—but all of them self-lacerating creatures of the *will*. A tormented idealist, Pound was interested in exemplary figures and their ideas. Lowell's instincts were for the underside of the familiar, for the weak motive at the heart of power. He was analytical and theatrical, where Pound was programmatic. But he did share with Pound a purgatorial sense of human history—one that the modern epic must pass through. Like Pound, he perceived time as a stalled machine, a tone cluster of states of mind across the centuries, darkened by madness, lust, ambition, age, the arrogance and intoxication of power—as Lowell's own mind had been darkened in his time.

Like Pound too, he hated the provincial, and always wanted a poetry that engaged all of his learning and passion, his wildness and civility, as well as the resources of history, culture, and nationalist spirit. That sense of history (the real, animating *life* of history) is, some would argue, more a European than an American concept—at least *literary* concept. These same critics might refuse *History* a place in the line that runs from Emerson and Whitman through our epic poems. This, in turn, reminds us of Lowell's own denials. In his talk of epic, where is there mention of that "greatest original practical example" of Whitman? *Is* there anything to be said—any pact to be made here?

Here is Whitman's reminder to himself when plotting *Song of Myself*: "Make no quotations and no references to other writers. Take no illustrations whatsoever from the ancients or classics . . . nor from the royal and aristocratic institutions and forms of Europe. Make no mention or allusion to them whatever, except as they relate to the new, present things—to our country—to American character or interests." One is doubly struck by such a passage. Once by its apparent antipathy to Lowell's sensibility and practice. And then, on second thought, struck by an odd similarity: taking illustrations from the past "as they relate to new, present things" is an apt definition of Lowell's chronicle in *History*. From his few references to Whitman, I would guess that, at some level, Lowell identified him with solipsism itself, and so feared and courted him as he would his own manic, mystic seizures. Or, one might say with more certainty, Lowell was deeply ambivalent about the American Romantic sublime, and the kind of epic poem that Whitman fashioned in *Leaves of Grass*, that prototype and constant model of the American epic, was one Lowell would have rejected. But I am not so sure.

This is not the place to recapitulate the classical norms and Romantic innovations in epic form; or the relationship between epic's "higher Argument" and the American sublime; or the economy of historical interpretation and visionary projection, the documentary and the vatic, in epic; or Whitman's own scriptural ambitions and decisive recasting of traditional epic by means of anti-epic devices. For a country with no history, no "autochthonous song," Whitman set out to create a tale of the American tribe that was, in Emerson's phrase, "the mirror carried through the street"—not merely held up to "the great and constant fact of Life" in these States, but moved through a changing subject; not held up to reflect the single heroic action, but turned continually outward onto the anecdotal panorama of American life, and inward on its own mercurial power. Whitman's epic hero was the divine average, that ensemble of representative men and women merged by and into the poet's own voice: anonymity given the identity of sublime song. If not always to the anonymous, American art does tend to the monumental, the idealizing, above all the abstract. Its epic hero, more often than not, is Emerson's Giant of Otherness, the genius of place. The "native American individuality" Whitman celebrated was, from one point of view, remarkably abstract: "In the center of all, and object of all, stands the Human Being, toward whose . . . evolution poems and everything directly or indirectly tend, Old World and New."

Lowell's poem, too, has a Human Being in the center of all, a representative man, the self-in-relationship. For all the specific gravity of its references, dramatic monologues, and autobiographical impressionism, in its way *History* is also an abstract poem—in the manner of Frank Parker's emblematic title page drawing, which deserves more study. Armor cast aside, a naked man sits within a classical ruin, studying a structure that could be a sepulcher or a plinth. Three other figures watch him: a skeleton and, overhead, a paternal sun and maternal moon. By its format and progress, the poem traces an emblematic, or archetypal story: that of Genesis itself, a man and a woman who are alternately the Great Parents, the hapless lovers, killer and victim, poet and muse. When Lowell says, in the sonnet called "Returning," that "No one like one's mother and father ever lived," he is offering an important clue about his poem—that its blend of memory and fantasy, its "voice alive with history," is an elaborate design to study certain *categories* of experience: recurrent, overlapping, determinant.

I think future commentaries on the poem will come to emphasize its submerged romance. To date, most readers have responded to *History* as they might to *Leaves of Grass* after the Civil War's terrible swift sword had cut into it—that is, after history's counter-sublime had reduced it to a harsher song. At the end of his life, Whitman called his book "the outcropping of my own emotional and other personal nature— an attempt, from first to last, to put a *Person*, a human being (myself, in the latter half of the Nineteenth Century, in America,) freely, fully and truly on record." Where *Notebook* could as easily have been entitled *Specimen Days*, so too do the 368 poems of *History* seem a kind of daybook—a free, full, and true record of Robert Lowell. But the interest and value of such a record will diminish in time, and unless we can begin to read *History* as something more than a ledger or mosaic we will be unable to save the poem from a slow death by footnotes. Its larger gestures, its *epic* gestures and patterns, are one lifeline.

From the beginning, the poet himself called this poem a "hybrid," meaning that it drew on as wide a variety of traditions and tropes as Lowell's "emotional and other personal nature" demanded. I have glanced at *History* with one eye on Pound and the historical epic, and another on Whitman and the romantic epic. I want, finally, to mention the classical epic. In his essay on epics, the one poet who obviously most engages Lowell's sympathy is Virgil—that most literary of epic poets, writing from the heart of the empire about the cruel cost of its triumph. Lowell saw America itself as a "Roman" empire— immense, crass, vital, crushingly powerful. And it might be more fair to *History* to read it as a combined Plutarch and Petronius. But I want to take the Virgilian model and hold it up to Lowell's poem. To do so is, again, to find a resounding echo. The traditional epic subject is *community*, it seems to me; and what distinguishes the epic are the tasks it sets itself, or its hero, to perform. They are two. One concerns the past, the other the future. The first task, a descent, is to visit the dead, to call on the ghosts, to reconcile with the fathers. The second task, ascending, is to found a city, to establish control. That is to say, an epic poem is one with a particular kind of *memory* and of *vision*. What and how he remembers or memorializes, and what and how he envisions his community— these are what make the epic poet. And they make sense of Lowell's *History* as well. The poem's first hundred pages are a kind of *katabasis*, back in time, back through Lowell's reading. It is a quest for those historical forces and cultural assumption that helped shape him; for those spots of time that fascinate or obsess him. That these larger forces are embodied in individuals-in-crisis rather than in events is characteristic of Lowell's temperament, as well as of the distinctly literary cast of this part of the poem. History is, after all, a series of biographies, a series of readings. Lowell's historical quest gives way, finally, to his struggle with the family romance, and his effort is to reconcile history with the self, and thereby gain control over both. This growth-of-a-poet's mind establishes the completed poem itself as that *place* of the future for the past.

ELIZABETH BISHOP

SOME NOTES ON "ONE ART"

The art of losing isn't hard to master;
so many things seem filled with the intent
to be lost that their loss is no disaster.

Lose something every day. Accept the fluster
of lost door keys, the hour badly spent.
The art of losing isn't hard to master.

Then practice losing farther, losing faster:
places, and names, and where it was you meant
to travel. None of these will bring disaster.

I lost my mother's watch. And look! my last, or
next-to-last, of three loved houses went.
The art of losing isn't hard to master.

I lost two cities, lovely ones. And, vaster,
some realms I owned, two rivers, a continent.
I miss them, but it wasn't a disaster.

—Even losing you (the joking voice, a gesture
I love) I shan't have lied. It's evident
the art of losing's not too hard to master
though it may look like (*Write* it!) like disaster.

The forms themselves seem to invite [some little depar-
ture from tradition], in our age of "breakthroughs." Take
the villanelle, which didn't really change from "Your eyen
two wol slay me sodenly" until, say, 1950. With Empson's
famous ones rigor mortis had set in, for any purposes be-
yond those of *vers de société*. Still, there were tiny signs.
People began repunctuating the key lines so that, each time
they recurred, the meaning would be slightly different. Was
that just an extension of certain cute effects in Austin Dob-
son? In any case, "sodenly" Elizabeth's ravishing "One Art"
came along, where the key lines seem merely to approximate
themselves, and the form, awakened by a kiss, simply tod-
dles off to a new stage in its life, under the proud eye of
Mother, or the Muse.

— James Merrill

> It is the poems you have lost, the ills
> From missing dates, at which the heart expires.
> Slowly the poison the whole blood stream fills.
> The waste remains, the waste remains and kills.

— William Empson

BISHOP WAS not often attracted to formal patterns. The key
words in various titles show her preference for the bracing
leads of rhetorical conventions (exercise, anaphora, argument,
conversation, letter, dream, a view) or for occasional premises
(visits, arrival, going, wading, sleeping). Twenty years separate
her two sestinas; her double sonnet "The Prodigal Son" ap-
peared in 1951, her ballad "The Burglar of Babylon" in 1964,
her last poem "Sonnet" in 1979. When she did write by for-
mula, her line stiffened toward the regularity of the pattern's
grid, her tone of voice gave over its intimacy. At the same
time, of course, her way with the line and her tone transfigured

each of the forms she worked in—none more so, as Merrill notes, than the villanelle.

A poet's debt is her starting point; her interest cancels it. Bishop's debt to Empson's "Missing Dates" is clear. His variations on "the consequence of life requires" are a study in slow poison. No less than Bishop's imperatives, his series of denials and definitions ("It is not. . . ," "It is . . .") serves as an instruction. And his contradictory rhyme *fills/kills* sets up Bishop's similar (but, because feminine, more difficult) *master/ disaster*.

Villanelles are inventions like triangles and their use is to cause "nature" to find its form only if it can do so in arbitrary human terms.

—A. R. Ammons

The art of life is passing losses on.

—Robert Frost

Sweet salt embalms me and my head is wet,
everything streams and tells me this is right;
my life's fever is soaking in night sweat—
one life, one writing! But the downward glide
and bias of existing wrings us dry—

Robert Lowell

THE EXEMPLARY poems are the grand Wordsworthian encounters—"At the Fishhouses," "The End of March"—that find their moral in their own slow pace. But I remain fascinated by those few poems—uncharacteristic, one might say, except that they are as central to an understanding of her work as anything else—that are *private* (or seem so), that defy decoding, are mysterious in their references and effect. The end of

"Roosters" is such a moment, but I am thinking of whole poems that are short, their obliquity (is threatened love the lurking shape?) wrought up to a pitch of extreme lyricism. I am thinking of "Insomnia," "The Shampoo," "Varick Street," "Conversation," "Rain Towards Morning," and "O Breath." "One Art" is in this mode too. It is directly, even painfully autobiographical (or seems so), yet more accessible than the earlier poems. It *shares* its subject with the person who reads and not just with the person written about. Perhaps it seems more accessible because of the quality of resignation that dominates. Or perhaps it is because of the form, that does not mask the experience but strips it of the merely personal. That is to say, the form characterizes the autobiography; in the arbitrary is discovered the essential. The villanelle serves as a field to explore the self's history, but also as a vantage point above it.

It is a familiar advantage in Bishop's poems, achieved by tone rather than by form: "awful but cheerful." Over the poems in *Geography III* could hang, sampler-like, the more dire motto of "The End of March": "Perfect! but—impossible." The nine poems in the book all exemplify that strain in Bishop—the strain native to Frost and Stevens as well—of dark knowing. "Cold is our element and winter's air / Brings voices as of lions coming down," says Stevens in "The Sun This March." That same element, the element bearable to no mortal, is where Bishop hears her voices. In its own way, "One Art" is their after-echo, the lyrical form a defense against extremes, against both perfection and impossibility.

Her title I take to mean "one art among others," as defense is the obverse of access. And I take "art" to mean "skill," but I want to come back to "art" in its other—primary? secondary? —meaning. What stays to puzzle is that the celebrated skill (a word we associate with *acquiring*) is for *losing*. The peculiar resonance of the phrase "the art of losing" is that the word has two meanings, transitive and intransitive. It can mean to mislay, or to fail. We hear the second meaning in the poem's first line, and the ghost of it throughout. "Lose" has other overtones: to elude, to stray, to remove, to be deprived. And etymologically (its root is to cut, loosen, divide) it's linked with pairs of terms that define the poem's emotional borders: analyze and solve, forlorn and resolve.

The catalogue of losses, from keys to continent, is a masterful sequence. The key starts a chain of being, the course of a life. Much is named without being specified. When I read "Then practice losing farther, losing faster," I hear—because of the mother's watch in the next stanza—"losing *father*." Then, the watch as an emblem of time is joined with the houses' containment of space. If the cities stand for society, then the rivers and continent stand in for nature.

Years foll'wing Years, steal something ev'ry day,
At last they steal us from our selves away;
This subtle Thief of Life, this paltry Time,
What will it leave me, if it snatch my Rhime?
—Alexander Pope

Love hath my name ystrike out his sclat,
And he is strike out of my bokes clene
For evermo; ther is no other mene.
—Geoffrey Chaucer

BEFORE THE terrible estrangement both recorded and enacted in the final stanza, there is an odd moment just ahead that cues it:

I lost two cities, lovely ones. And, vaster,
some realms I owned, two rivers, a continent.
I miss them, but it wasn't a disaster.

Elizabeth Bishop   143

The rhythm is exact, low-keyed, but the diction is queer. "Vaster" strikes a discordant note, not just because it is a forced rhyme-word, but because it is the first of three "literary" words (a usage Bishop avoided). The others are "realms" and "shan't," not including the "*Write* it!" that caps the sequence. They are words that seem out of place unless accounted for by some less obvious motive. I mean a reader's, not necessarily the poet's motive: the need to interpret, to allow the poem to make sharp departures from itself, and add layers of meaning. Any poet—any reader—so surprises himself, and form, that psychopomp, leads by its exigencies.

But "realms," secure in mid-line, is a deliberate choice. Is it a deliberate allusion? Brazil *was* a kingdom—but that's not it. "Realm" is a word from books, old books, and one use of it springs immediately to mind: "Much have I travelled in the realms of gold / And many goodly states and kingdoms seen." Keats' sonnet is about acquiring—a poem, a planet; a continent, an ocean; a *power*—in much the same way (and in roughly the same locale) Bishop's Brazilian poems are, and she may be alluding to having abjured the more exotic style of poetry she wrote during her Brazilian years in favor of the sparer style of her later poetry. But "realms" is a royal trope not just for style but for poetry itself, in Keats' and (perhaps? surely!) in Bishop's reckoning here. This being so, could the poem—one of its layered meanings, that is—be about the loss of poetic power, the failure of mastery? If that were the case, then the "you" addressed in the last stanza (and no wonder her "voice" is singled out) is akin to Apollo in Keats' sonnet— say, the enabling god, or familiar muse. That the poem traces its diminishments in so rigorously lyrical, even keening, a pattern; that it must force itself at the end to do what the poet no longer can do, to *Write*—there is the poignancy of this dejection ode.

But to say these days that a poem is "about writing" is both a critical cliché and a method to dismiss. Besides, the "you" of this stanza—her "joking voice" that mocks both mastery and disaster—has all the specific gravity (and general levity) of a real person. The loss of love here is not over and thereby mastered, but threatened: a possibility brooded on, or an act being endured. How Bishop dramatizes this threatened loss is uncanny. "I shan't have lied," she claims. Under such intense emotional pressure, she shifts to the decorous "shan't," as if the better to distance and control her response to this loss, the newest and last. And again, my mind's ear often substitutes "died" for "lied." In self-defense, lying makes a moral issue out of the heart's existential dilemma; a way of speaking is a habit of being. The real moral force of the stanza comes—and this is true in many other Bishop poems—from her adverbs: *even* losing you; not *too* hard to master. These shades of emphasis are so carefully composed, so lightly sketched in, that their true dramatic power is missed by some readers.

And then that theatrical last line—how severely, how knowingly and helplessly qualified! It reminds me of that extraordinary line in "At the Fishhouses," at three removes from itself: "It is like what we imagine knowledge to be." The line here begins with a qualification ("though"), goes on to a suggestion rather than the assertion we might expect of a last line ("it may look"), then to a comparison that's doubled, stuttering ("like . . . like"), interrupted by a parenthetical injunction that is at once confession and compulsion, so that when "disaster" finally comes it sounds with a shocking finality.

The whole stanza is in danger of breaking apart, and breaking down. In this last line the poet's voice literally cracks. The villanelle—that strictest and most intractable of verse forms—can barely control the grief, yet helps the poet keep her balance. The balance of form and content, of "perfect! But—impossible."

JOHN BERRYMAN

THE IMPEDIMENTS TO SALVATION

His work, as the chief outcome of the life, has the same character, and he recognized this character in the activity that produced it. . . . The poems have an enigmatic air and yet they are desperately personal. . . . He repudiated the sketches and resolved upon something different, a defiant attempt to create a masterpiece—ambitious, continuous, objective, faithful, and his own. Then he did it. . . . History, grammar, gods, an elaborate society, were nothing. A hero, so long as you didn't call him one and concentrated on his hanging shirt-tail, was worth having. . . . His people, in their stories, stay in your mind; but they have no existence outside. No life is strongly imaginable for them save what he lets you see. I think he is interested in them individually, but only as crisis reaches them. . . . His imagination was resolute in presenting him with conditions for fear; so that he works with equal brilliance from invention and from fact. . . . A domestic, terrible poem, what it whispers is: "I would console you, how I would console you! If I honestly could." . . . He was to describe this world with an Alexandrian stylization; with imagery ranging from the jungle up through war to medieval and hieratic imagery; with the last possible color, force, succinctness—without de-

stroying the illusion of fidelity. The banal story, that is, had to be given heroic and pathetic stature and yet not falsified. . . . . Of course he did write from inspiration, and of course he wrote also from close long observation, inquiry, study, and then he rewrote. He was like other men of genius, in short, often inspired and immensely deliberate. Yet this double explanation does not really account for the impression his work has always given, which might be put as follows: one is surprised that it exists at all—and one's surprise, if it diminishes, does not disappear with familiarity. . . . The reason it is not certain that he tried deliberately to be killed is that his fatigue and illness were such that nothing can be certain about his conscious mind. The two chief witnesses to his two suicidal exposures both speak of his semiautomatic, dreamlike state during them. . . . Death ends the terrible excitement under which he is bound to live, death resolves panic, death is "a way out," a rescue.

THESE ARE not comments about John Berryman, but by him, from what he called his "psychological biography" of Stephen Crane published in 1950 as part of the American Men of Letters series. The study was written during the brooding interval between his early and mature work, and to a greater extent than his critics have noticed Berryman seems to have been exploring there his own possibilities as well as Crane's. What he discovered in that distant and very different writer was finally for himself: the ambition to achieve a method by which to present and explore his deepest personal concerns. It is not a coincidence of scholarship that he came to see the basis of Crane's art in the oedipal conflict with the father who died when Crane was a boy—"The aggression against the father, the wish to be the father, and the solution for panic"—and its expression as "an action of his art upon the remembered possibility of death". The "irreversible loss"—the suicide of Berryman's father outside his twelve-year-old son's window—which the poet said motivates his *Dream Songs* is that same conflict, and the action of his art returns to find that same loss in himself: the death in his own life. But to use the tired term "oedipal conflict" is both misleading and reductive, at least insofar as it implies sexuality as the primary repression. In his later writings, Freud hinted at what his revisionists have more fully detailed: that consciousness of death is the primary repression and the instinct that drives us to transcend human limitation and vulnerability as well as the Father whose existence and authority represent our mortality. Norman O. Brown explicates the dilemma this way:

> The Oedipal project is not, as Freud's earlier formulations suggest, a natural love of the mother, but as his later writings recognize, a product of the conflict of ambivalence and an attempt to overcome that conflict by narcissistic inflation. The essence of the Oedipal complex is the project of becoming God—in Spinoza's formula, *causa sui;* in Sartre's *etre-en-soi-pour-soi.* By the same token, it plainly exhibits infantile narcissism perverted by the flight from death.

The ludicrous existential dualism, the seeming hoax of self and self-consciousness faced with defeat, decay, and death, results in an instinctive "project"—as Ernest Becker, in his *The Denial of Death*, summarizes it, "the flight from passivity, from obliteration, from contingency: the child wants to conquer death by becoming the *father of himself."* To view Berryman's work as such a project outlines the dimensions of his major books and approaches their ambition and achievement, as well as that of their unique style, a neurotic idiom poised to avoid or overcome the anxiety of his struggle with the self.

Berryman once described T. S. Eliot's poetic career as "a pure system of spasms," and he saw the similarity to his own long silences broken by work distinctly different from what had preceded it. His first "spasm" was *Poems* (1942) and *The Dispossessed* (1948), the results of his precocious apprenticeship. Berryman described himself when he said of Stephen Crane that "literary ambition unusually deliberate and powerful is manifest all through his early life." Of his days as a student at Columbia and Cambridge, a teacher at Harvard and Princeton, and as the young poetry editor of *The Nation*, Berryman noted in an interview: "I always wanted to be much older than I was, and from an early age I took to advising my seniors." If that admission betrays an ambivalent attitude toward the authority of tradition, his uneasiness was muted and respectful in these early poems. And even if he had not frequently spoken of his debt to W. B. Yeats and W. H. Auden in these books, their manner would have been apparent in the cerebral lyricism and scrupulous craft, the portentous symbols and assertive personifications, the presiding social and political concern of "the honourable and exhausted man" that Berryman adopted as his role here. But though he says he "began work in verse-making as a burning, trivial disciple" of Yeats, his project at the time was not "so much to resemble as to *be*" Yeats, so that his imitations can be seen as a displaced version of his ambition to create himself as a poet. It was the sort of compromise Berryman would make throughout his career. With a true poet's respect for his ancestors and a scholar's self-consciousness (Berryman always referred to himself as a scholar who wrote poetry) he rarely lapsed into a relaxed free verse, but fought his battles on prescribed ground, complicating older strategies, melting ancient armor into strange new shapes. As Donald Justice says:

> His subject was the self, often enough the self involved with history. But his personal exposures have a different feel about them than those of his contemporaries. No matter

how painful and honest they seem, they have first been subjected to the pressures of his art. Events, however catastrophic, are valued not so much for themselves as for what they can be made into, in words and music. The impersonality of art remains, therefore, as important as the personality of the poet.

The reason for this was best put by Theodore Roethke, in a notebook entry: "Form is a father: with all the ambiguities of father being operative."

These first books excuse themselves from the self shadowed by public events:

> The fox-like child I was or assume I was
> I lose, the abstract remember only; all
> The lightness and the passion for running lose
> Together with all my terror, the blind call
> At midnight for the mother. How shall we know
> The noon we are to be in night we are?
> The altering winds are dark and the winds blow
> Agitation and rest, unclear, unclear.
>
> ("At Chinese Checkers")

But there are times, inevitably, when the obvious efforts to display his personal and poetic maturity seem momentarily suspended by the pressure of the past. Among the several literary allegories in these collections are emotional allegories, dreamscapes that may be "the bitter and exhausted ground / Out of which memory grows" ("The Moon and the Night and the Men"). And Berryman realizes "We have a stake / In this particular region, and we look / Excitedly for situations that we know" ("Desire Is a World by Night"). Though his search is not excited, the situation he knows is his father's suicide. Where later poems allow him more awareness and his responses veer from rage to self-pity, the strenuous repression here permits only occasional confrontations, sudden, muffled expressions of loss, as here in "World's Fair":

> Suddenly in torn images I trace
> The inexhaustible ability of a man
> Loved once, long lost, still to prevent my peace,
> Still to suggest my dreams and starve horizon.
> Childhood speaks to me in an austere face.

Before anything else, his familiar "The Ball Poem" is an account of his own "dispossession" and the terms of survival:

> He is learning, well behind his desperate eyes,
> The epistemology of loss, how to stand up
> Knowing what every man must one day know
> And most know many days, how to stand up
> And gradually light returns to the street,
> A whistle blows, the ball is out of sight,
> Soon part of me will explore the deep and dark
> Floor of the harbour . . . I am everywhere,
> I suffer and move, my mind and my heart move
> With all that moves me, under the water
> Or whistling, I am not a little boy.

And as if to underline the point he refuses to make outright, Berryman follows that poem with another, "Fare Well," a nightmarish aubade to his father's still "moving shadow":

> What has been taken away will not return,
> I take it, whether upon the crouch of night
> Or for my mountain need to share a morning's light,—
> No! I am alone.
> What has been taken away should not have been shown,
> I complain, torturing, and then withdrawn.
> After so long, can I still long so and burn,
> Imperishable son!

Even in his earliest work, Berryman's essentially elegiac verse links in an "epistemology of loss" his father, and his friends, and so finally himself. *Poems* is dedicated to Bhain Campbell (1911–1940), a young poet with whom Berryman had shared an apartment in Detroit in 1939, and the epigraph reads:

> I told a lie once in verse. I said
> I said I said I said 'The heart will mend,
> Body will break and mend, the foam replace
> For even the unconsolable his taken friend.'
> This is a lie. I had not been here then.

As he stutters to repeat the false consolation, the contradiction of "here" and "then" predicts the focus of his later work.

In his review of *The Dispossessed* Randall Jarrell, with his usual acuity, singled out for discussion "The Nervous Songs," which along with "Canto Amor" pointed the direction in which Berryman was to develop his style. By remarking that "doing things in a style all its own sometimes seems the primary object of the poem," Jarrell had sited the center of Berryman's project, at least in its most abstract necessity. In *Love & Fame* Berryman remembers himself as a student reading R. P. Blackmur:

> 'The art of poetry
> is amply distinguished from the manufacture of verse
> by the animating presence in the poetry
> of a fresh idiom: language
>
> so twisted & posed in a form
> that it not only expresses the matter in hand
> but adds to the stock of available reality.'
> I was never altogether the same man after *that*.
>
> ("Olympus")

With a fresh idiom to make new reality was the accomplishment of *Homage to Mistress Bradstreet* and *The Dream Songs*, but before them he twisted and posed both his ability and experience in *Berryman's Sonnets*, his last and most self-conscious confrontation with fatherly form. Not published until 1967, they were written over the spring and summer of 1946, during which he carried on an adulterous affair with a married woman whom he names Lise (whose real name was probably Chris and whose pseudonym could be construed as "the Reader") and after which began his bouts with alcoholism and psychoanalysis. The poet's long hesitation to publicize the account of his Modern Love is symptomatic of the book's further inhibitions, especially when juxtaposed with such a similar sequence as Robert Lowell's *The Dolphin*. The retrospective poem which prefaces the *Sonnets* and questions "the right, upon that old young man, / to bare his nervous system," attributes the "original fault" of the poems to the sense that "wickedness / was soluble in art." It is not "wickedness" but guilt that is his subject, and the "art" that describes it an obsessive stylization that seeks at once to justify and distance it. Like other sonneteers, what Berryman sees in the girl is himself: "What you excite / You are, you are me." And since the poems were written ostensibly for himself, their narrative is encoded. The reader has only Berryman's own image of the woman, and can puzzle together the lovers' meeting (16, 70, 106), the pine groves where they make and lose their love (11, 64, 68, 71, 95, 115), the necessary deceptions (21, 25, 33), the "strange changes" of doubt (56, 57, 82, 83), and the affair's decline (96, 97, 101, 106, 107). If the poet himself was not, at least the poetry is more comfortable when singing of separation, both during and since the affair, "the shorn time we share." And that separation reflects the distance Berryman puts between the actuality and the account. "To become ourselves we are these wayward things," he says, and the self-consciousness that occasions guilt presents too the "wayward" parts he casts himself in—David, Aeneas, Lancelot, Tristan, Petrarch, Wyatt—played out in the traditional moral drama of love versus honor (31, 33, 45, 57, 69, 76, 98). The sequence's abstruse and ingenious imitations betray an edgy, deflecting intellectualization—art's effort to soothe rather than solve guilt.

The resolution lacking in Berryman's personal situation was perhaps the cause of the unsettled style of his *Sonnets*. The purposive allusiveness of his format fumbles for an inclusiveness that can balance both his experience and his self-conscious reflections on it, but it was not until his next "spasm," *Homage to Mistress Bradstreet* (1956), that his project found a decisive, "self created" style that later, in *The Dream Songs*, could include both simultaneously. *Homage*, in fact, is essentially a poem about style. Initiated as a dejection ode to the source of his declining powers, the poem transforms itself into an affirmation of self-discovery. Even at the costume drama level of historical narrative, Berryman's intense evocation of America's "first" poet is too self-absorbed—with, for example, the strange and strangely moving seduction scene—to be merely a dramatic tribute. Its sympathy is no less than identification: "We are on each other's hands / who care. Both our worlds unhanded us." Though Bradstreet lies "Deep / in Time's grave, Love's," she remains "a sourcing whom my lost candle like the firefly loves," so that Berryman's love for his predecessor becomes the poem's space across which their times gravely merge. How to become and survive as a poet in this New World's "barbarous place" where artists with "nightmares of Eden" can only ever be "strangers & pilgrims" is as much Berryman's concern as he imagines it was Bradstreet's. But at a deeper level of the poem, Berryman's own "Ambition mines, atrocious, in." Like *The Dream Songs'* soliloquy for two voices, the duologue is between Berryman and himself: "I am a man of griefs & fits / trying to be my friend." Or perhaps it would be better to say, between Berryman and his Interior Paramour, the muse purified of her sometime appearance as bitch-goddess—a role often forced on her by Berryman's own guilty relationships with the women whom he subjected, so to speak, to poetry. This poem's "pioneering" stakes out for him a language by which to articulate himself—he refers to both style and self when he speaks of "one enchained eager far & wild"—but which in this poem serves only to celebrate itself. Its bristling diction and buckled syntax attend a difficult birth; for clearly the description of Bradstreet giving birth is Berryman's own fathering of his poetic identity:

> Monster you are killing me Be sure
> I'll have you later Women do endure
> I can *can* no longer
> and it passes the wretched trap whelming and I am me
> drencht & powerful, I did it with my body!
> One proud tug greens Heaven. Marvellous,
> unforbidding Majesty.
> Swell, imperious bells. I fly.

That flight soared through 385 Dream Songs, which took off at least by 1955, and landed in 1968. He had found what Robert Lowell described as "a long, often backbreaking, search for an inclusive style, a style that could use his erudition, and catch the high, even frenetic, intensity of his experience, disgusts and enthusiasm." It is a style that draws on the Bible and *The Cantos*, the romances of Shakespeare and Chaplin, *Ulysses* and *The Lost Son*, Hopkins and Hart Crane and Cummings, blackface minstrel patter and alcoholic slur and babytalk. In this "monoglot of English / (American version)," Berryman had devised "a style stern wicked & sweet," "a song as fast as said, as light, / so deep, so flexing." And his pride in its uniqueness —"I perfect my metres / until no mosquito can get through" —is a conviction that this style is not merely the expression but the embodiment of his self. Its montage of voices and address catch up dreams, fantasies, memories, gossip, grudges and private jokes; its tone can veer from vulgar to exalted, manic to depressive; its narrative includes Berryman's binges, hospitalizations, travels, teaching, a broken arm, insurance forms, and his opinions on Vietnam and beer, poets and dentists: a maze of concentric circles of concern—the primary world of events, the secondary world of art, the private world of experience. *The Dream Songs* is a sprawling picaresque, a mock-epic, a wisdom work, a failed theodicy. But above all, Berryman is performing "operations of great delicacy / on my self," and probing "Our wounds to time." This haphazard chronicle of his continuing experience both prompts and props confessions of his involvement with the "Loss, deaths, terror" that are the poem's final subject. The dead who haunt the book are held as hostages against Berryman's own consciousness of death, each one a threatening reenactment of the crucial event in the poet's life.

It is obvious that the format for such an ambitious poem would have been in Berryman's mind for a considerable time before he actually began to write it. And if he was not already plotting *The Dream Songs* while at work on *Stephen Crane,* then at least several passages in that biography offer retrospective but leading clues for a reading of the poem. Clearly the title and general intention of *The Dream Songs*—"These Songs are not meant to be understood, you understand. / They are only meant to terrify & comfort"—derive from this description in the Crane book:

> Robert Graves, one of the shrewdest, craziest, and most neglected students of poetry living, laid out a theory of the origin of poetry once. A savage dreams, is frightened by the dream, and goes to the medicine man to have it explained. The medicine man can make up anything, anything will reassure the savage, so long as the manner of its delivery is impressive; so he chants, perhaps he stamps his foot, people

like rhythm, what he says becomes rhythmical, people like to hear things *again*, and what he says begins to rhyme. Poetry begins—as a practical matter, for use. It reassures the savage. Perhaps he only hears back again, chanted, the dream he just told the medicine man, but he is reassured; it is like a spell. And medicine men are shrewd: interpretation enters the chanting, symbols are developed and connected, the gods are invoked, poetry booms.

And Berryman's subsequent description of Crane is certainly the image of the poet in *The Dream Songs* as well: "Crane was not only a man with truths to tell, but an interested listener to this man. His poetry has the inimitable sincerity of a frightened savage anxious to learn what his dream means." That shrewd and crazy theory of Graves', which is Berryman's too, is similar to Freud's sense of the artist's conversion of his neurotic fantasies. The practical nature of both theories—"for *use*"—only underscores the similarity. For Berryman later elaborates his figure of the savage's dream by distinguishing between "rehearsal" and "investigation": "The poem can simply say what the dream (nightmare) was; at once it gets rid of the dream, and is solaced in hearing it said. An effect of style is undesirable. To *study* the dream, to embody it, as in a story —this is another matter." So too, compared with the seemingly "rehearsed" confessions of *Love & Fame*, those in *The Dream Songs* are "studied," projected investigations of the self's history, its past and present blurred together as in a dream.

Berryman is "a cagey John" in his preface to the book:

The poem, then, whatever its wide cast of characters, is essentially about an imaginary character (not the poet, not me) named Henry, a white American in early middle age sometimes in blackface, who has suffered an irreversible loss and talks about himself sometimes in the first person, sometimes in the third, sometimes even in the second; he has a friend, never named, who addresses him as Mr. Bones and variants thereof.

Why he needed Henry is problematical:

> Henry saw with Tolstoyan clarity
> his muffled purpose. He describes the folds—
> not a symbol in the place.
> Naked the man came forth in his mask, to be.

Henry's masking the naked Berryman is evidence of the poet's self-conscious uneasiness with his own experience, and along with the style of the poem itself such a transparent persona serves, by a minimal displacement, to baffle the anxieties of a more immediate presentation of self. Or in a more positive light, Henry is the sort of objectification of the self that occurs in dreams, just as the different voices of the poem and Henry's shifting identity—Henry House, Henry Pussy-cat, Henry Hankovich, Senator Cat, Mr. Bones, etc.—function like the mechanics of dream-work which can simultaneously include, condense and transform so much experience, both conscious and unconscious. As Berryman put it in an interview, Henry is his characterization of himself: "Henry both is and is not me, obviously. We touch at certain points. But I am an actual human being; he is nothing but a series of conceptions—my conceptions."

The derivation of Henry's name leads to one further speculation on his function. Readers have spotted Berryman's discussion of the name in *Stephen Crane*, or noted that "Henry Flower" is the alias of Joyce's Leopold Bloom, whose vulnerable, pathetic, self-delusive heroism Henry Pussy-cat shares. Berryman himself was more casual:

> My second wife, Ann, and I were walking down Hennepin Avenue one momentous night. . . . Anyway, we were joking on our way to a bar to have a beer, and I decided that I

hated the name Mabel more than any other female name,
. . . and she decided that Henry was the name she found
completely unbearable. So from then on, for a long time, in
the most cozy and affectionate lover kind of talk—we hadn't
been married very long at this time—she was Mabel and I
was Henry in our scene. So I started the poem.

Aside from the hints of self-hatred in that description, the very
flatness of the name—as flat as John Smith, which was Berry-
man's own name before he was adopted by his stepfather—
gives it a representative quality, and the influence of Whitman
on *The Dream Songs*, which the poet admitted, makes itself
felt here. At times, Henry is named "the New Man, / come to
farm a crazy land" and "a human American man," and when
in another exchange Henry mocks himself—"Reduce him to
the rest of us"—he is answered: "But Bones, you is that."
And he is. What Berryman displaces of himself makes room
for the rest of us; undoubtedly the poet was interested in
making a mid-century Representative Man whose Song of My-
self would both share and exemplify the lives of his audience.

The other and unnamed character in the poem is its Invisible
Man, the black interlocutor who addresses Henry as Mr. Bones.
His is the dark voice of mortality, an insistent refrain in these
Songs: "Mr. Bones, we all brutes & fools"; "Hear matters
hard to manage at de best, / Mr Bones. Tween what we see,
what be, / is blinds. Them blinds' on fire." And when, for
example, Henry resolves "I have to live," the black echo is:
"Now there *you* exaggerate, Sah. We hafta *die*." An obvious
but incorrect conclusion is that this interlocutor is, as Jerome
Mazzaro has written, "Henry's death urge." But just as the
Negro may derive from the character of Henry Johnson in
Crane's *The Monster*, where Berryman repeatedly refers to
him as a "rescuer," so too here he is an aspect of Henry's
"burnt-cork luck." Gabriel Pearson seems more exact in seeing

him as an emblem of survival: "The Negro is an expert in survival. He is familiar with death and yet somehow continually picks himself off the very floor, clambers out of the very basement of modern civilization. Supremely a victim, he escapes self-pity through joy in survival." Henry himself refers to his "mentor" as "the oldest one"—"black & ripe, a floater." And in addressing Henry as Bones, and so recalling his skeletal mortality, the Negro bares Henry's deepest self and urges a bitter stoicism similar to that of one of Berryman's own mentors, Philip Rieff:

> Character is the restrictive shaping of possibility. . . . The heaviest crosses are internal and men make them so that, thus skeletally supported, they can bear the burden of their flesh. Under the sign of this inner cross, a certain inner distance is achieved from the infantile desire to be and have everything.[1]

The dilemma which this "certain inner distance" dramatizes is, again, clarified by Berryman's reading of Crane, whose use of irony fascinated the poet. The role of the Ironical Man in Crane is that of the Negro in The Dream Songs, or as Berryman said: "a contest between the Alazon (Imposter) and the Eiron or Ironical Man: after vauntings and pretensions, the Alazon is routed by the man who affects to be a fool. The Imposter pretends to be more than he is, the Ironist pretends to be less." But as Henry becomes Bones, so too do both voices finally merge, the two aspects of Berryman's own personality—self-consciousness and instinct, Eros and Thanatos—inextricably one:

> Crane never rests. He is always fighting the thing out with himself, for he contains both Alazon and Eiron; and so, of course, does the reader; and only dull readers escape. As

comedy, his work is a continual examination of pretension
—an attempt to cast overboard, as it were, impediments to
our salvation. . . . There is regularly an element of pathos,
therefore, in his ironic (oppositional) inspection, and an ele-
ment of irony regularly in his pathos. A Crane creation, or
character, normally is *pretentious* and *scared*—the human
condition; fitted by the second for pathos, by the first for
irony.

The tone of the drama, in other words, is played out against
its plot; as Berryman portrays Crane's art, "it is for an ironic
inward and tragic vision outward that we value it most, when
we can bear it." That outward arc of tragedy cannot precisely
be called a plot: "it was not cliff hangers or old serials / but
according to his nature" that *The Dream Songs* maneuvers.
"Its plot," noted Berryman, "is the personality of Henry as he
moves on in the world, . . . areas of hope and fear that Henry
is going through at a given time." Or to use the term the poet
cites from Crane, "maps of accident." But if those "accidents"
are not consistent, they are congruent: "I sing with infinite
slowness finite pain." That pain is identical to Crane's "fate."
Having devised the drama of his characters, Crane, "watching
intently, tenderly, and hopelessly, blew Fate through it—say-
ing with inconceivable rapidity and an air of immense deliber-
ation what he saw." Helpless before what he saw, "the pattern
of justice in his art has to manifest itself as best it can under
the dreadful recognitions of honesty. Life is what it is. The
consequences of these recognitions, bitterness and horror, dis-
guise themselves in his grotesquerie of concept and style, his
velocity, his displacements of rage. Open, they would be insup-
portable." Berryman too, supported by his grotesqueries, man-
ifests his dreadful recognitions.

The fate blown through *The Dream Songs* is the ingredient

in Berryman's history that made his life "a handkerchief sand-
wich": his father's suicide, his own self-destructive urges, his
alcoholism, "the horror of unlove" at the root of his sexual
guilts, and even his art, which he calls his "life sentence":

> Failed as a makar, nailed as scholar, failed
> as a father & a man, hailed for a lover,
> Henry slumped down, pored it over,
> We c-can't win here, he stammered to himself.
>
> (184)

"Our intolerable problem" stammers through the Songs:
"There ought to be a law against Henry. / —Mr. Bones: there
is" (4); "Fate clobber all" (25); "We came toward the world,
did we not, accursed" (138). The broadest outline of Berry-
man's "accursed" concern details the impediments to salvation
—the existential dilemma of mortality:

> The cold is ultimating. The cold is cold.
> I am—I should be held together by—
> but I am breaking up
> and Henry now has come to a full stop—
> vanished his vision, if there was, & fold
> him over himself quietly.
>
> (85)

The inescapable fact that "the whole fault ends with death"
(144) leaves no "middle ground between things and the soul"
(385). The result is a radical and wrenching contradiction—
"grace & fear" (296)—on which Berryman broods. Shackled
to a "prostrate body, busy with your break" (165), "Henry
walked as if he were ashamed / of being in the body" (247), his
most obvious evidence. And from this, the trial proceeds with
"the 'I'm- / immortal-&-not' routine" (347), its tragedy usu-
ally checked with irony:

Supreme my holdings, greater yet my need,
thoughtless I go out.

(64)

This screen-porch where my puppy suffers and
I swarm I hope with hurtless love is now
towards the close of day
the scene of a vision of friendlies who withstand
animal nature so far as to allow
grace awhile to stay.

(106)

Today's Thanksgiving; that is, summing up
that which one bears more steadily than else
and the odd definite good.
I do this thrice a year; that is, I grope
a few sore hours among my actuals
for evidence of knighthood.

(163)

During those years he met his seminars,
went & lectured & read, talked with human beings,
paid insurance & taxes;

but his mind was not on it. His mind was elsewheres
in an area where the soul not talks but sings
& where foes are attacked with axes.

(352)

The no-man's-land between fact and fantasy, ruled by Freud's
terrible goddess Necessity, is any man's by birthright. The first
Dream Song laments that unfortunate Fall:

> What he has now to say is a long
> wonder the world can bear & be.
> Once in a sycamore I was glad

John Berryman 163

all at the top, and I sang.
Hard on the land wears the strong sea
and empty grows every bed.

But Berryman personalizes the anxiety by detailing "his complex investigations of death" (335), and especially of its toll among his friends—all poets, some distant figures like Roethke, Blackmur, and Plath; others intimate: Randall Jarrell and Delmore Schwartz. In fact, at the dead center of the book, Songs 146 through 161, is Berryman's most intense meditation on mortality, occasioned by Schwartz's death in obscurity:

> These lovely motions of the air, the breeze,
> tell me I'm not in hell, though round me the dead
> lie in their limp postures
> dramatizing the dreadful word *instead*
> for lively Henry, fit for debaucheries
> and bird-of-paradise vestures
>
> only his heart is elsewhere, down with them
> & down with Delmore specially, the new ghost
> haunting Henry most:
> though fierce the claims of others . . .
>
> 'Down with them all!' Henry suddenly cried.
> Their deaths were theirs. I wait on for my own.
> I dare say it won't be long.
> I have tried to be them, god knows I have tried,
> but they are past it all, I have not done,
> which brings me to the end of this song.
>
> (146)

As a man and a poet, Berryman had tried throughout his career to live in "the air where are / & can be, only heroes." That those heroes were invariably writers is an indication they served as transference projections for Berryman. The transference is more complex than the fact that he lived in the lives of his peers, so that his memories of Schwartz, for example, are those of himself as well: "I can't get him out of my mind, out of my mind / . . . I remember his electrical insight as the young man, / his wit & passion, gift, the whole young man / alive with surplus love." Besides serving his future, his transferences sought out a past; his elegies for Frost, Eliot, Hemingway, Williams and others reveal a longing for an artist-father in whose company he would himself be included by the art of the very poems he wrote to evoke them—a kind of necessary, controlling, and self-fulfilling projection. But with so much invested in others, their deaths are direct threats to Berryman: "This world is gradually becoming a place / where I do not care to be any more. Can Delmore die?" The consciousness of his own death is thus rubbed raw:

> The high ones die, die. They die. You look up and
> > who's there?
> —Easy, easy, Mr. Bones. I is on your side.
> I smell your grief.
> —I sent my grief away. I cannot care
> forever. With them all again & again I died
> and cried, and I have to live.
>
> —Now there *you* exaggerate, Sah. We hafta *die*.
> That is our 'pointed task. Love & die.
> —Yes; that makes sense.
> But what makes sense between, then? What if I
> roiling & babbling & braining, brood on why and
> just sat on the fence?

> (36)

When he sees them "all going away," Berryman describes his reaction as "Panic & shock, together," and this recalls his discussion of panic in *Stephen Crane*:

But panic is not so directly a form of fear as it is an overwhelming form of anxiety where control has failed and a regression occurs, driving the emotion back behind the point at which particular danger is occurring, toward an earlier general terror: toward what is called a trauma. As a response, that is, it exceeds any possible fear that can be felt for any conceivable particular danger, because it opens again some ancient vista.

Berryman's trauma intrudes clearly enough even in poems about others, as here in one about Randall Jarrell:

> Again, his friend's death made the man sit still
> and freeze inside—his daughter won first prize—
> his wife scowled over at him—
> It seemed to be Hallowe'en.
> His friend's death had been adjudged suicide,
> which dangles a trail
>
> longer than Henry's chill, longer than his loss . . .
> All souls converge upon a hopeless mote
> tonight, as though
>
> the throngs of souls in hopeless pain rise up
> to say they cannot care, to say they abide
> whatever is to come.
> My air is flung with souls which will not stop
> and among them hangs a soul that has not died
> and refuses to come home.
>
> (127)

That anxious last line speaks of the difficulty Berryman had in resolving the effect of his father's suicide: "death grew tall / up Henry as a child," and "It all centered in the end on the suicide." That "Something black somewhere in the vistas of his heart" goads a variety of panicked and contradictory responses. Since they all involve a boy's arrested image of his father's adult strength, there is a sense in which the steady, mortal voice of the Negro interlocutor might be the poet's father. In *Stephen Crane*, he remarks that "as the Negro rescues the Crane-mask, the boy, he represents not only Crane but Crane's father," and in *The Dream Songs*, hapless Henry and the Negro who "rescues" him come to read like a dialogue between Berryman and the memory of his father, kept ironic to distance the pain and diminish the realization. Berryman wavers among feelings of abandonment (76), admiration (145), rage (384), and self-pity. But beneath these tense contradictions lies the real feeling—one which Berryman would not be able to articulate until he returned to confront it in his unfinished novel *Recovery:*

'New problem. Did I myself feel any *guilt* perhaps—long repressed if so, and mere speculation now (defense here)— *about Daddy's death?* (I certainly picked up enough of Mother's self-blame to accuse her once, drunk and raging, of having actually murdered him and staged a suicide.) Lecturer lately on children's blaming themselves for father drunk (=What did I do to make Daddy angry and get drunk?). BLANK, probably odd. He *was* drinking heavily, all four of them were in those last weeks, nightmarish quarrels. Gundeath at dawn, like Hemingway's, imitating his father. Does my fanatical drinking emulate his, and my fanatical smoking (both "manly")? So possible it wasn't rage/self-pity, but guilt, that were simply driven underground for a year (Why? if so) to emerge after all and cripple my prep school years . . . . How many models can a grown man survive?' . . . Tall handsome Daddy, adored and lost so soon!

It is the failing effort to repress this guilt with which the poet faints at the end of this Song:

I'll sing you now a song
the like of which may bring your heart to break:
he's gone! and we don't know where. When he began
taking the pistol out & along,

you was just a little; but gross fears
accompanied us along the beaches, pal.
My mother was scared almost to death.
He was going to swim out, with me, forevers,
and a swimmer strong he was in the phosphorescent Gulf,
but he decided on lead.

That mad drive wiped out my childhood. I put him down
while all the same on forty years I love him
stashed in Oklahoma
besides his brother Will. Bite the nerve of the town
for anyone so desperate. I repeat: I love him
until *I* fall into coma.

(143)

It is this same guilt which motivates the best-known Song:

There sat down, once, a thing on Henry's heart
so heavy, if he had a hundred years
& more, & weeping, sleepless, in all them time
Henry could not make good.
Starts again always in Henry's ears
the little cough somewhere, an odour, a chime.

(29)

The father whom he unconsciously feared he had driven to
death had "left Henry to live on" with loss and guilt, and the
manner of that survival is finally the focus of *The Dream
Songs. Recovery*—its title the central theme of all Berryman's
work—provides the poet's own evaluation of his Songs: "Good
deal of authentic mania there, black and blue wit, pain—the

fellow going on to fresh defeats, flappable, flappable. Surviving however." The book opens by setting its own minimal goal in an equation of confession and loss: "I don't see how Henry, pried / open for all the world to see, survived." The adulthood forced on him by the suicide has never been grown into: "Now Henry is unmistakably a Big One. / Funnee; he don't feel so. / He he just stuck around." And those child's eyes that see "the whole implausible necessary thing" are left glazed in a time "when the word / 'happy' sheds its whole meaning, like to come and / for memory too." For Berryman lived his forward life back in memory—"memoried, / like a remaining man"— each loss linked with the death, each success with the guilt. The scattered childhood, the deaths of friends, the failure of marriages, the lack of recognition, the later reputation, the alcohol, the wards, all make "a disadvantage of surviving." Inevitably, these are times he "pauses to wonder why he / alone breasts the wronging tide" and considers his father's example, as if survival were a retribution. But on the whole he is "prepared to live in a world of Fall." "We wake & blunder on, / wiser, on the whole"; the surprise of these Songs is that their hero can so often "recover & be whole."

Berryman was an escape artist, but seemed in the last two books published during his lifetime to have abandoned the enabling tricks and disguises of *The Dream Songs*. In a late interview he remarked:

> . . . it didn't resemble any verse I had ever written in my entire life, and moreover the subject was entirely new, solely and simply myself. Nothing else. A subject on which I am an expert. . . . I am a scholar in certain fields, but the subject on which I am a real authority is me, so I wiped out all the disguises and went to work.

Love & Fame (1970) was written with the intensity of the Dickinson lyrics which influenced it—Berryman finished the book in three months—and involved a shift in style as radical as that in Lowell's *Life Studies*. Some of it is plainly prose. But generally, the style of this book, and of *Delusions, Etc.*, is closer to the "new musics" envisioned in an early Berryman poem:

> New musics! One the music that we hear,
> this is the music which the masters make
> out of their minds, profound, solemn & clear.
>
> And then the other music, in whose sake
> all men perceive a gladness but we are drawn
> less for that joy than utterly to take
>
> our trial, naked in the music's vision,
> the flowing ceremony of trouble and light,
> all Loves becoming, none to flag upon.
>
> ("Canto Amor")

The naked trial of *Love & Fame*, its flattened style and obsessive details, make it the most exposed and intimate collection—which is perhaps one factor contributing to the general puzzlement and disappointment which surrounded its publication. Though some critics defended its intentions—Jerome Mazzaro, for instance, drew the interesting comparison with Augustine's *Confessions* which he saw as its model—most readers found its sexual anecdotes and empty boasting tedious. One critic spoke for the majority: "John Berryman's poetry ripened from dignified impersonality to comic egoism, and declined from that into sober self-exploitation."

Berryman was sufficiently stung by his "uncomprehending" critics to append to the book's revised second edition a "Scholia" which explained its continuity with his previous work—especially in its use of the dissolving personality, "here, that of the mature poet omnipotent and that of the aging man deprived and powerless." Each of the book's four sections Berryman terms "movements criticizing backward the preceding"—an ironic mode similar to that of *The Dream Songs*, though here tone substitutes for the variety of voices. But to understand properly the purpose of his confessions and his irony, *Love & Fame* must be read as the first part of a larger work which includes *Delusions, Etc.* Together, their pattern forms a deliberate plan, one which Berryman then tried again in *Recovery*. The novel's autobiographical hero, Alan Severance, explains it: " 'Maybe if I can find' (he wrote in his Journal) 'and reveal this cluster of unknown horrors, underlying even them in me I will find God' and he felt okay." Considering that *Delusions, Etc.* (1972) was written during the same "spasm" that produced *Love & Fame* and that the second book's provisional title was *Trips to the Interior*, the poet's intention in *Love & Fame* is clearer: to reveal a cluster of horrors, the bondage of the self's history, in order to free what "underlies" to find God, to write himself out of exterior experience as a preparation, a purgation, for the trip to the interior. Again, his study of Crane is helpful:

> A refuge is a serious matter; and no human being is very strong. The careful student J. A. K. Thomson observes that, tracing the Ironical Man to his beginnings, we "find him, not the remote and fastidious Intellectual, but someone far more elemental, simple, grotesque, and pitiful." This habit of mind—which one possesses by nature or not at all; it cannot be learned—is a form of *lying low* before the Divine Jealousy.

And before he "lies low" in *Delusions, Etc.*, Berryman has glaringly revealed his past in *Love & Fame*—its very intimacy a form of exaggeration which he works to deflate in the process of purging himself of it. To write "for *use*," to uncover the "real" life occluded by the delusive accumulation of events and ambitions, to begin again with rejections that necessitate enumeration, to re-father himself—this is the point of the seem-

ingly coy or contradictory poem "Message" which restates
Berryman's project in *Love & Fame:*

Amplitude,—voltage,—the one friend calls for the one,
the other for the other, in my work;
in verse & prose. Well, hell.
I am not writing an autobiography-in-verse, my friends.

Impressions, structures, tales, from Columbia in the Thirties
& the Michaelmas term at Cambridge in '36,
followed by some later. It's not my life.
That's occluded & lost.

The first poem, "Her & It," dramatizes the dilemma of the
last infirmities of his mind and heart. By dreaming of a girl he
once loved—a real girl, and his muse, and his lost loves and
wives—Berryman emphasizes (so his "Scholia" explains) "his
insecurity about his fame (over-brandishing) [which] matches
his insecurity over his 'true' (exposed as false by his repeated
infidelity to it) love he is so proud of, and we have before us an
existential man, wishing to be (twice—cf. title) what is impos-
sible to quicksilver (Luther's word for man's heart) Man." He
is the "current noisy pseudo-world-figure fixated on a local
ancient unidentifiable whisper":

Time magazine yesterday slavered Saul's ass,
they pecked at mine last year. We're going strong!
Photographs all over!
She muttered something in my ear I've forgotten as we
   danced.

What was once mumbled on a dance floor is identified with a
more ancient whisper which Berryman answers in his "Eleven
Addresses to the Lord," but his first section of *Love & Fame*
deals only with "my inordinate desire," allowing little con-
science and minimal consciousness: "It is supernal what a youth

can take / & barely notice or be bothered by / which to him older would work ruin" ("Down & Back"). There is a nervous edge to the brags, and the jumpy, associative narration heaps up ancedotes and sins with impatience. At times, a context is offered like slides hurriedly clicked on, off:

> Magical mourning blues, at the Apollo & on records.
> Victoria, Bessie. Teagarden. Pine-top Smith
> the sightless passionate constructor.

> Anti-semitism through the purblind Houses.
> News weird out of Germany.
> Our envy for any visitor to the Soviet Union.
> The shaking incredible transcripts of the Trials. . . .

> Ping-pong at the Little Carnegie,
> the cheapest firstrate date in the Depression city.
> A picture of me in *The New York Times*
> with a jock-strap on, & socks & shoes,

> taken during the Freshman-Sophomore Rush . . .
>   ("Nowhere")

The technique here reflects the polymorphous perversity of his ambition, caught between "Shirley & Auden"—a frantic search for ideal loves and heroes:

> I had, from my beginning, to adore heroes
> & I elected that they witness to,
> show forth, transfigure: life-suffering & pure heart
> & hardly definable but central weaknesses

> for which they were to be enthroned & forgiven by me.
>   ("The Heroes")

An eccentric friend, a Renaissance scholar, sixty-odd, unworldly, he writes limericks in Medieval Latin,

stood up in the rowboat fishing to take a leak
& exclaimed as he was about it with excitement

'I wish my penis was big enough for this whole lake!'
My phantasy precisely at twenty:
to satisfy at once all Barnard & Smith
& have enough left over for Miss Gibbs's girls.

("Two Organs")

He read poetry then as he says Pound wrote it: "zeroing in on
feelings, / hovering up to them, putting his tongue in their ear,
/ delicately modulating them in & out of each other" ("The
Heroes"). When he "grunted, over lines and her" ("Images of
Elspeth"), he is pursued by The Other Lover, whether the man
who cuts in while he dances ("Cadenza on Garnette") or the
poets with styles their own:

I didn't want my next poem to be *exactly* like Yeats
or exactly like Auden
since in that case where the hell was *I?*
but what instead *did* I want it to sound like?

("Two Organs")

In a sense, these are both images of his "perforated daddy, /
daddy boxed in & let down with strong straps, / when I my
friends' homes visited, with fathers / universal & intact"
("Freshman Blues"). The concern, finally, is for identity: "I
dreamt at times in those days of my *name* / blown by adoring
winds all over" ("My Special Fate").

The second section moves on to "the outspread opening
world," to the "Images, memories, of a lonely & ambitious
young alien" ("The Other Cambridge") during his year at
Clare College, Cambridge. His voyage begins with wide-eyed
irony:

Yeats, Yeats, I'm coming! it's me. Faber & Faber,
you'll have to publish me some day with éclat
I haven't quite got the hang of the stuff yet
but I swamp with possibility

("Away")

But the succeeding narrative of his "unwilling monkhood" is
less reflexive, more continuous and concerned than the first
section. As Berryman "strolled to look & see, & browsed, &
began to feel" at the University of Newton and Milton and
Wordsworth, he becomes more aware of how he responds to
the world and why: "Along with my hero-worship & wish for
comradeship / went my pride, my 'satanic pride' " ("Monk-
hood"), both based on "Fear. Of failure, or worse, *insignifi-
cance*" ("Friendless"). His desires grow more focused: "Will I
ever write properly, with passion & exactness, / of the damned
strange demeanours of my flagrant heart? / & be by anyone
anywhere undertaken?" ("Monkhood"). And that concern for
acceptance—the longing for unearned approval—still allows
him to confess, "I stand ashamed of myself," of his arrogance
and assumptions—the shame at his public excesses which later
gave way to guilt and to the release of the poem itself:

When I was fiddling later with every wife
on the Eastern seaboard
I longed to climb into a pulpit & confess.
Tear me to pieces!

("Views of Myself")

Like his one-a-day poems, his casual affairs—"Once, when
low, I made out a list—it came to 79" ("Thank You, Chris-
tine")—swell both pride and desperation, which are resolved
in the final four poems which describe his deeply-felt affair
with an English actress whom he once names "Lesbia." Signif-

John Berryman 175

icantly too, the rival is defeated: "By six-fifteen she had prom-
ised to stop seeing 'the other man.' / I may have heard better
news but I don't know when" ("Tea").

Having stared down his past, Berryman uses the third sec-
tion as a final purge. Like Keats, he can say "then on the shore
/ Of the wide world I stand alone and think / Till love and fame
to nothingness do sink." He is alone here—"I am busy tired
mad lonely & old" ("Damned")—and often too garrulous as
he looks on the wide world to settle scores with history, politics
and social unrests. In all he finds, "Woe quotidian, woe a
crony" ("Relations"), and each is dismissed with the same
despairing irony he finds to scuttle his own history. It is the
consciousness of death that motivates both the realizations and
the ironies—the death that makes everything beyond the self
meaningless and which presently threatens the self as well.
This section begins with "The Search," a scholar's parodic
version of his later discovery:

> And other systems, high & primitive,
> ancient & surviving, did I not neglect,
> sky-gods & trickster-gods, gods impotent,
> the malice & force of the dead.

> When at twelve Einstein lost belief in God
> he said to himself at once (as he put it later)
> 'Similarly motivated men, both of the past & of the present,
> together with their achieved insights,
> *waren die unverlierbaren Freunde'*—the unloseable friends.

The reference to Einstein is, of course, a personal allusion; as
Berryman says in a later poem, "my father's suicide when I
was twelve / blew out my most bright candle faith." That
ancient vista which has drawn him toward "the unloseable
friends"—ideal love and high art—opens now on a final pur-
gation and ascent toward the Divine Jealousy. The section

concludes with a group of poems whose titles alone describe as well as a synopsis would their sequence and purpose: "A Huddle of Need," "Damned," "Of Suicide," "Dante's Tomb," "Despair," "The Hell Poem," "Death Ballad," " 'I Know,' " "Purgatory," "Heaven," "The Home Ballad." Berryman begins his divine comedy in that dark wood of despair:

> It seems to be DARK all the time.
> I have difficulty walking.
> I can remember what to say to my seminar
> but I don't know that I want to.
>
> I said in a Song once: I am unusually tired.
> I repeat that & increase it.
> I'm vomiting.
> I broke down today in the slow movement of K. 365.
>
> ("Despair")

and centers it in a hospital where the poet is confined, surrounded by the victims of addiction to alcohol and heroin no less fatal than his to love and fame.

What emerges are the "Eleven Addresses to the Lord," which celebrate his release from lifelong delusions, from history's certain defeats into eternity's possible salvation in "Rest or transfiguration":

> You have come to my rescue again & again
> in my impassable, sometimes despairing years.
> You have allowed my brilliant friends to destroy themselves
> and I am still here, severely damaged, but functioning. . . .
>
> Whatever your end may be, accept my amazement.
> May I stand until death forever at attention
> for any your least instruction or enlightenment.
> I even feel sure you will assist me again, Master of insight
> & beauty.

John Berryman   177

The religious nature of his humiliation was influenced by the procedures of Alcoholics Anonymous Berryman detailed in *Recovery;* here too he lifts "up / sober toward truth a scared self-estimate" ("A Prayer for the Self"). But, as he told an interviewer, it is a God of rescue rather than of righteousness that obsesses the poet—"what has been for many years one of my favorite conceptions. I got it from Augustine and Pascal. It's found in many other people too, but especially in those heroes of mine. Namely, the idea of a God of rescue. He saves men from their situations, off and on during life's pilgrimage, and in the end. I completely bought it, and that's been my position since." This God of rescue he calls an "ingenious & beneficial Father":

> I am afraid,
> I never until now confessed.

> I fell back in love with you, Father, for two reasons:
> You were good to me, & a delicious author,
> rational & passionate. Come on me again . . .

Berryman's restored faith, in other words, has rescued his own father, whose suicide had ruined his faith in himself and caused the guilts that forced false love and empty fame. And in praising "a delicious author, / rational & passionate," he praises not only God and his father, but the accomplishment of himself, his project.

Delusions, Etc. is really just an over-extension of *Love & Fame,* a prolonged celebration of "my newly simple heart," along with an account of his faith's culmination in religion and of his resumption of Roman Catholicism. In a group of poems about transference heroes (Washington, Beethoven, Emily Dickinson, Georg Trakl, and Dylan Thomas) his "Beethoven Triumphant"—which is some proof of Berryman's poetic strength at the shaky close of his career—speaks of his own late style and stance: "Back from an over-wealth, the simplification of Necessity." As severe as the psalmist or the prophets, Berryman continues his awe at the release granted him by the "Adonai of rescue":

> However, lo, across what wilderness
> in vincible ignorance past forty years
> lost to (as now I see) Your sorrowing
> I strayed abhorrent, blazing with my Self.
>
> I thought I was in private with the Devil
> hounding me upon Daddy's cowardice
> (trustless in stir the freeze: 'Do your own time').
>
> ("Matins")

And poems like "The Form" and "Back" search out the pattern of that Necessity in his past, and so the ways of a Will in which he has found the peace of sonship: "If He for me as I feel for my daughter, / being His son, I'll sweat no more tonight / but happy hymn & sleep" ("Compline"). But increasingly with this book one thinks the poet protests too much. And if, as Freud would hold, Berryman's sense of salvation is the projected nostalgia of his infancy, his unresolved trauma intrudes a new series of doubts and anxieties—the menace of "panic" —which undercuts the book's celebration. As A. Alvarez noted in his review, "Berryman's religious verse seems like a willed, nervous defense against the appalling sadness which permeates the real poems at the heart of the book." That sadness is, first of all, the persistence of self-conscious doubt: "Father, Father, I am overwhelmed. / I cannot speak tonight. / *Do* you receive me back into Your sight?" ("A Prayer After All"). But that is a doubt grounded in guilt:

> I feel myself a deep & old objection.
> You gave me not a very able father,

joyless at last, Lord, and sometimes I hardly
(thinking on him) perform my duty to you.

Ah then I mutter 'Forty-odd years past.
Do I yet repine?' and go about your business,—
a fair wind and the honey lights of home
being all I ask this wind-torn foreign evening.

("Overseas Prayer")

This interminable trauma, in turn, revives the threat of death
—an aging man's intimations of mortality: "We're running
out / of time & fathers, sore, artless about it" ("Tampa Stomp").
And the gap, which time widens and art cannot close, between
Berryman and his father, strains his faith in God. "I know You
are there. The sweat is, I am here" ("Certainly Before Lunch").
That "here" is his familiar, non-existent "middle ground," the
existential swamp of self:

Problem. I cannot come among Your saints,
it's not in me—'Velle' eh?—I will, and fail.
But I would rather not be lost from You—
if I could hear of a middle ground, I'd opt:

a decent if minute salvation, sort of, on some fringe.
I am afraid, afraid. Brothers, who if
you are afraid are my brothers—veterans of fear—
pray with me now in the hour of our living.

("Nones")

The pun in "the hour of our living" equates it with death, and
the Necessity of God's will becomes confused with that of
death. This account of his elation grows less ambiguous than
hysterical:

It is plain to me
Christ underwent man & treachery & socks

& lashes, thirst, exhaustion, the bit, for my pathetic &
  disgusting vices,
to make this filthy fact of particular, long-after,
faraway, five-foot-ten & moribund
human being happy. Well, he has!
I am so happy I could scream!
It's enough! I can't BEAR ANY MORE.
Let this be it. I've had *it. I can't wait.*

("The Facts & Issues")

Simplified, that Necessity braces the purified version of his
resignation to it:

> Age, and the deaths, and the ghosts.
> Her having gone away
> in spirit from me. Hosts
> of regrets come & find me empty.
>
> I don't feel this will change.
> I don't want any thing
> or person, familiar or strange.
> I don't think I will sing
>
> any more just now;
> or ever. I must start
> to sit with a blind brow
> above an empty heart.

("He Resigns")

The allusion there is less to the Yeats line than to the first
Dream Song: "Once in a sycamore I was glad / all at the top,
and I sang. / Hard on the land wears the strong sea / and
empty grows every bed." And that echo measures the distance
he has survived but failed to close in an occluded life. The
actions of art upon the remembered possibility of death seem,

at last, to dislodge his "favorite conception," "the idea of a God of rescue," and to recover his terrible conclusion in *Stephen Crane:* "Death ends the terrible excitement under which he is bound to live, death resolves the panic, death is 'a way out,' a rescue." The empty bed. The empty heart. To escape such emptiness Berryman leapt into it on January 7, 1972, abandoning the artful bridge of confessions his project had constructed to span a lifelong struggle. A few months before he died, he told a friend what he would like inscribed on his headstone: beneath his name and dates, let them carve: "FantASTic! FantASTic! Thank Thee, Dear Lord!"

ENDNOTE

1. Philip Rieff, "The Impossible Culture: Oscar Wilde & the Charisma of the Artist," *Encounter* (September 1970), 35:40–41.

SYLVIA PLATH

SHORT CIRCUITS
AND FOLDING MIRRORS

READ TOGETHER, Aurelia Schober Plath's edition of her daughter's *Letters Home* and Edward Butscher's overheated, undiscriminating, yet interesting biography, *Sylvia Plath: Method and Madness*, remind one of the strong "period" quality of this poet's life and attitudes. McCarthyism, heavy petting, the military-industrial complex, *The New Yorker*, bomb shelters, the vocationalism and domesticity, the unfocused neuroses and emotional hyperbole—these suggest the era: Plath's ambitions and anxieties were redolent of the ruthless vanities and sad defenses of Eisenhower's America. The most extensive and convincing interpretation of Plath's work—Judith Kroll's elaborate, even pedantic *Chapters in a Mythology: The Poetry of Sylvia Plath*—reinforces this sense by reading the career in terms of the then fashionable murk of Robert Graves's White Goddess mythologies. In Plath's "mythicized biography," Kroll contends, the poet's autobiographical impulses were subsumed by archetypal patterns and strategies that at once revealed, organized, and articulated her experience in poetry. In impressive detail, Kroll traces through Plath's sources and imagery the poet's pursuit of the Muse as both the subject of her work and its inspiration. There is no doubt that Plath exploited various back-of-the-brain protocols as a ready-made source of images and plots that focused the facts of her own life.

Kroll's is a symptomatic response to this poet, though more intelligent than most. The establishment of a cult, with accompanying distortions of attention, inflated claims, and rapt explications, normally attends the appearance and aftermath of any "period" poet. (I do not mean that as a pejorative term; among others, Shelley, Arnold, Hart Crane and Frank O'Hara seem to me equally "period" poets, whose sensibilities uniquely captured—and whose work continues to recover for later readers—their culture's tone, values, and issues.) I suspect that, in retrospect, Plath will have emerged as the most distinctly "period" poet of her generation. Already she is viewed as a cultural, as well as a literary, phenomenon. Alternately heroine or victim, martyr or scapegoat, she has been symbolized and exploited so hauntingly in the cultural consciousness that it is difficult not to read her life—with its gestures of defiance, compulsion, and despair—rather than her work, in which those gestures are re-imagined. But Plath is also an especially representative figure of the directions and dynamics of poetry in the early 1960s. And I think that can be seen nowhere more clearly than in a stylistic reading of her work, of the ways in which she absorbed and altered the poetic climate then prevailing. In the dedicatory poem to *Nones*, which was published at about the time Plath first began writing verse, Auden caught the official tone exactly when he spoke of a "civil style" vitiated by "the wry, the sotto-voce, / Ironic and monochrome." Her initiation into such a situation, her attempts to master it while achieving an individual voice, the methods she used to dismantle or energize such a polite inheritance, and her shift to a more daringly expressionistic and highly inflected verse—all of these are aspects of a larger trend then occurring in poetry. But in a poignantly foreshortened way, Plath got there first, so that her career remains paradigmatic. Its force and permanence reside less in her subjects than in her rapidly evolving relationship to style, and in her final accomplishment of a form that combines its prosody, imagery, and tone with an abiding authority.

PLATH WAS an assiduous apprentice, and put herself resolutely through the traditionalist paces. However predictably feeble the results were, she did acquire a degree of technical expertise and fluency, so that by the time she considered herself a professional she had ready answers to an interviewer's question about her sense of craft:

> Technically I like it to be extremely musical and lyrical, with a singing sound. I don't like poetry that just throws itself away in prose. I think there should be a kind of constriction and tension which is never artificial yet keeps in the meaning in a kind of music too. And again, I like the idea of managing to get wit in with the idea of seriousness, and contrasts, ironies, and I like visual images, and I like just good mouthfuls of sound which have meaning. . . . At first I started in strict forms—it's the easiest way for a beginner to get music ready-made, but I think that now I like to work in forms that are strict but their strictness isn't uncomfortable. I lean very strongly toward forms that are, I suppose, quite rigid in comparison certainly to free verse. I'm much happier when I know that all my sounds are echoing in different ways throughout the poem.[1]

What is curious in that hurried litany of modernist pieties is that her attention was as often fixed on the possibility of error as of achievement. And indeed, her early poetry consistently portrays her abilities rather than her experience; in fact, that is frequently the explicit subject of the poems themselves: "Hardcastle Crags," "The Ghost's Leavetaking," "Black Rook in Rainy Weather," "A Winter Ship," "Ouija," "Snake-charmer," "Moonrise," "On the Difficulty of Conjuring Up a Dryad." These are all poems that worry the difficulty of aligning reality and vision, and "vision" in *The Colossus* is a term with no mystical force. It is Plath's word for art itself—a transcendent, idealized heterocosm, ordered and self-reflexive. It is, in other words, the well-wrought poetics of the modernist masters and their New Critics: Yeats, Stevens, and Auden, as domesticated and institutionalized by Brooks-and-Warren. *The Colossus* is not merely the poetry of an ambitious but cautious beginner; it is a summary of the prevalent mode, and Plath's imagination, though equal to its forms and discretions, was not yet strong enough to assert a personality apart from the mimed voice. She followed the rules of the game, and generally set low stakes.

Her first collection betrays the novice's self-consciousness. It is a poetry of chosen words, of careful schemes and accumulated effects; its voice is unsteady, made up. It leans heavily on its models; there are broad hints of help from Stevens, Roethke, even Eliot. The refinement of this poetry derives not only from its being influenced or allusive. There is also a kind of awkward delicacy to it—which may come from her identification of herself with what she thought was a genteel line of women poets like Marianne Moore and Elizabeth Bishop, or may be connected with her insistent academicism. Whatever the reasons, there is an inhibited quality to the verse's perspectives, as well as a distinctly literary cast to many of the poems that borrow Oedipus or Gulliver, Byron or Medea, Gabriel or Lucine for their authority. Another symptom is the stiff, stale diction that rattles around in so many of these poems: words like "cuirass," "wraith," "descant," "bole," "bruit," "casque," "ichor," "pellicle." This is a language found nowadays only in the columns of a Thesaurus—an underlined copy of which Ted Hughes remembers always on his wife's knee at the time, as if she were more interested in the unusual than in the appropriate word. One need only compare her "Sow" to "View of a Pig" by Hughes—who early became and always remained the strongest influence on her work—to sense the more natural ease with which he urges and controls his language and the power it draws from strangeness. His dead pig retains a menacing vitality, as Hughes narrows his regard, pares his description, and concentrates on essentials. Plath, on the other hand, fusses with piggy banks and parslied sucklings, a constantly shifting metric, long sentences, and a glut of adjectives—all of which dilute her argument and blur the poem's occasion and subject.

In 1958, at a time when she was as devoted to drawing as she was to verse, Plath wrote to her mother, "I've discovered my deepest source of inspiration, which is art"—not an unusual discovery for any young poet. But she was not referring only to the origins of poems, though she drew on Breughel's *The Triumph of Death*, Rousseau's *Charmeuse de Serpents*, and DeChirico's *The Disquieting Muses*, among others. I take her to have meant her method as well. It is not merely those expected *Gemäldegedichte* that would lead one to call most of the poems in this book *compositions*. Throughout, she is attracted to textures and shapes, to landscape, primary colors and gradated shades, grounded figures, and above all, to design. These are, of course, concerns and effects that enact the then dominant aesthetic, with its stress on correctness and perspicuity, on elaborated forms, on the observing eye and ordering mind.

The pictorial bias in *The Colossus* has, in turn, inevitable stylistic consequences. "Man in Black" is a convenient example:

> Where the three magenta
> Breakwaters take the shove
> And suck of the gray sea

To the left, and the wave
Unfists against the dun
Barb-wired headland of

The Deer Island prison
With its trim piggeries,
Hen huts and cattle green

To the right, and March ice
Glazes the rock pools yet,
Snuff-colored sand cliffs rise

Over a great stone spit
Bared by each falling tide,
And you, across those white

Stones, strode out in your dead
Black coat, black shoes, and your
Black hair till there you stood,

Fixed vortex on the far
Tip, riveting stones, air,
All of it, together.

The poem is in the rhyme scheme that most frequently appears
in Plath's early poetry, slanted terza rima. (It seems typical of
this poet that she favored one of the most stylized and difficult
verse forms in English, and then worked against its strictures.
It is as if she wanted to take advantage of a tradition, but
without ever seeming to do so.) The entire poem—and this is
unusual for Plath—consists of just one long sentence. The
careful, pointed exposition is clearly blocked in hard edges, not
unlike those drawings by Plath I have seen that are heavy,
dark, flat. This poem's "narrative" has preceded the opening
stanza, its one character is outline and absence, and all its
details converge toward the last, abstract stanza (which seems

to echo Wordsworth), where the mysterious human figure alone establishes the relationships among the objects that, in random ensemble, comprise the scene. It is, in other words, a poem about the poet; a poem about itself, its single sentence containing the whole. But notice too that each of its shifts of direction or attention is signaled by "and." This is a characteristic of Plath's early poems—this, or her constant use of an appositional format, usually a metaphor per line. Such tactics count on a *succession* of ideas, objects, or equivalents to structure a poem, and not on their *interdependence*, relationships that a more complex syntax, for instance, would demonstrate. Plath's technique tends to give the same lexical value to the different parts of the poem, and thus produces a flattening or equalizing effect—like a painting with no perspective.

Instead of animating her poems by the intricacies of arrangement, she tries to invest them with a kind of verbal and metrical energy, almost as if to distract the reader from their meanings, to veil their deeper significance and flourish instead their versified foreground. Levels of diction, from the colloquial to the exalted, are jumbled. Parts of speech are regularly interchanged, forceful predicative words are especially favored as substitutes. And though rhyme schemes (or, occasionally, syllables) are employed to steady a stanza, the metric of any one line within that stanza is erratic and aggressive. Accents may be syncopated, but most often are just heaped up. Plath does the same thing with adjectives, which abound. The combination results in a blistered, hectoring line that lacks any real subtlety or persuasion. She doesn't like to play on or with words; she rarely uses enjambments successfully or ingeniously. She is concerned, then, primarily with the length, the intensity, and the patterning of her lines and poems, and not with their modulation or variety.

Ted Hughes once said that most of Plath's early poems turn on "the opposition of a prickly, fastidious defence and an imminent volcano"—an antagonism, finally, between the disciplines of her art and the demands of her experience. "Poem for a Birthday," the sequence that concludes the British edition of *The Colossus*, seems her first calculated effort to discover rather than impose the form of her experience. Despite its reliance on Roethke, there is a new assurance to the verse that permits strong tonal effects and interesting elliptical cuts. Perhaps that is because these poems are not dominated by the representational eye but by the presentational vagaries of the unconscious. Again, I suspect the influence of Hughes. It was at about this time that he turned her attention away from studying poetry toward mystical and anthropological texts; away from formal literary exercises and more seriously toward horoscopes, the tarot, the ouija board, improvisations, meditational devices, and free association games. In its own way, each is a ritualistic yet unstructured procedure to release experience from the unconscious, to which one would give voice rather than shape. This corresponds with Plath's own sense of poetic strength, which was invariably bound up with the notion and sensation of release. After the birth of her two children, she began to write with an increasingly confident maturity, just as later her separation from her husband delivered her into a final creative fury—in October 1962, the month after her separation, she wrote at least twenty-six poems. *The Bell Jar* seems to have had a kind of purgative function for its author, and her simultaneous discovery of the confessional poetry of Robert Lowell and Anne Sexton—which provided her the necessary examples of how to include her life in poetry—she also described in terms of release.

Each is a release *into* the self, into emotional and psychological depths either cultivated by or thrust upon her. And at the same time, she was prompted to free her work of the inhibitions, both psychological and stylistic, that had restricted her first book. It is very difficult to analyze in clear, progressive detail a stylistic "development" such as Plath's, which matured in only a few years and could change radically over several months. Still, her so-called "transitional" collection, *Crossing the Water*, can be read as a record of her experiments to secure the rapid advances she had made since *The Colossus*. Take, for instance, the opening stanza of "Finisterre":

> This was the land's end: the last fingers, knuckled and
> rheumatic,
> Cramped on nothing. Black
> Admonitory cliffs, and the sea exploding
> With no bottom, or anything on the other side of it,
> Whitened by the faces of the drowned.
> Now it is only gloomy, a dump of rocks—
> Leftover soldiers from old, messy wars.
> The sea cannons into their ear, but they don't budge.
> Other rocks hide their grudges under the water.

Plath's use of a word like "cannons" is familiar enough, but those rocks that "hide their grudges under the water" are new; they mark a shift from the striking word to the startling image. And furthermore, this is an image whose impact is calculated, controlled, and coaxed from the opening line's clutching hand of land. The poem's effects, in other words, are less immediate and transient. The brace of a rhyme scheme is gone, and the lines are irregular in length. Both those decisions seem a part of Plath's desire to approximate the rhythms of speech. Her poetry is never exactly conversational, but "Finisterre," if not the "direct, even plain speech" that Hughes says she was soon striving for in an effort to escape the rhetoric of the official High Style, has at least the effect of a soliloquy's heightened naturalism—an effect that her radio script "Three Women" displays brilliantly, though it comes at the expense of the theatrical. In her last work, Plath intensified that voice, but it always remained a dialogue between the mind and itself.

Although several of the "transitional" poems—say, "The Babysitters" or "In Plaster"—are too prosaic, they are merely the failures of Plath's otherwise successful project to give her poems a more dramatic posture, not merely by manipulating a poem's rhythms and imagistic resources, but by providing a situation for its voice. "Face Lift" and "Parliament Hill Fields," are fine examples of Plath's new awareness of plotting a poem, implying a character—of accumulating significance within the poem's own narrative. It was a necessary step toward the refracted events and mysterious presences in *Winter Trees* and *Ariel*. What, in the late poetry, seems blurred by psychic disjunctiveness is given its force by the hard exactness of tone, and the poems in *Winter Trees*—poems like "Purdah," "Childless Woman," "By Candlelight," and "Thalidomide"—have a heightened, penetrating force that her poems of midpassage lack. There is something more than the psychological realism of accommodating narrated facts into poetry, or of using the poem itself to discover her experiences rather than merely to record or fantasize her feelings about them. By the time one reads *Winter Trees*, one hears a voice grown markedly more inflected—usually with an angry irony:

> O maiden aunt, you have come to call.
> Do step into the hall!
> With your bold
> Gecko, the little flick!
> All cogs, weird sparkle and every cog solid gold.
> And I in slippers and housedress with no lipstick!
>
> ("The Tour")

And the tone of voice comes increasingly to determine the line breaks, now a collusion of image and breath:

> Do not think I don't notice your curtain—
> Midnight, four o'clock,

Lit (you are reading),
Tarting with the drafts that pass,
Little whore tongue,
Chenille beckoner,
Beckoning my words in—
The zoo yowl, the mad soft
Mirror talk you love to catch me at.

("Eavesdropper")

Increasingly in her later work, as here, the voice becomes both the rhythmical principle and the context for meaning. In poems like "By Candlelight" or "The Other" the syntax of accusation or inquiry or reaction, the disjunctive details of private experience, and the spliced images of her surrealist tendencies, begin to merge into what can be called a characteristic poem. In *Crossing the Water*, for example, "Last Words" or "A Life" still display the tension of the will doing the work of the imagination. But in a later poem like "The Other," the willfulness yields to a purified, demonic energy:

You come in late, wiping your lips.
What did I leave untouched on the doorstep—

White Nike,
Streaming between my walls!

Smilingly, blue lightning
Assumes, like a meathook, the burden of his parts.

The police love you, you confess everything.
Bright hair, shoe-black, old plastic,

Is my life so intriguing?
Is it for this you widen your eye-rings?

One way to appreciate the stylistic breakthrough of *Ariel* is to trace some of the recurrences of a single concern—her father, The Father—to its treatment in the book's most famous poem, "Daddy." The plain-prose version is in *The Bell Jar*, whose narrator, Esther Greenwood, "was only purely happy until [she] was nine years old," when her father—who had come "from some manic-depressive hamlet in the black heart of Prussia"—had died. And Esther, on the psychotic verge of suicide, "had a great yearning, lately, to pay [her] father back for all the years of neglect, and start tending his grave." It is only a simple sense of loss, of the horrible distance between the living and dead, that is revealed:

> At the foot of the stone I arranged the rainy armful of azaleas I had picked from a bush at the gateway of the graveyard. Then my legs folded under me, and I sat down in the sopping grass. I couldn't understand why I was crying so hard.
>
> Then I remembered that I had never cried for my father's death.
>
> My mother hadn't cried either. She had just smiled and said what a merciful thing it was for him he had died, because if he had lived he would have been crippled and an invalid for life, and he couldn't have stood that, he would rather have died than had that happen.
>
> I laid my face to the smooth face of the marble and howled my loss into the cold salt rain.

Immediately after this scene, Esther returns from the graveyard, swallows the pills, hides in a cellar hole, and lies down to death: "The silence drew off, baring the pebbles and shells and all the tatty wreckage of my life. Then, at the rim of vision, it gathered itself, and in one sweeping tide rushed me to sleep." Given the point of view, the emotion here is left distanced and unaccountable, and is told with the restraint that Plath uses throughout the novel to draw out slowly its cumulative effects of disorientation and waste. But the images of stone and sea, sleep and escape, quarry and fear, that structure her account are important. In a memoir written for a 1963 broadcast, "Ocean 1212-w," Plath broods on her relationship with the sea and her earliest self: the miracles of immersion and completion. The birth of her younger brother then defined for her "the *separateness* of everything. I felt the wall of my skin: I am I. That stone is a stone. My beautiful fusion with the things of this world was over. The tide ebbed, sucked back into itself." And later, at the end: "My father died, we moved inland. Whereon those nine first years of my life sealed themselves off like a ship in a bottle—beautiful, inaccessible, obsolete, a fine, white flying myth."

To watch this myth, these images, resumed in the poems discovers Plath, at first, refining and deepening her metaphor with the precisions of verse. In "The Colossus," the girl clambers in helpess self-absorption over the mammoth ruins of her father:

> Thirty years now I have labored
> To dredge the silt from your throat.
> I am none the wiser.
>
> Scaling little ladders with gluepots and pails of Lysol
> I crawl like an ant in mourning
> Over the weedy acres of your brow
> To mend the immense skull-plates and clear
> The bald, white tumuli of your eyes.
>
> A blue sky out of the Oresteia
> Arches above us.

The figure is right: the immense size symbolizing her incest-awe, its ruined fragments projecting her ambivalent feelings. But the mystery of loss and betrayal, the secretive sexual fantasies, the distortions of knowledge and memory, are left unexplored, dependent solely on the poem's figurative force:

Nights, I squat in the cornucopia
Of your left ear, out of the wind,
Counting the red stars and those of plum-color.
The sun rises under the pillar of your tongue.
My hours are married to shadow.
No longer do I listen for the scrape of a keel
On the blank stones of the landing.

It is *The Bell Jar*'s suicidal darkness she curls into here, longing to be reborn into return; it is the same sea that threatens suitors. The same sea that washes through "Full Fathom Five": "Your shelled bed I remember / Father, this thick air is murderous, / I would breathe water." The same stone in "The Beekeeper's Daughter," a poem addressed to "Father, bridegroom": "My heart under your foot, sister of a stone." The same dark exclusion that ends "Electra on Azalea Path":

I am the ghost of an infamous suicide,
My own blue razor rusting in my throat.
O pardon the one who knocks for pardon at
Your gate, father—your hound-bitch, daughter, friend.
It was my love that did us both to death.

In all of these early poems, the images are retired to approximate the experience, but their equivalents cannot manage its depth and intricacies. But "Daddy"—the title alone indicates that she will write out of the experience directly—is suddenly strikingly different, even as its details are finally aligned. The echoes we are meant to recall sound with a first force: "black shoe / In which I have lived like a foot / For thirty years, . . . Marble-heavy, a bag full of God, / Ghastly statue, . . . a head in the freakish Atlantic." The language and movement of "Daddy" are entirely new: instead of slow, careful gestures, the poem races its thickly layered and rhymed syncopation into some strange, private charm to evoke and exorcise a demon-lover. The short lines—which Plath reads with tremulous contempt in her recording of the poem—have a formulaic quality appropriate to the murderous ritual that the poem enacts: "Daddy, I have had to kill you. / You died before I had time." But what is most extraordinary about this poem is the complexity of experience that it includes. If "The Colossus" deals with remorse, "Daddy" deals in guilt. The poem veers between love and hate, revenge and regret, Eros and Thanatos. Imagining herself as a Jew and her father as a Nazi, or her husband as a vampire and herself as a maiden, the poet languishes in a need for punishment to counter the loss of love. The ambivalence of identification and fear is used to reveal more than "The Colossus" even hints at:

> Every woman adores a Fascist,
> The boot in the face, the brute
> Brute heart of a brute like you. . . .
>
> At twenty I tried to die
> and get back, back, back to you.
> I thought even the bones would do.
>
> But they pulled me out of the sack,
> And they stuck me together with glue.
> And then I knew what to do.
> I made a model of you,
> A man in black with a Meinkampf look
>
> And a love of the rack and the screw.
> And I said I do, I do.

The paranoid's identification of the persecutor with the rejected father, the macabre *Liebestod*, the "model" marriage that confirms tortures finally felt in a real marriage, the degradation of her father (which doubles as the origin of guilt in the murder of the primal father) as a form of self-loathing, the loss of her father and husband like two suicides that leave the poet furiously fingering her scars—"Daddy" astonishes a reader by the fury of its hurts.

The strong poetic personality that emerges in "Daddy" should remind a reader that the accomplishment of *Ariel* is first of all a stylistic one—what Ted Hughes calls its "crackling verbal energy." The exuberance is of a special sort. One would hesitate to term it "American," except that Plath herself did in a 1962 interview: "I think that as far as language goes I'm an American, I'm afraid, my accent is American, my way of talk is an American way of talk." The crucial dynamics, the sharp, quick tonal contrasts, the biting precision of word and image, the jaunty slang, the cinematic cutting, the high-power montage—these are what she is pointing to. Even in poems, like "Tulips," with quieter long lines, she sustains a new tension of menace and propulsion:

> My body is a pebble to them, they tend it as water
> Tends to the pebbles it must run over, smoothing them
>   gently.
> They bring me numbness in their bright needles, they bring
>   me sleep.
> Now I have lost myself I am sick of baggage—
> My patent leather overnight case like a black pillbox,
> My husband and child smiling out of the family photo;
> Their smiles catch onto my skin, little smiling hooks.

In the book's best poems, the lines are pared down, at times to a stark, private code, but always with purity and exactness. Paradoxically, this taut, new control often creates effects of singular primitivism—the sense we have when encountering language used for rituals that precede literature, that impersonally participate in something more than they are. The seeming impersonality of the surfaces of the *Ariel* poems, as distinct from their private origins, derives from Plath's abundance and abandon, from the sense of autopsy she creates. There are several ways this has been achieved.

Though there are a few strong poems that employ two-line, pistonlike stanzas, her favorite stanza remained the tercet. The *Ariel* stanza must have developed from her earlier habit of terza rima, with its visual probity and stylized uniformity. But the freedom and variety of her new stanzas perfectly match the skittish, inflected voice that projects them. The lines in poems like "Lady Lazarus" and "Fever 103°" can be extended or retracted at will; often they prefer the shortness capable of sustaining a single word or phrase or fragment, giving it the prominence and strangeness of isolation. The thrusting surprise of line lengths is particularly apt for the continually shifting forms of address in, say, "Lady Lazarus," which jumps from invocation to question to command. It is steadied somewhat by the irregular use of rhyme, both internal and external, which establishes an aural "pattern" juxtaposed with the visual one. And Plath's canny use of repeated words and formulas has the same effect—appropriate to a poem that is less about suicide itself than about her obsessive, suicidal hatred of men and marriage, about loathing and self-hatred:

> So, so, Herr Doktor.
> So, Herr Enemy.
>
> I am your opus,
> I am your valuable,
> The pure gold baby
>
> That melts to a shriek.
> I turn and burn.
> Do not think I underestimate your great concern.

Ash, ash—
You poke and stir.
Flesh, bone, there is nothing there—

A cake of soap,
A wedding ring,
A gold filling.

Herr God, Herr Lucifer,
Beware
Beware.

Out of the ash
I rise with my red hair
And I eat men like air.

The aural sense of recurrence and the syntactic and visual irregularities together create an unsettling experience, one from which we have no time for distance as the poem, like many of Plath's late poems, rushes forward to exhaust itself. Where her early work was, in every sense, contained, *Ariel* operates at levels altogether more instinctual, uncertain, expelled. In these poems, there is less attention paid to explicit argument or rationale, to conceit or epiphany. To expropriate what her poem "Mystic" asks and answers, "Does the sea // Remember the walker upon it? / Meaning leaks from the molecules." Meaning, that is to say, derives not from the walker but from the water. The poet is not presider but medium, and the poem is not the expression of meaning but its conjuring context. And, for this effect, it is clearly her imagery Plath depended on in this book—the relentless succession of metaphors that seek out equivalence rather than comparison, identity rather than similarity. When such a technique seems unduly compulsive, as it does in "Cut," the result is dully self-indulgent. But a poem like "Edge" demonstrates brilliantly Plath's ability to induce a process—rather than construct a product—by the juxtaposition of paradoxical images rendered with the force of statement; the smiling corpse, the illusory necessity, the children as serpents (the Greek symbol of Necessity), the rose and the moon's night flower. During the course of this poem, the images blend with and become one another, a series of folding mirrors shifting in value and meaning—from the dead woman to the moon considered as female, an eerily animated dead stone dressed as the corpse is. And which is which?

These are the kinds of nondiscursive "deep images" that Robert Bly and James Wright were also exploring, though in *Ariel* Plath has done so with more conviction. Their progammatic "irrationalism" depends too heavily on accidental correspondences, avoiding as it does both metaphor and argument. Plath's approach was more enlightening, less erratic, and she was more successful than either Bly or Wright in getting beyond the mere physicality and discrete epiphanies of traditional imagism. Then too, poems like "Getting There," "Medusa," or "Little Fugue" make extensive use of the surrealism that poets like Robert Lowell would later turn to as, in Lowell's phrase, the "natural way to write our fictions," or the radical method of capturing the *natural* unreality of experience and of creating a new knowledge of it. Even the source of *Ariel's* subject matter—no longer established themes in the suggested settings, but fragments of the occasional, accidental, domestic, or unconscious—has come to dominate much of the better work now being written. I am suggesting, in short, that Plath prefigured many of the decisive shifts in poetic strategy that occurred in the decade following her death. It is difficult to study her brief career for the kinds of substantial thematic complexities and continuities that one reads in Roethke or Lowell. But, considered from a stylistic viewpoint, Plath was as important an innovator as either of those poets. Her consistency and importance lie in her experiments with voice and the relationships among tone and image and address—axes after whose stroke the wood rings.

ENDNOTE

1. From an interview conducted by Lee Anderson, April 18, 1958, now in the Lee Anderson Collection of Recorded Poets at the Yale Collection of Historical Sound Recordings, Yale University Library.

W. D. SNODGRASS

THE MILD, REFLECTIVE ART

IT IS NOT difficult to believe W. D. Snodgrass's boast that he is descended, on one side of his family, from Robert Herrick, and on the other from Robert Burns. His lyricism is not only the most consistent among the confessional poets, it is the most insistent: "without some sort of external modification, like conventional stylistics, "he has written," it is extremely difficult to create a structure and tone complex enough to keep the language alive at all points." His syllabics and stresses and rhyme schemes are not meant to chasten his subject, but to balance its emotional demands and accommodate contradictory experiences and feelings: a language "alive" to the life it records. That life, in its meter-making argument, does not touch the extremes of madness or longing that aggravate the work of Sexton, Lowell, Plath, and Berryman. His family is not burdened with fame or wealth; his history is not haunted with attempts at suicide or perfection. Just as his verse is the successor to the severe, homely lyrics of Hardy and Frost, so too his losses and betrayals are the familiar ones, circumscribed by the small-town society to which our playwrights and novelists have accustomed us. In his poem "These Trees Stand . . . ," Snodgrass describes his own poetry when he tells of a night nurse on ward-rounds and "the mild, reflective art / Of focusing her flashlight on her blouse." The light he shines back on his own life reflects a sincerity, both technical and moral, that never excludes subtlety: complex but not complicated. The same strictness with which he measures his song is apparent in the lines he draws to trace his self, his story. In an early essay on D. H. Lawrence, Snodgrass predicts the direction of all his own later work: "To know one's needs is really to know one's own limits, hence one's definition."[1] The need for love which limits trust, the need for growth which limits security—the dilemmas that gather definition, itself continually revalued in his effort to say, with Parolles, "Simply the thing I am / Shall make me live."

Quoted on the dust jacket of *Heart's Needle* (1959), Robert Lowell wondered at Snodgrass' poetic origins: "He flowered in the most sterile of sterile places, a post war, cold war midwestern university's poetry workshop for graduate poets." Snodgrass' first models were consistent with such an atmosphere and curriculum; the congealed symbolism and obliquities of Empson and early Lowell. But his stylistic shift was more of an adjustment than a rejection:

> [The teachers at Iowa] were marvelous teachers, though at a certain point, I felt that they were teaching me to write learned, symbol-laden poems that any good modern poetry committee could write. They all thought I was wrong, and were really concerned for me. And they said, "You mustn't do this, you got a brain, you can't write this kind of tear-jerking stuff." But above all they had really taught me how to pack a poem with meaning, and from that it's a fairly easy jump to how to pack a poem with feeling, which to me tells a lot more. They were worth opposing. . . . You know, I had people like Robert Lowell, Berryman, all those people came there to teach, and they were worth fighting, too.[2]

This kind of respectful impatience began with his reading, the jaded quality of which drove him back to the poet's private intentions and personality which, in turn, revalued the poem:

> I remember when I was in school, we were all taught to write obscure, brilliant, highly symbolized poems about the loss of myth in our time, and, you know, it suddenly began to occur to me that I didn't care about the loss of myth in our time; frankly, I was glad to be rid of the stuff. . . . But we were all writing poems about what we thought "The Waste Land" was about. None of us had bothered to find out that "The Waste Land" isn't about that at all. We thought it was about that because you could make doctoral dissertations by talking about all the learned allusions in "The Waste Land" and how it was about, you know, the need for a "meaningful myth" in our lives; nobody had noticed it was about Eliot's insane wife and his frozen sex life. He had helped disguise this, with Pound's assistance, by his editing of the poem. We believed people's doctoral statements about the poem. We believed Frost and Eliot when they said their poems were about other things than their own sex lives, and we can now look at the poems and see that that just isn't so at all.

The way he listened developed into the way he spoke, though as with other confessional poets it was the force of example which allowed his discovery. Some of these examples were local and personal; a young poet at Iowa named Robert Shelley was one:

> Just as I was writing imitation Lowell, he was writing imitation Hart Crane. Then all of a sudden he struck on a very simple, direct, lyrical style that really floored me—it was exactly the sort of poem all the critics were saying you couldn't write because our age was too fragmented or com-

plicated or something. He only finished half a dozen of those poems, however, before he committed suicide. So all of a sudden, his style came onto the market—we were all very fond of him and now it seemed not only permissible but even a good thing to take that style he'd only begun and go on to develop it.[3]

A more recognizable influence was that of Randall Jarrell, whose own last books, *The Woman at the Washington Zoo* (1960) and *The Lost World* (1965), were decidedly more relaxed and autobiographical than his earlier work, and whose muted, civilized voice—along with those of Ransom and Roethke—Snodgrass came to recall:

> Lowell was my teacher at Iowa, but I'd been writing like him even before he came there (I think). I worked with Jarrell at a writer's conference in Boulder, Colorado and he helped jar me out of that style. I showed him the same poems that practically all the best critics (Warren, Ransom, etc.) had liked and he didn't like any of them. He liked, instead, a piece I'd paraphrased from Ovid and two of Rilke's *Sonnets to Orpheus* (which later appear with a larger group of them in *After Experience*). So I began to suspect that it might really be better to simply say it, straight out, simply and directly. I could see that even with my modern heroes, Rilke and Rimbaud, there was always either a sense of direct surface narrative or else a musical and lyric thrust to carry you through the poem—meantime, I was beginning to suspect that when most of us there at Iowa put the subrational up on the surface of the poem (as Rimbaud, for instance, had done) we were not making any discoveries that he hadn't already made.[4]

Rimbaud's poem "*Mémoire*," for example—Snodgrass' translation of which appears in *After Experience*—sinks its pretext beneath fragmented symbolic equivalents. Snodgrass doesn't refuse to use symbols; in fact, he depends on them frequently, just as he employs satire or parable or personae, if that is what a particular poem requires. But, unlike Rimbaud, he foregrounds the actual experience drawn from life, always allowing subject to dominate symbol, and trusting his musical substructure to carry the expressive, unconscious force of both his pretext and his poem. In a rather formal statement about his work, he puts it this way:

> . . . the poet's voice must embody not the expedient certainties of his daily life and belief, but rather in its style, in its way of treating details and images (how discrete are they, how firm, how extensive?), above all in its sounds, its subrational structure of aural textures and rhythms. It is here he must hope to find those meanings which may remain beyond the consciousness of his own period, but which may be deep enough to endure into the consciousness of another. [5]

Snodgrass' reliance on a kind of notational expressiveness was likewise determined by examples "beyond the consciousness of his own period":

> But I think my chief influences were musical. The last-century Germans you speak of came to me chiefly through musical settings—especially Mahler's *Kindertotenlieder*. I tried translating some of these and while my teachers like Lowell and Engle could help me very much on those poems which they truly loved and understood, they wouldn't let *me* write such poems. A second big influence there was a set of Spanish and Italian songs of the 16th and 17th centuries by Hugues Cuenod which appeared just then—I still remember the first day I heard them—my hair simply stood on end. And I wanted to do something as directly and stridently passionate. At least I thought that would be a real

and significant blunder—to go on writing as we had been wasn't important enough even when it worked.[6]

The qualities he cites in the song literature—simplicity and passionate directness, sustained by the unobtrusive subtlety of their settings—are among the most distinctive characteristics of Snodgrass' own verse and version of the confessional impulse. One might even assert the direct influence of the *Kindertotenlieder* on the "Heart's Needle" sequence. The poems by Friedrich Rückert were written after the deaths of two of his young children, and their settings by Mahler have become associated with the death of his own youngest daughter shortly after he completed the song cycle. Rückert's texts stress not so much the death of his children as the emptiness their loss has left, and Mahler's music points up the poignance of the poems by its restraint. The sequence closely links variations of grief, each with its own distinct tone and rhythmical structure, heightened by the music's unembarrassed and delicate pathos.

The convergence of these influences can only be considered as part of the transformation of Snodgrass' style, because style —in his phrase, "that quality of voice which suggests qualities of mind"—is finally, for this poet, a moral and psychological concern. The "sincerity" he sought for the texture of his verse made similar demands on his subject, and having discovered *how* he could speak, he had further to discover what he needed to say. The value of the poem as product was inextricably bound up with the process of its composition: to compose is finally to expose. "Am I writing what I *really* think?" was the question—the criterion—that insisted itself. Abandoning rhetorical disguises meant forgoing psychological defenses as well:

> For I believe that the only reality which a man can ever surely know is that self he cannot help being, though he will only know that self through its interactions with the world around it. If he pretties it up, if he changes its meaning, if

he gives it the voice of any borrowed authority, if in short he rejects this reality, his mind will be less than alive. So will his words.[7]

The effect of this demand for self-knowledge on the compositional process may be a reason for Snodgrass' relatively small body of work, and is reflected in the rigor with which he pursues the nuances of both an experience and its voice. His generalized account of his procedure with any given poem implies the sincerity he calls for, even as it provides a miniature of his career itself:

> In working on an actual poem I almost always find myself starting it much the way we were taught at Iowa. I make a very compacted, intellectualized, and obviously symbolical poem with a lot of fancy language in it. But then, as I go on working at it, the poem happily becomes plainer and longer, and seems much more "tossed off." The first version often seems very labored and literary and intellectual. The final version, if I'm lucky, will seem very conversational, and sort of "thrown away." It will also be much longer.[8]

The process, in other words, is one of "realizing" an experience back towards the casual immediacy with which it first occurred.

This commitment to a relentless probing and revelation is not easily achieved, and in Snodgrass' case derives from psychotherapy, which provided both its stimulus and model. The simultaneous discovery of self and voice, and of the sincerity necessary to both, is evident in this account by the poet of his therapy at the University Hospital in Iowa City:

> In many ways that therapy really consisted of just stating and restating the problem until you finally got it in your own language—until then, you really hadn't said anything. So long as you were talking about "castration anxiety," etc.,

you were acting so superior to the problem, that you belied the very existence of the problem in the way you set out to describe it. Until you said that in your own language, you hadn't really accepted its existence, much less dealt with *your* experience of it (as opposed to someone else's abstractions about it).

Or to say the same thing another way, I began to notice that one of the two of us in that room sounded like a psychiatry textbook and it wasn't *him*. (Perhaps I should note that he—the doctor—wasn't *really* in the room at all because the whole thing was part of an experimental technique.) Anyway, all this led me to question the tone and the subject matter of my poems. I was surprised to notice that my doctor wasn't much interested when I talked about those abstractions; he sat up and took notice when I talked about my daughter. He wasn't inclined to question me about those things where I could sound impressive; more often he asked me how I was planning to pay my rent.

I'd gone into that therapy because (partly) I'd not been able to write for two years. I recall that my doctor specifically asked me if that wasn't because I wasn't writing about things I cared enough about to get me past the resistance.

I might also comment that some years later I went into deep analysis in Detroit. That, of course, affected my work but in ways that were less obvious (if, perhaps, more far-reaching). It had a very large hand in the poems I did based on paintings.[9]

Week after week, alone in a strangely familiar room, speaking out loud to himself, over and over, the guilts and fears and inadequacies, until his language caught their reality, and problems became self. The formality of his verse underscores the authority of his struggle, and if the effect of song is finally—with whatever self-consciousness—celebratory, then Snodgrass reminds himself and his readers of Rilke's words: "for the poet whose aim is praise, the great test is how much of the world's misery and sorrow can be digested into that praise."[10]

There was considerable misery to be digested by Snodgrass before the praise and prizes which greeted the eventual publication of *Heart's Needle*. The isolation of his decision and the discouragement by his teachers were prolonged over the five years he worked on the "Heart's Needle" sequence, begun in 1953:

> When I started writing these poems, my teachers were concerned for me and didn't like the poems at all. Lowell, I recall, was particularly distressed. But several years later I sent the whole cycle of poems to Donald Hall and Louis Simpson who were editing their first anthology—they got very excited about them and Hall showed the whole group to Lowell, who entirely changed his mind about them. He got me a publisher later when no one else would publish my book and, in general, he opened all the doors for me. He later wrote me to say that he took those poems as one of his models in the *Life Studies* pieces.[11]

By this time, Snodgrass had absorbed his training sufficiently to use it rather than be used by it, and had eliminated from his final collection its aspects of "insincerity." While a few poems in the book—"MHTIS . . . OU TIS," "Orpheus," "Riddle"—are stiffer than the rest, and so seem throwbacks, none is merely an exercise.

The three poems which open *Heart's Needle* comprise an initiatory account of the poet's return home, both chronological and spiritual, from World War II on. "Ten Days Leave" is a study in disorientation and alienation, the artificiality of the past and detachment of the present, much like Hemingway's story "Soldier's Home." His specific model, though, was probably William Meredith's 1944 poem "Ten-Day Leave," whose stanza scheme and central dream-metaphor Snodgrass adopted for ironically different purposes. The war-jarred poet returns in person to his service dream of home:

> Supposing it were just his old mistake?
>
> But no; it seems just like it seemed. His folks
> Pursue their lives like toy trains on a track.
> He can foresee each of his father's jokes
> Like words in some old movie that's come back.

But his new awareness stumbles over the inadequacy of metaphor to restore the familiar; the poem proceeds by analogy, each stanza testing—*like, as if, supposing, seems, recalls*—a dreamscape at which he wonders: "How real it seems!" It is the principle of unreality that dominates until resolved in the third poem, just as the perspective shifts from the "he" of this poem, to "we" in the next, and finally to "I" in the third. "Returned to Frisco, 1946" resumes the stance and structure of "Ten Days Leave" to describe his last landing. As soldiers, they had "scrambled like rabbits / Up hostile beaches," and now, under the twisted banner of Owen's "old lie," they assault "our first life," "our old lives." But the new enemy seems like his own family; the new fear, like his old habits. The liberty he had fought to give others and been granted himself leaves him

> Free to choose just what they meant we should;
> To turn back finally to our old affections,
> The ties that lasted and which must be good.
>
> Off the port side, through haze, we could discern
> Alcatraz, lavender with flowers. Barred,
> The Golden Gate, fading away astern,
> Stood like the closed gate of your own backyard.

The illusion of choice is left bewildering in this poem, since Snodgrass came to find, through psychotherapy, that it depends on a sense of self-identity that can at once accept and transcend the past. "ΜΗΤΙΣ . . . ΟΥ ΤΙΣ," dedicated to the psychiatrist he never saw, R. M. Powell, works the returning soldier motif into the story of Odysseus. Like the Greek hero, the poet's "defiant mind" allowed him escape from the dark cave and return to a self centered with a guilt that proves reality:

> Unseen where all seem stone blind, pure disguise
> Has brought me home alone to No Man's land
> To look at nothing I dare recognize.
> My dead blind guide, you lead me here to claim
> Still waters that will never wash my hand,
> To kneel by my old face and know my name.

The quest for his "name," a definition discovered through needs and limits, continues throughout the book—in "Home Town," "A Cardinal," "These Trees Stand . . . ," and "April Inventory"—and serves as the light by which he reflects on his personal and social relationships.

The next twelve poems explore the ruins of his first marriage, and the reconstruction of his life with new love. This section opens and closes with similar poems—"At the Park Dance" and "Home Town"—which dramatize the poet's isolation, after the shocks of war and divorce, from his accustomed community. The virtue he makes of this necessity is his resolve to learn from the experience. The last stanza of "Home Town" abandons the poem's narrative of habitual fears and desires pursued on small-town curbs, and the poet turns inward to ask himself the anxious question:

> Pale soul, consumed by fear
> of the living world you haunt,
> have you learned what habits lead you

to hunt what you don't want;
learned who does not need you;
learned you are no one here?

This is the lesson also learned in "Orpheus" and in "The Marsh," where Snodgrass explores the emotional underworld and swamp of his first marriage. As Orpheus, the poet descends to ask Time and Experience for the woman he can only remember but not now love. Though he accuses himself of "mistrust," by figuring the experience into a self-justifying myth, complete with a bleak, modernist cityscape, Snodgrass evades the pain by means of the pattern, so that the actual experience is diminished in its detail, though its self-pity is coddled by the high style:

It was the nature of the thing:
No moon outlives its leaving night,
No sun its day. And I went on
Rich in the loss of all I sing
To the threshold of waking light.
To larksong and the live, gray dawn.
So night by night, my life has gone.

This theme is more convincing in later poems to his daughter, where the loss that allows song is combined with a more realistic guilt.

The companion poem to "Orpheus" is "Papageno," which employs the same rhyme scheme to present the complementary poet: folkloristic rather than mythological, a birdcage replacing the lyre. And this poem sets the tone and style for those that follow: gentle, witty, lyrical, wondering, celebratory. It is not "my stealthy flute" that can "whistle up a wife"; love, in the person of his second wife Janice, to whom the poem is dedicated, finds him:

I beat about dead bushes where
No song starts and my cages stand
Bare in the crafty breath of you
Night's lady, spreading your dark hair,
Come take this rare bird into hand;
In that deft cage, he might sing true.

The "Night's lady" is no longer the Eurydice he could not lead back, but the Papagena who saves him from death—even though Snodgrass' description seems confused with that of Pamina, daughter of the Queen of the Night in Mozart's *Die Zauber-flöte*. This entire group of poems rises from "the burned out bed / of ashes" ("September in the Park") to tell about recovery and renewal. Guilt is not only purified through sacrifice but through more vitalistic and seasoned cycles which turn memories into hopes, and which naturalize the necessity of suffering. Despite the self-addressed caution in "Seeing You Have . . . ," Snodgrass grounds these poems in joy, and in "Riddle" even turns his pride into a series of conceits—self-consciously echoing the metaphysical poets—and puns on the "divorce" that has united the lovers. And while poems like "Winter Bouquet" and the two titled "Song" are domestic and erotic, "The Operation"—another of the hospital poems favored by the confessionalists—works toward its simple recognition through ritual (robes to arena to angel to bowl) and allusion (Pierrot and Christ). It is a remarkable poem, blending the realistic and the visionary into an account of his struggle towards the still point of a confident marriage: his wife's gift crystalizing the dark, rushing world he watches through it:

I lie in night, now,
A small mound under linen like the drifted snow,
Only by nurses visited, in radiance, saying, Rest.
Opposite, ranked office windows, glare; headlamps, below,

Trace out our highways; their cargoes under dark
                                    tarpaulins,
Trucks climb, thundering, and sirens may
Wail for the fugitive. It is very still. In my brandy bowl
Of sweet peas at the window, the crystal world
Is inverted, slow and gay.

If the first two groupings of the book's poems deal with
Snodgrass' sense of "new life," with himself after his return
from war, and with his second wife after his divorce, then a
third group—"A Cardinal," "The Campus on the Hill," "These
Trees Stand . . . ," and "April Inventory"—move still further
out to sift the continuing life of his social and professional
relationships. "A Cardinal" is the book's pivotal "crisis poem,"
Snodgrass' version of "Resolution and Independence," which
both sums up the poems that precede it and summons up those
that follow and exemplify it. The first part of the poem—the
opening twelve stanzas—presents the heartache and drowsy
numbness of the poet, not half in love with easeful death but
stunned by the mediocre, post-war technocracy and stunted by
his inability to signify his presence as a poet in it. The question
forced on him—what is *mine?*—is worked through a series of
contrasts: poet/nature, poet/city, nature/city. The "marketable
praise," "this heavy prose / of factories and motors" deadens
his own "scared silence," "blank pages" and unmarketable
rhymes. Realization cannot lessen alienation; though he hears
"the ancient pulse of violence" throbbing beneath suburban
advertising jingles, his own sense of helplessness in a society
whose enterprise freely excludes him—even as the insects and
birds withdraw from the woods in which he seeks a meaningful
solitude—leave him voiceless: "Meantime, I fuss with phrases
/ or clamp my jaws in silence." The second part of the poem
abruptly introduces its symbolic cardinal—the bird-figure fa-

miliar to poetry from Shelley's skylark to Stevens' sparrow—
though it is less a symbol in the sense of embodying an abso-
lute correspondence than a focus for the poet's modulating
awareness of himself. Snodgrass' own predicament screens his
first, Jacobean understanding of the "Old sleek satanic cardi-
nal," no different from industrialized vultures and whose song,
like theirs, is a "Hosannah to Appetite." But the poet goes on
to realize his "Darwinian self-pity," and to listen again to the
cardinal as "he outspeaks a vital / claim to know his needs"
and "sings out for survival." What the cardinal says is, of
course, what Snodgrass is learning of himself:

> The world's not done to me;
> it is what I do;
> whom I speak shall be;
> I music out my name
> and what I tell is who
> in all the world I am.

Mere appetite is changed to assertion, itself a style in which the
self is to be discovered. The uselessness of poetry is converted
into the importance of self. Here is the end of the poem:

> All bugs, now, and the birds
> witness once more their voices
> though I'm still in their weeds
> tracking my specimen words,
> replenishing the verses
> of nobody else's world.

Just as he has listened to learn, so too he speaks to his daughter
in the paired poem of assertion "These Trees Stand . . . ,"
where he urges his separation from her as an example, in a
touching lesson of pride in the absurdity of isolation:

Your name's absurd, miraculous as sperm
And as decisive. If you can't coerce
One thing outside yourself, why you're the poet!
What irrefrangible atoms whirl, affirm
Their destiny and form Lucinda's skirts!
She can't make up your mind. Soon as you know it,
Your firmament grows touchable and firm.
If all this world runs battlefield or worse,
Come, let us wipe our glasses on our shirts:
Snodgrass is walking through the universe.

The other two poems in this group also take up the question of survival, set in the stale academic atmosphere of Fifties America. "The Campus on the Hill" details Snodgrass' frustration at Cornell, where he had moved to teach after Iowa, and at the version of survival among his students. While the world breaks around them, they hope to survive by staying inert:

They look out from their hill and say,
To themselves, "We have nowhere to go but down;
The great destination is to stay."
Surely the nations will be reasonable;
They look at the world—don't they?—the world's way?
The clock just now has nothing more to say.

That last line, and the poem's title, are meant to recall Edwin Arlington Robinson's villanelle, "The House on the Hill":

And our poor fancy-play
        For them is wasted skill:
There is nothing more to say.

There is ruin and decay
        In the House on the Hill:
They are all gone away,
There is nothing more to say.

That same empty disgust is Snodgrass' attitude here, and his condemnation is severe, even as it seems to depend in part on his own helplessness. A much richer account of the same situation is Snodgrass' best known poem "April Inventory"— richer because more personal. The satire is muted and includes himself, so that his survival sounds more authentic. This elegy for *d'antan* opens with the cruelest month reminding of nature's renewal which taunts his steady decline: "In thirty years I may not get / Younger, shrewder, or out of debt." But unlike those isolated manipulators, the "solid scholars" who have gotten "the degrees, the jobs, the dollars," he has sought values which recover self, has pursued his arguments in human incidents:

> I taught my classes Whitehead's notions;
> One lovely girl, a song of Mahler's.
> Lacking a source-book or promotions,
> I showed one child the colors of
> A luna moth and how to love.

> I taught myself to name my name,
> To bark back, loosen love and crying;
> To ease my woman so she came,
> To ease an old man who was dying.
> I have not learned how often I
> Can win, can love, but choose to die.

This humility before the primacy of the self's needs allows Snodgrass a pride in his losses, which the Roethkean last stanza moralizes:

> Though trees turn bare and girls turn wives,
> We shall afford our costly seasons;
> There is a gentleness survives
> That will outspeak and has its reasons.

W. D. Snodgrass   219

> There is a loveliness exists,
> Preserves us, not for specialists.

Everything he has learned through these poems is relearned in the second half of the book, the "Heart's Needle" sequence, ten poems to Cynthia, his daughter by his first marriage, one for each of the seasons during the two and a half years, from the winter of 1952 until the spring of 1955, of his divorce and remarriage.[12] As both a completely other person and still a part of himself, his daughter provides Snodgrass a unique occasion to confront his selfhood at a point where all its relationships converge. That point is also an extremely painful one—a point where, like the trapped fox, he has had to gnaw off his own paw to escape, where legal estrangement becomes existential estrangement, where he cannot explain his maturity to her innocence and so has to revalue both, where the limits of self-pity and bitterness cannot be distinguished from the needs for growth and regret. To maintain such a developing complexity within the scheme of a single poem is a difficulty Snodgrass overcomes, first of all, by the voice he has achieved. William Heyen once described it as "urgent but controlled, muted but passionate, unassuming but instructive." And in addition to his voice, there is the verse; each poem is given an independent rhythmical structure—sometimes elaborate, sometimes simple—which varies the angle of feeling and perception, and can accommodate rather than avoid his revelations of loss and resolve. At the same time, the poems are closely linked, not only by the central relationship which they trace, but by a series of motifs—bed, snow, fox, trap, bird, color—which recur, gathering new meanings into old. And these techniques combine finally to portray a world of self-willed, separate individuals whose shared—and disillusioned—experience makes possible a tentative but necessary union. What Snodgrass says in the first poem could be used to summarize his technique throughout:

> And I have planned
>
> My chances to restrain
> The torments of demented summer or
> Increase the deepening harvest here before
> It snows again.

The introductory poem offers the bleak background of his daughter's childhood. Born during the Korean War, she did not warm the frigidity of his marriage, a cold war in its own terms:

> Child of my winter, born
> When the new fallen soldiers froze
> In Asia's steep ravines and fouled the snows,
> When I was torn
>
> By love I could not still,
> By fear that silenced my cramped mind
> To that cold war where, lost, I could not find
> My peace in my will. . . .

That inverted reference to Dante introduces to the sequence the important theme of will, which necessitates his own actions and his attempt to teach his daughter that their consequences are important in ways she may come to understand for her own life. The second poem translates an actual occurrence into a parable, giving it a form in which the child can understand her own experience. The garden which father and daughter have planted, and which she has unwittingly walked on and over-watered, recapitulates her own childhood: "Child, we've done our best." And the advice he offers, which predicts their separation, catches up his own failure as well:

Someone will have to weed and spread
    The young sprouts. Sprinkle them in the hour
When shadow falls across their bed.
You should try to look at them every day
    Because when they come to full flower
        I will be away.

The third, fifth and ninth poems of the sequence are the most bitter, and the third is perhaps the most painful since it describes the first shock of separation from his daughter. The middle of the poem distances the event by recalling newspaper accounts of the Korean War as metaphors of the failed marriage and its victim:

We read of cold war soldiers that
Never gained ground, gave none, but sat
    Tight in their chill trenches.
Pain seeps up from some cavity
Through the ranked teeth in sympathy; . . .

It's better the poor soldiers live
    In someone else's hands
Than drop where helpless powers fall
On crops and barns, on towns where all
    Will burn. And no man stands.

The eerie stillness of this violence then draws back a time "I tugged your hand, once, when I hated / Things less; a mere game dislocated / The radius of your wrist." The necessity now to "appease another"—a mother—extends the game-image, as the poet tries to hold back the reality of loss, to hope he is saving what he surrenders: "It may help that a Chinese play / Or Solomon himself might say / I am your real mother." With the fourth poem, the separation has settled into its awkward round of visits, and the tension between the poet and the father is strained as Snodgrass mocks the golden-lads-and-girls-all-must myths by which we try to make sense of dislocation:

> We huff like windy giants
> scattering with our breath
> gray-headed dandelions;
> Spring is the cold wind's aftermath.

The grief he feels and has caused is linked to a guilt at his inability to perform either role, which the last stanza gently displaces:

> Night comes and the stiff dew.
> I'm told a friend's child cried
> because a cricket, who
> had minstreled every night outside
> her window, died.

The fifth poem completes the first half of the cycle, bringing it around again to winter and the dark, closed landscape of his separation, and to the same images of the first poem:

> Winter again and it is snowing;
> Although you are still three,
> You are already growing
> Strange to me.

What is strange to him is her growth apart from him:

> You chatter about new playmates, sing
> Strange songs; you do not know
> *Hey ding-a-ding-a-ding*
> Or where I go
>
> Or when I sang for bedtime, *Fox*
> *Went out on a chilly night*,
> Before I went for walks
> And did not write.

And it forces him to concede, as does the fox, "the paw, / Gnawed off, he cannot feel; / Conceded to the jaw / Of toothed, blue steel."

But this realization, which informs the second half of the cycle, is one in which Snodgrass will discover his own motives. This begins with the lengthy sixth poem, the background and composition of which Snodgrass himself has described in his essay "Finding a Poem" and need not be repeated here. But it is important to note the patterns which his recognition assumes. The poet is meditating on the time passed since his daughter's first acceptance of life at birth: "You took your hour, / caught breath, and cried with your full lung power." A series of metaphors follows to describe the marriage breakup— birds whose nests were flooded, trees ruined in storms—and the survival by sacrifice:

> Crews
> of roughneck boys swarmed to cut loose
> branches wrenched in the shattering wind, to hack free
> all the torn limbs that could sap the tree.

The "July Fourth" storm he mentions—an Iowa City tornado of 1953—recalls subliminally his own sister's death on that date of the asthma his daughter suffers from: "Your lungs caught and would not take the air." His sister's refusal of breath had been a denial of life, and Snodgrass now fears Cynthia will not choose her own life:

> Of all things, only we
> have power to choose that we should die;
> nothing else is free
> in this world to refuse it. Yet I,
> who say this, could not raise
> myself from bed how many days
> to the thieving world. Child, I have another wife,
> another child. We try to choose our life.

By casting the present dilemma into the shadow of the past, Snodgrass has discovered as well the dimensions of his own decision, and has come to understand the necessity, for himself and his daughter, to choose the unavoidable. If he cannot grant her his presence to learn by, he can offer his daughter his example: to turn betrayal of others into trust of self, denial into decision. The balance thus achieved, for himself and in his relationship, is apparent in the seventh poem:

> Here in the scuffled dust
>   is our ground of play.
> I lift you on your swing and must
>   shove you away,
> see you return again,
>   drive you off again, then
>
> stand quiet till you come.
>   You, though you climb
> higher, farther from me, longer,
>   will fall back to me stronger. . . .
>
> Once more now, this second,
>   I hold you in my hands.

The eighth is an account of the new "household" set up by the two. No longer the romantic one of constancy, where a small girl plots with her father to catch a star, "pull off its skin / and cook it for our dinner," their relationship has all the realism of packed lunches and "local restaurants." Though the ending reiterates only regret and resentment, his acceptance is one by which loss gives strength:

> As I built back from helplessness,
>   when I grew able,
> the only possible answer was
>   you had to come here less.

W. D. Snodgrass   225

Though the "sweets" they eat on her visits leave "cavities," their anxious motto has become "We manage."

The ninth poem relapses to the blank bitterness of early poems:

> A friend asks how you've been
> and I don't know
>
> or see much right to ask.
> Or what use it could be to know. . . .
>
> Nothing but injury will grow,
> I write you only the bitter poems
> that you can't read.

But the scene of remembrance—before cases of posed stuffed animals in a Natural History Museum—reveals the self-hatred at the roles and feelings he finds himself locked into at his worst. The "little bobcats" arched in their "constant rage" remind the poet that it was here, the year before, that his daughter and stepdaughter "pulled my hands / and had your first, worst quarrel, / so toys were put up on your shelves . . . I forced you to obedience; / I don't know why." The reason lies in the epigraph from Simone Weil with which Snodgrass prefaced his essay on Dostoyevski: "A harmful act is the transference to others of the degradation which we bear in ourselves. That is why we are inclined to commit such acts as a way of deliverance." If acceptance is its own deliverance, then the poet is, for the moment, caught in a refusal to yield to himself:

> The window's turning white.
> The world moves like a diseased heart
> packed with ice and snow.
> Three months now we have been apart
> less than a mile. I cannot fight
> or let you go.

The last poem resolves the relationship; it is the final changed return, rich with natural and seasonal imagery, and steadied by the most constant rhythm in the cycle: "The vicious winter finally yields" and "our seasons bring us back once more." Her return, like that of the spring and its rites, has occurred often enough for him finally to believe it is desired rather than allowed, and the sequence ends with their escape into themselves and each other:

> If I loved you, they said, I'd leave
> and find my own affairs.
> Well, once again this April, we've
> come around to the bears;
>
> punished and cared for, behind bars,
> the coons on bread and water
> stretch thin black fingers after ours.
> And you are still my daughter.

At the same time Snodgrass was writing *Heart's Needle*, he published a few poems about his parents and their responsibility for his sister's death. They appeared under various pseudonyms because Snodgrass did not want them to come to his mother's attention, and they were only gathered finally in a small, expensive, limited private edition called *Remains*, published in 1970 under the anagram S. S. Gardons, for whom Snodgrass had devised a cryptic life and disappearance. His reluctance is understandable, considering the terrible honesty with which these portraits are drawn, but as he asks in an essay on Ransom, "How could one be a first-rate artist without offending, deeply, those he most loves?" These are raw poems, but not heartless: their forgiveness persists in their understanding. The rage of his memories and the intensity of his analysis are controlled in a verse which turns a revenging wit into a search for origins. His own survival—prior to that of war and divorce—has depended on escape, just as his alternative self, his sister, retreated beyond will into a suicidal surrender. This book is Snodgrass's unflinching view of the remains.

The opening pair of poems—"The Mother" and "Diplomacy: The Father"—assumes the personalities of each parent to reveal their unconscious motives. A perverse inversion of her nature and role is the key to "The Mother," and Snodgrass uses careful conceits and turns of phrase to spot this, as in her view of her own children:

> Born of her own flesh; still, she feels them drawn
> Into the outer cold by dark forces;
> They are in love with suffering and perversion,
> With the community of pain. Thinking them gone,
>
> Out of her reach, she is consoled by evil
> In neighbors, children, the world she cannot change,
> That lightless universe where they range
> Out of the comforts of her disapproval.

The type of the devouring mother is apparent in the dark, poisonous images of cave—"labyrinth of waste, wreckage / And hocus-pocus"—and spider:

> And the drawn strands of love, spun in her mind,
> Turn dark and cluttered, precariously hung
> With the black shapes of her mates, her sapless young,
> Where she moves by habit, hungering and blind.

Though she feeds on her own family to nurture imaginary hurts, Snodgrass sketches her as a driven creature in that last line. In the companion poem, his father is one of the sapless, black shapes, and Snodgrass uses his Polonius-like voice and advice to reveal and dismiss him simultaneously, though with more regret than he can manage for his mother, if only because his father seems trapped in more awareness of his situation. The comparative self-justification—"as in yourself" is the second line of every stanza in this speech to his son—urges power, which stresses his own impotence, and force, which uncovers his lack of passion. The compromises he has made to live with his wife and world are still tinged with possibilities despaired of:

> Friend, this is lonely work. Hankerings will persist
> for true allies, those you love; you will long
> some days to speak your mind out or just assist
> someone who, given that help, might grow strong
> and admirable. This is your black hour,
> the pitiless test.
>
> But think back: what did they ever do for you?
> As in yourself,
> so in those who take your help, your thought, your name,
> seek out their old strengths, their hidden talents
> to aid and abet, to buy out. Your fixed aim,
> whatever it costs you, must still remain a balance
> of power in the family, the firm, this whole world through.

What his father has missed is himself and the qualities of self Snodgrass had learned in *Heart's Needle*: love, trust, growth, passion, dedication. Against these he measures his father; against his father, himself. Yet in his own way, this father has provided an example in reverse for Snodgrass' sense of his own fatherhood, and this draws the two men into a complex similarity. In his father's last words to him, Snodgrass points up that connection to himself, and to those who recall his relationship to his own daughter:

> Your life's the loving tension
> you leave to those who'll still take your instruction.
> You've built their world; and air of soft suspension
> which you survive in, as cradled and sustained
> as in yourself.

The following four poems center on the events and causes surrounding his asthmatic sister's death. "The Mouse" is a memory poem, recalling the course of their childhood together, how they would weep over a dead mouse, as in Hopkins' "Spring and Fall: To a Young Child." And later he cannot weep and knows why: by expanding the memory into metaphor, he describes their avenging fury of a mother as a cat

> That pats at you, wants to see you crawl
> Some, then picks you back alive;
> That needs you just a little hurt.
> The mind goes blank, then the eyes. Weak with dread,
> In shock, the breath comes short;
> We go about our lives.
>
> And then the little animal
> Plays out; the dulled heart year by year
> Turns from its own needs, forgets its grief.
> Asthmatic, timid, twenty-five, unwed—
> The day we left you by your grave,
> I wouldn't spare one tear.

The poet's prose version of these events, if less vivid, is more direct:

> It seemed to me that she, disapproving the life around her and unwilling to find any other, had withdrawn into a very destructive and self-deceiving relationship with her mother. This, of course, had satisfied none of her real needs, but she was unable to change her course; she developed a severe case of asthma. . . . When her problem became progressively worse and she reached the age at which it must have been clear that she would never marry or have any independent career, she took the logical last step. On the morning of the Fourth of July. . . , her heart simply quit beating. To die on Independence Day seemed an act of terrible and destructive

blamefulness, yet this may have been, in its way, the easiest solution of her dilemma—she had died spiritually (that is, as an animal moved by aims and opinions) years before.[13]

This too is the subject of the book's most powerful poem, "Fourth of July," with its stark narrative and weary, end-stopped lines, choked on the smoke that seeps through the city, his home and family, which compose a land of the dead. The public celebration counterpoints the private numbness:

> She stopped a year ago today.
> Firecrackers mark the occasion down the street;
> I thumb through magazines and keep my seat.
> What can anybody say? . . .
>
> It is a hideous mistake.
> My young wife, unforgivably alive,
> Takes a deep breath and blows out twenty-five
> Candles on her birthday cake.

The ironic contrast between the two women—the sister he could not rescue, and the wife who rescued him—barely allows him to tolerate his own angry resignation:

> It is an evil, stupid joke:
> My wife is pregnant; my sister's in her grave.
> We live in the home of the free and of the brave.
> No one would hear me, even if I spoke.

This is the same voicelessness as in "A Cardinal," and again is caused by the obscuring of the self: his sister's life, and the poet's identity among an oppressive family. When he does speak, he does so away from his parents—at the public isolation of a funeral, or the privacy of a bedroom, or in a poem. "Viewing the Body" and "Disposal" are macabre descriptions of his dead sister and her empty room, and the poet's violence

—in her casket she lies with "Eyeshadow like a whore"—
emphasizes his outraged sense of waste.

The final two poems are the remains of the family tragedy:
its survivors, his parents and himself. "The Survivors" is his
last glance back, searching for what he has already found: "We
wondered what might change / Once you were not here; /
Tried to guess how they would rearrange / Their life, now you
were dead." Everything is overgrown or disrepaired, and the
two stone lions on the front steps have their eyes patched with
cement. Blind too are the ghostly parents, who attend at a dead
ritual of separation:

> Only at night they meet.
> By voiceless summoning
> They come to the living room; each repeats
> Some words he has memorized; each takes his seat
> In the hushed, expectant ring
>
> By the television set.
> No one can draw his eyes
> From that unnatural, cold light. They wait.
> The screen goes dim and they hunch closer yet,
> As the image dies.

If "Nothing is different here," then the last poem, "To a
Child," stakes out the life he has made for himself by means of
a warning prayer to his daughter. The poem is familiar because
it is close to those in "Heart's Needle"—though muted by the
mood which the other poems in *Remains* cast over it—and is,
in fact, a spin-off of the sixth poem in the earlier sequence. In
"Finding a Poem," Snodgrass recalls revising first drafts of that
poem, and the deletions he felt necessary: "Finally, I had to
give up my lines about stone-skipping and the Sunday lovers
on the riverbank. This nearly broke my heart, but I promised

myself to work them into a later poem." They settle finally
into "To a Child":

> Still, I guess we often choose
> Odd spots: we used to go stone-dapping
> On the riverbanks where lovers lay
> Abandoned in each others' arms all day
> By their beached, green canoes;
> You asked why they were napping.

The odd spot he and his daughter have come to is a field for
"our talk / About the birds and the bees." That talk is preceded
by stanzas describing episodes and lessons in the forms of
natural love. In their own way they rehearse the facts of life,
the facts of his own and of their life together:

> And I mailed you long letters
> Though you were still too young to read; . . .

> They threw my letters out.
> Said I had probably forgotten. . . .

> We have watched grown men debase
> Themselves for their embittered wives

> And we have seen an old sow that could smother
> The sucklings in her stye,
> That could devour her own farrow.
> We have seen my sister in her narrow
> Casket. Without love we die;
> With love we kill each other.

As in the ending of "Heart's Needle" Snodgrass attempts to
affirm life in the face of his child's imagining herself dead. The
earlier poem closed with the example of self-affirmation; this
poem is more tentative, more desperate:

I sit here by you in the summer's lull
Near the lost handkerchiefs of lovers
To tell you when your brother
Will be born; how, and why.
I tell you love is possible.
We have to try.

Nine years elapsed between *Heart's Needle* and the publication of *After Experience* (1968). Perhaps that length of time itself accounts for the variety of work in the later volume, but Snodgrass was probably also intent on displaying his interests and achievements apart from those confessional. The diversity of *After Experience* is reminiscent of the example of Snodgrass' old master Lowell. Nearly half of the book is occupied with twenty-four translations and a series of long poems which are interpretative recreations of the subjects and energies of five impressionist paintings. And of the remaining poems, several are set pieces, which their titles alone indicate: "A Character," "Flash Flood," "Exorcism," "Edmund to Gloucester," "The Men's Room in the College Chapel," "Powwow," and his academic satirical allegory "The Examination." The influence of Vietnam is felt in an increased political note to the work, in such poems as "Inquest" and "A Visitation."

Snodgrass seems, then, intentionally to have restricted his confessional impulse, but it does shape a significant portion of the book even though the poet's use of it has changed along with his intervening experience. The book's title hints at Snodgrass' personality in these poems: it is wary, hard-edged, guarded, perhaps more pessimistic, certainly more *experienced*. The shift between first and second books has been from awareness to understanding.

The title poem is an extreme example of the essentially dramatic nature of this process. In his effort to demonstrate the final similarity between two seemingly opposed views of life, Snodgrass alternates the phrases of two speakers: the first is Spinoza, the opening of his essay "On the Improvement of the Understanding"; the second is a lecture Snodgrass says he heard in the Navy on the most effective way to kill a man in hand-to-hand combat. The brutal details of ripping off "the whole facial mask" undercut, but do not destroy, the philosopher's exalted argument; the purposes of Snodgrass' juxtaposition are closer to a comment he once made in an interview: "Your ideas are normally just the way you disguise your feelings so that you can do what you want without admitting you're doing it. All right, so our disguises are a part of us. . . . Most people, by taking off their clothes, don't demonstrate much except that they aren't very interesting. . . . I'm much more interested in the kinds of disguises we put on all the time. Our disguises can reveal a lot more about the way we feel."[14] What Snodgrass says here was put more succinctly by Valéry: "There is no theory that is not a fragment, carefully prepared, of some autobiography." This is why the poem's last stanza points its accusation at the poet himself, as well as at the reader:

> And you, whiner, who waste your time
>   Dawdling over the remorseless earth,
> What evil, what unspeakable crime
>   Have you made your life worth?

This is finally the function of the book's "ideas," and the effect of its probing hesitancy: Snodgrass sets (his critics would say, reduces) his actual experience to a moral scrutiny, in order to discover and evaluate the real feelings and motives beneath the disguises and rationalizations, the autobiography beneath the theory. His concern is not for belief, but for character, and if this deprives the book of the immediacy of *Heart's Needle*, it does lend a larger, more penetrating perspective which is apparent when the poems in *After Experience* about his daughter and his first wife are compared with earlier ones.

The cumulative narrative arrangement of poems in *Heart's Needle* was concentrated and consistent. In this book, it is more oblique, but a reader can still easily follow the chronology of events in Snodgrass' experience: his uneasy relationship with his daughter, the troubles in his second marriage, the love affairs, the professional disappointments. What Snodgrass has done, though, is to intersperse his narrative poems with lyrical, depersonalized ones, which serve as choric interludes by framing his experiences with more distance. In fact, the opening poem of the collection, "Partial Eclipse," seems addressed, at first, to the generalized "you" of the traditional lyric, until later we see it, along with the three, more direct poems that follow it, as a continuation of the "Heart's Needle" address to his daughter. They would be harsh poems, if they were not hardened. In the "eclipse" of their relationship that time has clouded over, "Something, one glint was left," and in the next poem ("September") even that dims:

> I hoped to spot that small Green Heron
> We saw together down the marsh
> This August. He'd gone off on an errand.
>
> Then too, of course, this *is* September.
> The newts in the creek had gone, already.
> I don't know where. I can't remember
> Your face or anything you said.

The next two poems seek the reasons in the girl's own emerging maturity. What disturbs the poet, in "Reconstructions," is the way in which her parents' characters are reconstructed in the child:

You offered me, one day, your doll
To sing songs to, bubble and nurse,
And said that was her birthday;
You reappeared then, grabbed her away,
Said just don't mess with her at all;
It was your child, yours.

And earlier this summer, how
You would tell the dog he had to "Stay!"
Then always let him sit
There, ears up, tense, all
Shivering to hear you call;
You turned and walked away.

There is a measure of self-disgust in this realization since in reflecting her father's behavior, she reminds him of what he has made her "real" existence for himself, of his own "reconstructions": "I memorize you, bit by bit, / And must restore you in my verses / To sell to magazines." The final poem in this group, "The First Leaf," merely elaborates this guilt:

Next year we'll hardly know you;
Still, all the blame endures.
This year you will live at our expense;
We have a life at yours, . . .

You move off where I send you;
The train pulls down its track.
We go about our business;
I have turned my back.

The "enduring blame," what time can and cannot erode, is also the occasion for the poems about his first wife, "Mementos, 1" and "Mementos, 2." Both involve the accidental discovery of a memory—a photograph and a dress, the first in a desk drawer, the second in "the third-flood closet," both suggesting the dark, hidden nature of the unconscious. The photograph in "Mementos, 1" is at once his idealized memory and the evidence of his immaturity:

> you stand
> Just as you stood—shy, delicate, slender,
> In that long gown of green lace netting and daisies
> That you wore to our first dance. The sight of you
> stunned
> Us all. Well, our needs were different, then,
> And our ideals came easy.

His later "needs" were determined by growth and the imperative escape from marriage's "lies, self-denial, unspoken regret," which forced his sense of reality and the genuine "first meeting." The blame that endures is a helpless one, and is here transferred to a poignant longing: "I put back your picture. Someday, in due course, / I will find that it's still there." In "Mementos, 2," his discovery of "that long white satin gown / and the heavy lead-foil crown" his wife once wore as the local "Queen of the May" stirs erotic memories—roots, hair—that embitter other memories of her neurotic fears that his love "might stain" her. "Yet the desire remains," and in that contradiction he finds forgiveness of a sort:

> I thought of our years; thought you
> had had enough of pain;
> thought how much grief I'd brought you;
> I wished you well again.

A series of poems go on to detail the difficulties in his second marriage, and the poet's strong sense of will—his ability to make a life for himself—is shaken by undercurrents of fatalism: "The curse is far from done; / When they've taken your daughter / They can take your son" ("The Platform Man").

Even his affairs are hedged in by circumstance or doubt; there seems a self-sought claustrophobia in "A Friend" and "Leaving the Motel," where moral conclusions are either forced or suspended.

Two other poems in *After Experience* deserve mention in a discussion of Snodgrass' confessional work. "Leaving Ithaca" looks back to a poem like "April Inventory," and is in many ways more winning. It is a more modest and relaxed poem, yet more carefully worked. Dedicated "to my plaster replica of the Aphrodite of Melos," the poem turns this battered and mended piece of kitsch into his enduring symbol of Love, around which other loves have lived and died: "Well, we must both look secondhand. / Lady, we've cost each other":

> Now, of course, we have to move again
> And leave the old house roughhewn as we found it,
> The wild meadows and unworked fields around it—
> No doubt it would have spoiled us to remain.

The poet's survival depends on the persistence of love, as in a line addressed to both the statue and his wife: "Lady, we are going to have another child." The echo of his earlier affirmations is fainter and more defeated, but continues Snodgrass' most urgent and appealing uses of his experience as exemplary:

> We'll try to live with evils that we choose,
> Try not to envy someone else's vices,
> But make the most of ours. We picked our crisis;
> We'll lose the things we can afford to lose
>
> And lug away what's left in orange crates. . . .

This same tenacity structures the narrative of "A Flat One" (hospital slang for a corpse), an extensive revision of a poem written for John Berryman at Iowa, about the death of Fritz Jarck, an old World War I veteran in a VA hospital where

Snodgrass was working at the time. It is a cunningly detailed poem, complete with a Foster Frame bed and autoclave, that builds to a crucial self-examination on a man's moral and human response to pain and the suffering of others. The poet's initial resentment is selfishly uncomprehending:

> Old man, these seven months you've lain
> Determined—not that you would live—
> Just to not die. . . .
>
> They'd say this was a worthwhile job
> Unless they tried it. It is mad
> To throw our good lives after bad;
> Waste time, drugs, and our minds, while strong
> Men starve. How many young men did we rob
> To keep you hanging on?

But he hesitates into his discovery: "You stayed for me—/ Nailed to your own rapacious, stiff self-will." Stretched out on a Foster Frame bed would have given the old man a crucified look, but that reference is less important than the fumbled conclusion, where the poet lurches to learn what he has since taught himself to exemplify:

> I can't think we did *you* much good.
> Well, when you died, none of us wept.
> You killed for us, and so we kept
> You, because we need to earn our pay.
> No. We'd still have to help you try. We would
> Have killed for you today.

We would have killed for you today.

Something vicious lurks under the sentiment, and it recurs in several poems throughout *After Experience*. "Edmund to Gloucester" gives voice to the villain of a "bitched world." Like the book's title poem which undermines its own consolations, "The Men's Room in the College Chapel" explores the place of sex and excrement that lies subversively beneath high-minded beliefs. In "Inquest," with its villanelle-like pattern insisting on its obsessive repetitions, the speaker cross-examines his mirrored reflection. The figure—in the mirror, in the speaker's conscience, and in his subconscious, both in this poem and in the one following, "A Visitation"—is clearly Adolf Eichmann. Snodgrass is fascinated, here as elsewhere, with choked-back guilts and justification's twisted reasoning. Feelings he first discovered in himself and in his marriages he begins to notice in—or project onto—history itself: in either a person or a people, forces move in "implacably to rule us, unaware."

Such poems could be said to have led to *The Fuehrer Bunker*, a project that has preoccupied Snodgrass for two decades since *After Experience*. But in fact, the roots of the project go back much further. When he first enrolled in the writing workshop at Iowa, he intended to study playwrighting, not poetry. Even earlier he had begun to make a play out of Hugh Trevor-Roper's *The Last Days of Hitler*. The dramatization got nowhere, but the idea was rekindled in the early seventies when Snodgrass began fashioning monologues for the leading actors in the drama of the last month of the Third Reich. Twenty of them were published as a book-length poem-in-progress in 1977. Others followed, and in his *Selected Poems 1957–1987* Snodgrass chose a new grouping of fifteen, along with a note to say that the cycle now consists of over seventy poems, which have been variously drawn on for staged performances.

Perhaps the final shape and purpose of the poem will eventually come clear. (I hesitate to call it a play; though possibly conceived as a sort of anti-*Faust*, its dramaturgy is too weak, and its details too impacted, for it to hold the stage. A closet drama, then—or bunker drama.) In a note to the 1977 edition, Snodgrass wrote that his intention went beyond a mere account of the horrifying details: "The Nazis—like some others one may have encountered—often did or said things to disguise from the world, and sometimes from themselves, their real actions and intentions. My aim is to investigate the thoughts and feelings behind the public facade which made those actions necessary or even possible. My poems, then, must include voices they would hide from others, even from themselves." But even that explanation is vague, and the question remains: is the poem a stuffed owl? (A question made more pointed still by the project that subsequently engrossed the poet—a long sequence called *The Death of Cock Robin*. Most of these poems are written in doggerel; all are related to paintings by DeLoss McGraw, and spoken by a character called "W. D." With a few exceptions, like the bravura "A Darkling Alphabet," these latest poems are not only a disappointment but a puzzle: why would a poet with such gifts, even in his search for diversity and new "voices," deliberately parody those gifts and wreck a career?)

The Fuehrer Bunker is best read, I think, as a peculiar extension of Snodgrass' earlier work. There are two couples in the poem, Hitler and Eva Braun, and Joseph and Magda Goebbels. They stand as perverse extremes of traits the poet had earlier documented in his own experience. Adolf Speer (whom Snodgrass interviewed as part of his research) functions as a kind of bad seed/wise child of these marriages, and as close to a stand-in for the author himself as we're given. We are encouraged to make these connections by the epigraph that now prefaces the sequence: "Mother Theresa, asked when she first began her work of relief and care for abandoned children, replied, 'On the day I discovered I had a Hitler inside me.' " But aren't such comparisons too slick? They risk trivializing the tragic life of history, and distorting the true dimensions of the domestic life as well.

The grotesque delusions of his cast (Bormann's mushy letters home, Eva Braun singing "Tea for Two," Magda Goebbels' villanelle to explain murdering her own children) are his theatrical focus, but his subject finally is, in Arendt's now overused phrase, the banality of evil. That banality now outweighs the more intriguing parallels to themes in Snodgrass' previous books, but they are crucial. Snodgrass himself has pointed out that the Nazi leaders were each failed artists, and as a distorted analysis of the artistic temperament the poem can take its place as a kind of *Inferno*, written after but to be read before the purgatorial confessions of *Heart's Needle*. During their conversations, Speer told Snodgrass: "We were like the Greeks when they got to Asia Minor and had all that limitless space before them." *The Fuehrer Bunker* is a poem about *limits*, from the point of view of those who won't or can't recognize them.

Turning to *The Fuehrer Bunker* is not unlike the experience, after having read Hardy's exquisite lyrics to his dead wife, of then turning to read *The Dynasts*. Myself, I search the second half of the *Selected Poems 1957–1987* for poems like the 1986 sequence called "A Locked House," which involves the breakup of a marriage. "Mutability," "The Last Time," and "A Locked House" itself would be reckoned among Snodgrass' strongest work. In the last-named poem, he remembers driving home with his wife as they worried, needlessly, about their locked house and secure marriage. But with the years things happened "none of us ever guessed," and the house stands again locked, but because abandoned rather than waiting:

> The house still stands, locked, as it stood
> Untouched a good
> Two years after you went.
> Some things passed in the settlement;
> Some things slipped away. Enough's left

That I come back sometimes. The theft
And vandalism were our own.
Maybe we should have known.

The painful memories these poems sift for moral bearings
have consistently resulted in Snodgrass' best work. Though, as
they demonstrate, he has not entirely forsaken the confessional
mode, he has sharply modified it for his own purposes. For a
poet so concerned with survival, perhaps this was a necessary
tactic after the enormous success and influence of *Heart's Needle*.
But it is his confessional poetry that remains as the heart of his
achievement. In "April Inventory," he mentions teaching his
classes "Whitehead's notions." One of those notions is that
"the canons of art are merely the expression in specialized form
of the requirements for depth of experience." At its best, Snod-
grass' mild, reflective art has specialized in precisely that depth
of experience.

ENDNOTES

1. W. D. Snodgrass, "A Rocking-Horse: The Symbol, the Pattern,
the Way to Live" (1958), *In Radical Pursuit*, p. 133 (New York:
Harper & Row, 1975).

2. "W. D. Snodgrass: An Interview," *Salmagundi* (Spring-Sum-
mer 1973) 22–23:165.

3. WDS to JDMcC, from a letter dated May 28, 1973.

4. *Ibid.* The "paraphrase from Ovid" referred to is "Europa,"
which was never collected but appears in *Botteghe Oscure* (1953),
12:325–27.

5. Quoted in William Martz, ed., *The Distinctive Voice*, p. 256
(Glenview, Ill., 1966).

6. WDS to JDMcC, from a letter dated May 28, 1973.

7. W. D. Snodgrass, "Finding a Poem" (1959), *In Radical Pursuit*,
p. 32.

8. Philip L. Gerber and Robert J. Gemmett, eds., " 'No Voices Talk to Me': A Conversation with W. D. Snodgrass," *Western Humanities Review,* (Winter 1970), 24(1):71.

9. WDS to JDMcC, from a letter dated February 6, 1974. See "Poems About Paintings," *In Radical Pursuit,* pp. 63–97. Snodgrass' critical essays are all strongly psychoanalytical in their method as well, and often distinctly autobiographical in their account of his approach to an understanding of the texts involved. *In Radical Pursuit* includes readings of *A Midsummer Night's Dream, Don Quixote,* the *Inferno,* and the *Iliad,* and with each he is concerned to reveal and explore "the unconscious areas of thought and emotion" in these expressions of their artists' personalities. By equating exegetical criticism with consciousness and even ideology, Snodgrass' purposely "radical" stance demonstrates the continuity and integrity of his relationships to texts—whether lived, written, or read. The true work of art is finally an "important act in our lives," and like every other such act is "both propelled and guided by the darker, less visible areas of emotion and personality." See also "Poetry Since Yeats: An Exchange of Views," *Tri-Quarterly* (1965), 4:100–11.

10. W. D. Snodgrass, "Four Gentlemen; Two Ladies," *The Hudson Review* (Spring 1960), 13(1):130.

11. WDS to JDMcC, from a letter dated May 28, 1973.

12. It is interesting to note that Snodgrass had originally titled each poem in the sequence. On a typescript of "Heart's Needle" sent to Theodore Roethke on August 25, 1957 (and now in The Theodore Roethke Collection, Suzzallo Library, University of Washington), Snodgrass wrote the following titles over each of the poems, and under each added the season it recounts:

1. The Cold War (Winter 1952)
2. Planting (Spring 1953)
3. The Separation (Summer 1953)
4. Evening Visitation (Autumn 1953)
5. Loss of Feeling (Winter 1953)
6. Reviving (Spring 1954)
7. Fledgling (Summer 1954)
8. Ferment (Autumn 1954)

9. Deadlock (Winter 1954)

10. Returning (Spring 1955)

These titles have the simplicity of lieder titles, and are another indication of the influence of such songs on Snodgrass's sequence. I am indebted for this information to William Heyen and Richard Blessing.

13. This is drawn from the version of "Finding a Poem" as it originally appeared in the *Partisan Review* (Spring 1959), 26(2):280. In reprinting the essay in *In Radical Pursuit,* Snodgrass repressed this section, withdrawing the painful family privacy from public view, and says only that his sister was "closely involved with her family" and that "It would be hard to say *why* she died."

14. "W. D. Snodgrass: An Interview," p. 161.

JAMES MERRILL

ON *WATER STREET*

CUSTOMARILY, a collection of James Merrill's poems begins with a short lyric that anticipates by announcing them the concerns and tone of the whole book. The thematic departures and presiding patron of *The Country of a Thousand Years of Peace* are introduced in the opening title poem. "The Nightgown" in *Nights and Days*, "Log" in *Braving the Elements*, and "The Kimono" in *Divine Comedies* are each a conceit—as much an invocation of powers as a retrospective commentary on the act of writing itself—that sounds a keynote to be struck in important poems throughout the different books. *Water Street*, published in 1962 and a watershed in his development as a poet, is unusual in this regard for having no proleptic lyric. Instead, the book's longest and major poem, "An Urban Convalescence," comes first. Its pride of place is understandable; Merrill himself has called the poem "a turning point" in his career. In its grand way, then, it announces not only the preoccupations of *Water Street* but a decisive change in the poet's thinking about the emotional and technical capacities of verse.

If *Water Street* had been organized along the lines of his other collections, then Merrill might have placed the second poem, "From a Notebook," first in the book. Its very title points toward the volume's effective origins, and its figures for speech — the writer as Narcissus over his frozen pond or before a mirror's "dreamless oval," as steel-shod skater tracing loops and spirals on the page's "fresh / Candor" — are no less eloquent for being familiar. But I suspect the more fitting prelude to *Water Street* would have been a poem that could double as its dedication — "For Proust." Like "From a Notebook," it too is a poem about writing, but an altogether more virtuosic and substantial one. The poem presumes to tell a story: one of Proust's midnight forays into the world to capture a detail for his novel, his rendezvous at the Ritz with a woman who might but never does hum "the little phrase," and his exhausted but enriched return to his study. But much more is illustrated by the poem than its exemplary anecdote. We might be alerted to this by the rare rhyme scheme (each quatrain's median couplet is an identical rhyme) that emphasizes the notion of repossession or by the evidence of a very Proustian foreshortening — whereby, for example, the conjured friend is at first "a child," then three stanzas and a conversation later has a white lock in her hair, and in the last stanza is replaced by, or transformed into, the "old, old woman" who tends him. "For Proust" is a deft portrait of, and tribute to, the novelist; it is also a summary of his novel's leading motifs and a succinct interpretation of the method of his *recherche*. The balance, in fact, between the writer's life and his art — what Merrill calls here "the painful sum of things" — is the poem's ballast. Throughout, the emphasis is on pain — on neurasthenia and anxiety, on betrayal and inadequacy — until that pain is strangely intensified by its conclusion:

> Back where you came from, up the strait stair, past
> All understanding, bearing the whole past,
> Your eyes grown wide and dark, eyes of a Jew,

You make for one dim room without contour
And station yourself there, beyond the pale
Of cough or of gardenia, erect, pale.
What happened is becoming literature.

Feverish in time, if you suspend the task,
An old, old woman shuffling in to draw
Curtains, will read a line or two, withdraw.
The world will have put on a thin gold mask.

His retreat is his great responsibility. By "bearing the whole past," he gives life to what is over, forgotten or misunderstood. "What happened"—that is, what he had experienced once and tried another time to understand—is given a continuous existence by and in his art. And that task, though fatal, redeems: the haggard life mask glows, first with fever, finally with immortality. "The thin gold mask," writes Richard Howard, "is not a defense against reality, nor a concealment from it; it is a funerary enduement which will withstand and redeem the wreckage of a life." It is clever of Howard so to have merged— or to have allowed the final image to contain—both the artist and the world. Certainly the poem encourages such a reading. Proust enters his "one dim room" as if it were a tomb, so that his sacrifice—the sacrifice of himself into his novel—seems to merit the honor of a royal death mask. But it is the world, not the artist, that puts on the mask. On a literal level, the last line simply refers to the world beyond Proust's curtained window, a world then putting on the gold mask of dawn.[1] But more is implied. What is happening has become literature; image subsumes event. The world *will have* put on a rich finish—its outlines familiar but its appearance transfigured—when so portrayed by the artist and then so seen by his reader. The presence in this last stanza of the "old, old woman" is also suggestive. Again on a literal level, she is a conflation of Proust's servant Céleste Albaret, of his beloved mother, and of his grandmother. But she is, too, the world itself, that "ancient, ageless woman of the world" who presides over the close of "Ephraim." In a sense, then, it is she who puts on the thin gold mask, as earlier she had worn other masks: the conjured friend's, a child's, the loved one's. She has been both muse and material, and at the end it is the old woman who "will read a line or two." Are not an author's muse and his ideal reader two aspects of the same figure?

"For Proust," then, is as much a celebration of the natural yet mysterious sources of art as it is an evocation of the frail but godlike powers of the artist. Both those subjects are taken up in *Water Street*. And Proust himself, long Merrill's most deep-rooted influence, may be seen to have replaced Hans Lodeizen—the tutelary spirit of *The Country of a Thousand Years of Peace*—as the patron of this book. Hans was the Young Man taken out of time, cultivated but impersonal, a hero because a martyr, perfected because unfulfilled. Proust, on the other hand, is the more human figure and the more mature artistic model. Struggling against time in order to recover it, he is at once at the heart of the world and the perpetual outsider, the internal exile. Merrill seeks to live by Proust's great laws in *Water Street* and to adapt his novel's methods for poetry. Questions of scale and intimacy and intermittence, of the ability to create and to characterize the self, of the alchemical function of metaphor to change the lead of private experience into the gold of archetypal art—for all these questions and others Merrill sought an answering verse in this book. Where Proust sought his answers, in the primary worlds of childhood and the sensual life, so, too, does Merrill seek his. More than half the poems in the book are concerned with childhood, with family or domestic scenes. The specific and circumscribed settings of poems like "Getting Through" or "A Tenancy" are their new advantage. "The Water Hyacinth," for example, is addressed to his maternal grandmother (whose elegy is the following poem, "Annie Hill's Grave"), juxtaposing old memories of her and of hers with present realities of age and illness. The ingenuous tone with which the poem opens is secured from slackness by the strong affection in its direct address and by an easy and convincing naturalness that is new in Merrill's voice:

> When I was four or so
> I used to read aloud
> To you—I mean, recite
> Stories both of us knew
> By heart, the book held close
> To even then nearsighted
> Eyes. It was morning. You,
> Still in your nightgown
> Over cold tea, would nod
> Approval. Once I caught
> A gay note in your quiet:
> The book was upside down.

From that point on, the poem deals with what else is now "upside down," time having overturned all but such memories. The poem increases in syntactical complexity as it broadens the scope of its concern. And to resolve the poem, Merrill combines his perspectives to focus on a remembered detail that is both historically exact and symbolically apt. The water hyacinth, imported at the turn of the century when she was honeymooning, later choked the St. John's River near his grandmother's native Jacksonville:

> A mauve and rootless guest
> Thirsty for life, afloat
> With you on the broad span

It would in sixty years
So vividly congest.

Other of Proust's discoveries and maneuvers are present as
well, either as compositional aids or emotional attitudes. There
is a new attention to motivation, the use of involuntary mem-
ories, the deployment of interlocking images, a heightened
awareness of the imperfection of the present and the transience
of the past. They animate the best poems in *Water Street*—
"An Urban Convalescence," "A Tenancy," and "Scenes of
Childhood." But I would group the book with Merrill's early
work because, while these three poems are superior to anything
in his two previous books, and by their innovations help define
the direction and force of his subsequent work, they are not
matched by the remainder of the book. In comparison with *The
Country of a Thousand Years of Peace*, this book may even
seem a slighter one; there are fourteen fewer poems, and a
narrower range. There is a delicacy at work in *Water Street*
that gives several poems charm ("Five Old Favorites," "The
Lawn Fete of Homunculus Artifex"), and a heartiness that
gives others some bite ("Roger Clay's Proposal," "The Recon-
naissance"), but neither quality makes any of those poems very
significant. Not until *Nights and Days* can he sustain for the
length of an entire book the originality and intensity that mark
the three important poems in *Water Street*.

Leading off the book as it does, "An Urban Convalescence"
occupies a position analogous to that of "Beyond the Alps" in
Robert Lowell's *Life Studies*, a book published three years
before *Water Street* and one whose crucial autobiographical
emphasis may well have helped Merrill to fashion the circum-
stantial intimacy of his own poem. In both poems, life changes
to landscape, as Lowell put it: both are trains of thought that
end in Paris, Merrill's in memory, Lowell's in anticipation.
"Beyond the Alps" is a pivotal poem in Lowell's work. It stands

as a renunciation of his tortured and hieratic Catholic beliefs, preliminary to the secular cast of *Life Studies* with its pathetic portraits of impotence and madness. Though *Water Street* has none of the novelistic coherence of *Life Studies*, and certainly none of its anguish, "An Urban Convalescence" stands in a similar relation to Merrill's previous work. It too signals a rejection. More by its example than by any declaration, it abjures an earlier belief or mode, in this case the baroque preciosity, the feints and baffles of *First Poems* and *The Country of a Thousand Years of Peace*. The style of those books is gestural: taut or spiraling, all running colors and arrested development, preferring ecstasy to refinement, contradictions to continuities. The best of that style—its brio, its lavishness, its fondness for paradox—remains in *Water Street*. Its ornate excesses and riddles do not. Modest set pieces such as "To a Butterfly" or "The Parrot Fish" serve to remind one of how few such emblematic poems there actually are in the book and of how Merrill is now less content with intellectual conceits and more dependent on phenomenal details, vivid and familiar, than he was before.

To compare "Saint" or "The Charioteer of Delphi" in *The Country of a Thousand Years of Peace* with "Angel" in *Water Street* accentuates the difference. The former poems, metrically constrained, deal in extreme states of soul, in rapture, despair, havoc. The free verse of "Angel" is altogether more relaxed and genial and corresponds to the poem's witty amiability. Like the earlier poems, it too explores the themes of learning and mastery but takes up those themes in a context of the commonplace. It too measures the self against an idealized image, but far from lamenting the distance between them, it delights in their comic disparity. Like the statues of Sebastian and the charioteer, the guardian angel above the poet's desk—conceivably a postcard—has an iconic presence but is no martyr with whom the poet longs to identify himself. This angel, a sort of anti-muse, is both ironic and unaware, self-important yet humorously miniaturized:

> Above my desk, whirring and self-important
> (Though not much larger than a hummingbird)
> In finely woven robes, school of Van Eyck,
> Hovers an evidently angelic visitor.
> He points one index finger out the window
> At winter snatching to its heart,
> To crystal vacancy, the misty
> Exhalations of houses and of people running home
> From the cold sun pounding on the sea;
> While with the other hand
> He indicates the piano
> Where the Sarabande No. 1 lies open
> At a passage I shall never master
> But which has already, and effortlessly, mastered me.

The angel's silent reproach makes him seem at first like Stevens' angel surrounded by paysans, the necessary angel of earth come to lead the poet to the promised land of reality. Inside, composing, mastered by another artist's music, the ephebe is directed to the world beyond his window—the world Proust transcended by absorbing. But the lexical ambiguity in the first line, whereby the poet's metonymous desk is itself "whirring and self-important," is the clue. The moral the angel next draws is only a projection, an "as if," of the poet's own frustration and self-doubt:

> He drops his jaw as if to say, or sing,
> 'Between the world God made
> And this music of Satie,
> Each glimpsed through veils, but whole,
> Radiant and willed,
> Demanding praise, demanding surrender,

How can you sit there with your notebook?
What do you think you are doing?'

The poet sees himself poised between the world and his art, cut off from the one, incapable of the other. The world having been described as a work of art (a "crystal vacancy," and the sun pounding on the sea as if on a piano note) and Satie's Sarabande given the divine status of mastery, they reinforce each other and, by their self-sufficiency, "Radiant and willed," combine to accuse the poet of precisely what he has not—or not yet, not until "Angel" is over—been able to create. At this point in the earlier two poems, the speaker would have turned disconsolately back in, or been stung into reminiscence. But Merrill is in a puckish mood here. A teasing decorum settles the score, as the poet turns back to his page. Neither his piano playing nor his writing are yet connected, or legato, he has said, but by the last line the completed poem serves to confound the angel's conscience and the poet's doubts:

> However he says nothing—wisely: I could mention
> Flaws in God's world, or Satie's; and for that matter
> How did he come by *his* taste for Satie?
> Half to tease him, I turn back to my page,
> Its phrases thus far clotted, unconnected.
> The tiny angel shakes his head.
> There is no smile on his round, hairless face.
> He does not want even these few lines written.

Merrill's avoidance of melodrama in this poem, of emotional impasse or baroque expedients, is characteristic of *Water Street* as a whole and of a new bearing in his work to come. His poems now tend to insist on questioning their own assumptions, on tempering headstrong convictions with heartfelt reservations, on maintaining a revisionary attitude toward both experience and his feelings about that experience. The effect, for all the opportunities it gives the poet to vary a poem's pace and to manipulate a reader's responses, is one of emotional honesty, an openness that belies the very artistry used to achieve it. This quality becomes a hallmark of Merrill's best poems, which accommodate their own second guesses. A poem, though intricately worked, will sometimes seem a series of fresh starts, each more precise and more resonant than the last. As a man comfortable with the subtleties of imagery, the speaker of these poems is used to threading the maze of his thoughts, will not trust himself too readily and, because he can explain them, is not surprised by his mind's play or his language's darting eloquence. What I call here a poem's "emotional honesty" should not be mistaken for the frankness of the confessionalists. It may be, as Valéry noted, that a man knows too little of himself to reveal to us, in his "sincere" confessions, much more than we could easily have guessed without his telling us. *Water Street* is not itself autobiographical in any documentary sense. Unlike the sometimes flat transcripts of Ginsberg or Lowell, it does not serve up the raw events of Merrill's "outer" life or the overdetermined accidents of his emotional dealings. Nor does it even draw very specifically and consistently on his own biography, as "The Book of Ephraim" will later do. Yet there seems a candid intimacy to this book that is absent from his earlier work and is the distinction of his later. In an interview Merrill once shrugged off confessional poetry as "a literary convention like any other, the problem being to make it *sound* as if it were true." It is, in other words, a manner rather than the matter of a poem that confers its intimacy. But this is not only an affair of style: certain nuances of tone, adjustments of perspective, the forging of private experience in the hearth of myth and fable, pattern and drive. It is also a demand for a probity prior to the poetry, which the style must reinforce. Whatever Merrill may reserve from the reader, we feel he has not deceived himself. His most affecting poems, from *Water Street* on, succeed not because of how they expose or suppress the facts of his life but because they rely on an intellectual scrupulosity while searching out the truths of the heart.

WATER STREET begins, in "An Urban Convalescence," with a recovery. The title implies an illness that is never specified in the poem, as are the paralysis in "The Thousand and Second Night" or the virus in "A Fever." There may have been— probably was—an actual illness, but for the sake of the poem, it is more metaphoric than real, a spiritual condition rather than a physical ailment. From one point of view it can be seen as the Proustian creative malady. In this view the invalid and the artist share and feed on a hypersensitivity that is denied the "normal" man. And like the convalescent who seeks out reviving stimulants, the artist as *homme nerveux* seeks out— and is sought out by—new sensations that, however slight, stir old, ramifying memories, as they certainly do in this poem. But from another point of view we might see it less as an enabling difficulty than as a disabling facility. And I think Merrill names the problem, albeit covertly, in a turn of phrase so "facile" as to be distracting. "The sickness of our time" very nearly translates, after all, the *maladie du temps* that pervades the speaker's consciousness and the poem's impulses toward escape, stability, reassurance. Hampered by the existential horror of mortality, the sickness unto death that is time itself, the only convalescence possible involves a new understanding of his life that would allow the speaker to reconcile himself to loss and limitation.

That it is an urbane convalescence might be expected, but an *urban* one? We have great recuperative odes, from Coleridge to Ashbery, with rural or retired settings, and we are used by now to the sort of urban pastoral that Frank O'Hara perfected.

But Merrill's poem—though an arcadian pattern can be per-
ceived, with its garlands, tendril, fruit, roots, the Champs-
Elysées themselves—deliberately leaves behind the pastoral
world of natural resources and idealizing fictions, and seeks its
remedy elsewhere. The poem begins outdoors:

> Out for a walk, after a week in bed,
> I find them tearing up part of my block
> And, chilled through, dazed and lonely, join the dozen
> In meek attitudes, watching a huge crane
> Fumble luxuriously in the filth of years.
> Her jaws dribble rubble. An old man
> Laughs and curses in her brain,
> Bringing to mind the close of *The White Goddess*.
>
> As usual in New York, everything is torn down
> Before you have had time to care for it.
> Head bowed, at the shrine of noise, let me try to recall
> What building stood here. Was there a building at all?
> I have lived on this same street for a decade.

The opening is done in quick, broad strokes. Within a dozen
lines the setting is vividly sketched in and the speaker's char-
acter outlined. He is delicate, disoriented, literate. The scene
itself—which could hardly astonish a New Yorker but might
startle a *penseroso* isolated a week with his own thoughts—is
nearly grotesque. What in the trade is called "construction
work" is an image—one that Lowell later used effectively in
"For the Union Dead"—that serves two purposes. On the one
hand, it establishes the poem's premise by symbolizing the
uncaring ravages of time and of a discontented civilization.
That theme with its attendant images—of demolition and frag-
mentation, of convulsive change and wasting—is quintessen-
tially the theme of modern poetry itself. If Merrill did not have
Baudelaire's "*Le Cygne*" in mind while writing "An Urban

Convalescence"—which is unlikely for one so well versed in French poetry—then at least a reader might recall the earlier poem's lament that *"la forme d'une ville / Change plus vite, hélas! que le coeur d'un mortel."* Baudelaire goes on to contrast the shifting cityscape with the permanence of private memories:

> Paris change! mais rien dans ma mélancolie
> N'a bougé! palais neufs, échafaudages, blocs,
> Vieux faubourgs, tout pour moi devient allégorie,
> Et mes chers souvenirs sont plus lourds que des rocs.

In Merrill's poem there are no *chers souvenirs* of New York. The mad external destruction both reflects the speaker's illness and mental confusion and is a projection of it. But at this point the second meaning of the image is active, for Merrill's New York is less Eliot's Unreal City than it is Baudelaire's *cité pleine de rêves*. Who fumbles luxuriously in the filth of years but the dreamer or the analysand? If not so pointed or clinical in its associations, then the image of "construction work" does signal a turn inward, and if not a conscious excavation of the self, then a willingness to permit the operations of involuntary memories. This purposiveness on the speaker's part is under-scored by the religious imagery that dominates the passage. He joins the apostolic "dozen / In meek attitudes," his "Head bowed, at the shrine of noise." There is less irony in those terms than there may seem at first, and the pattern is continued through the rest of the poem, whose crisis-quest format would dictate such images. The speaker who sets out as a *flâneur* soon enough becomes a passionate pilgrim—and therefore, like the invalid, a type of the artist himself, a type familiar from Wagner or from Henry James.

This realization leads us to yet another layer of references in these stanzas. The laughing, cursing old man in the crane brings to mind—to the speaker's mind—the close of *The White*

Goddess, that cranky "historical" grammar of poetic myth by Robert Graves. Merrill may simply be referring to the book's discussion of the ties between the crane and Apollo, to whom the bird is sacred—even as it is also associated with the creation of the alphabet and, by extension, of poetic language. But the allusion may be more complicated. What also comes to mind is the Work of the Chariot. In his peroration, Graves harangues the modern world's mechanistic, patriarchal, and repressive order, its spokesman the left-handed satirist who curses—a word he derives, questionably, from the Latin *cursus*, "a running, especially the circular running of a chariot race," a *cursus contra solem*. The satirist is opposed to the bard, a recurrent figure in the history of poetry and the only true poet in Graves' reckoning. He is distinguished by his devotion to the White Goddess—who is about to appear in Merrill's poem, with "white gestures," in a cab. For Graves, she is the aboriginal Triple Goddess who is both enchantress and inspirer, Mother and Muse, the only theme of the true poet's song. And her son is Apollo, the poet-god-victim who celebrates her. In her guise as Moon, she appears as child (New Moon or Spring), as woman (Full Moon or Summer), as hag (Old Moon or Winter). Is it merely coincidental that these are the three apparitions of woman in Merrill's "For Proust"? I doubt it. There are a great many affinities between *The White Goddess* and Merrill's work in general—so many, in fact, that it would be impractical for me to pursue them here. Even if we ignore the intricate connections between Graves and Merrill, or between *The White Goddess* and "An Urban Convalescence," it is crucial to comprehend that the speaker thinks of what he sees *in terms of* a theory of poetry and is reminded of a book that seeks to answer a single question: how is the poet inspired? That is the question that Merrill's poem poses, too. When the speaker says, "I have lived on this same street for a decade," he means to be rueful about his inattentiveness. But

Merrill himself means something more. A decade had passed between *First Poems* and *Water Street*, so that in an important sense he is referring to, and bringing into question, the kind of style and material he had "lived on" to date. The next stanzas disrupt the surface of his musing with a rush of ghostly memories:

Wait. Yes. Vaguely a presence rises
Some five floors high, of shabby stone
—Or am I confusing it with another one
In another part of town, or of the world?—
And over its lintel into focus vaguely
Misted with blood (my eyes are shut)
A single garland sways, stone fruit, stone leaves,
Which years of grit had etched until it thrust
Roots down, even into the poor soil of my seeing.
When did the garland become part of me?
I ask myself, amused almost,
Then shiver once from head to toe,

Transfixed by a particular cheap engraving of garlands
Bought for a few francs long ago,
All calligraphic tendril and cross-hatched rondure,
Ten years ago, and crumpled up to stanch
Boughs dripping, whose white gestures filled a cab,
And thought of neither then nor since.
Also, to clasp them, the small, red-nailed hand
Of no one I can place. Wait. No. Her name, her features
Lie toppled underneath that year's fashions.
The words she must have spoken, setting her face
To fluttering like a veil, I cannot hear now,
Let alone understand.

The lithe poetic line here is particularly effective. The stops and starts, the florid reverie, the mesh of associations, render perfectly a mind both consciously working to recall and being seized by memories beneath thought, the speaker's equilibrium having already been unsettled by his illness and by the racket. The first stanza here sets up a model of memory, and the second is an example of its involuntary force. While trying to summon up a whole, a detail appears—not the building, but an ornamental garland that may or may not have been carved on the building that might have stood there. Why that garland, and when did it "become part of me"? How is the phenomenal world internalized and spiritualized? How does the incidental sensation leave a memory trace that, later, is involuntarily recalled as the catalyst for still other memories? Proust says of the uneven paving stones: "the fortuitous and inevitable way in which the sensation had come about determined the truth of the past it resurrected and of the images it set in motion." So Merrill's poem proceeds fortuitously and inevitably, by a series of imagistic links—lintel dissolving to cheap engraving used to wrap a real bouquet given to the woman in a taxi a decade ago in another city on just such a day as this. . . . That he cannot remember who *she* is, that he dismisses her condescendingly as one of "that year's fashions," and that the whole scene has ominous overtones (it is "Misted with blood," the engraving is "crumbled to stanch" the flowers clasped in her "red-nailed hand"), suggest that the memory is an especially painful and still injurious one. If this is what Freud called a screen memory, then the incident may be a substitute for something that happened much further back in time or more recently still (and so may be connected with his illness). But it is left deliberately, insistently vague—almost as if to suggest and include all those possibilities.

At a low point in *The Captive* Marcel comes to a realization: "Nothing assured me that the vagueness of such states was a sign of their profundity." And the same would be true of this poem as well unless we read it more metaphorically than pathologically. Marcel eventually triumphs by turning his memories into art. Art is also the real focus on the stanzas above. What he remembers, surely: the carving, the engraving, the cinematic girl. And the descriptive language, too, stresses the artificial: "calligraphic," "cross-hatched rondure," "gestures," "fashions." More important, the memory assumes a mythic dimension. The woman is the embodiment of an idealized city, a dreamy Paris of *temps perdu*. Whether she is Graves' white goddess or a veiled figure more in the manner of Cocteau than of Keats, she is a muse. And even as she fades, she is Eurydice to this poet's Orpheus. In any case, it is a fugitive vision, a failed or incomplete memory. But it serves to remind him of the nature of memory itself, and of a life, a person, the past—which is what the next stanza portrays:

> So that I am already on the stair,
> As it were, of where I lived,
> When the whole structure shudders at my tread
> And soundlessly collapses, filling
> The air with motes of stone.
> Onto the still erect building next door
> Are pressed levels and hues—
> Pocked rose, streaked greens, brown whites.
> Who drained the pousse-café?
> Wires and pipes, snapped off the roots, quiver.

The memory of the woman that draws him deeper into the past only to undo it had demonstrated how private experience is shaped by myth—the lesson of art itself. The woman's resemblance to Eurydice tells us a great deal about the man who so remembers her. That strain continues here, if we imagine the speaker imagining himself as Orpheus climbing the stair of Hades, that realm of roots. Orpheus' music made the stones dance; here his "air" dances with "motes of stone." Later, having failed, he faces a maenad-like "shrieking," his "eyes astream" like Orpheus' singing head. But this, perhaps, is to bring to the forefront what was only meant to be lurking. A specific myth is less important than the cast of mind. The first half of this poem works its way by suggestions, by overlapping and cumulative images and allusions that continually add meanings while resisting a single intention. The real street he "lived on" in the opening stanza, for instance, is here replaced by memory's imaginary house "where I lived." It is the fabled house of art, but rather than make that explicit, the poet characteristically shies away, and all is melted into air, into thin air. The motes of stone in his mind's eye become again the soil of his seeing, and exposed in that are its very roots—which, with a blink, become the wires and pipes of an actual dwelling and the fanciful cordial of its various stories. The initial question "Was there a building there at all?" has been answered by the revelations of memory, and the question now is "Who drained the pousse-café?" "Drain" means not just to empty but to drink or *approfondir*, and it is self-evidently the poet who has, without having realized it, taken in his own past, who heard then and understands now.

"Well, that is what life does." This next line, which clears the poem's throat before introducing a dwindling, moralizing coda to its first half, is typical of Merrill's manner. The poem began with a jolt, turned inward with a shudder, and has come back quivering. Now the catchphrase—the same sort of cliché or journalistic language the poet will later regret having to use—stabilizes the situation. But its shrug disguises a literal truth. That *is* what life does: destroys and restores, *aboutir à un livre:*

> Well, that is what life does. I stare
> A moment longer, so. And presently
> The massive volume of the world
> Closes again.

Upon that book I swear
To abide by what it teaches:
Gospels of ugliness and waste,
Of towering voids, of soiled gusts,
Of a shrieking to be faced
Full into, eyes astream with cold—

With cold?
All right then. With self-knowledge.

There is much about the design and tone of "An Urban Con-
valescence" that is reminiscent of Henry James—of "The Jolly
Corner," say, or parts of *The American Scene*. Merrill's con-
valescent is one of James' poor sensitive gentlemen. The fateful
"inner detachment" of John Marcher in "The Beast in the
Jungle" comes strongly to mind in this connection. Marcher—
whose very name links him with Merrill's walker—is blocked
from life by his sense of "being kept for something rich and
strange" and suffers, as Merrill's speaker does not, a terrible
failure of human energy. Both men are ill, though: Marcher
with his compulsive fantasy, Merrill's speaker with his own
sort of inhibiting delicacy or inner detachment. Only when it
is too late does Marcher read "the open page of his story,"
"the sounded void of his life": "This horror of waking—*this*
was knowledge, knowledge under the breath of which the very
tears in his eyes seemed to freeze. Through them, none the
less, he tried to fix it and hold it; he kept it there before him so
that he might feel the pain. That at least, belated and bitter,
had something of the taste of life." Merrill's stanzas above,
while similar to Marcher's realization, have none of its despair.
They resolve *in time*, not only to face up to the world of brutal
experience, but to acknowledge the "ugliness and waste," those
oxymoronic "towering voids" and "soiled gusts" in his own
life and character as well. It is on himself that he means to cast
a cold, self-knowing eye.

If the poem had ended here, it would have seemed determined rather than conclusive, too abrupt and even forced. The poem's second half, however, extends and fulfills it. In *First Poems* the long poem "Variations and Elegy: White Stag, Black Bear" has a somewhat similar (though reversed) structure. After the six intricately metered variations, the more loosely written elegy is a resumption of the material already set out, but its fantasia tends to wander from, when it is not circling around, the initial terms of the poem. The concluding seven quatrains of "An Urban Convalescence," on the other hand, are an altogether more brilliant stroke. While nearly parodying details from the first half of the poem, they manage to recapitulate its narrative, in the process revealing its unsuspected delusions and depths. To begin with, the speaker moves indoors —or rather, back indoors: from exposure and commitment to enclosure and doubt, from what life teaches to what art questions. The quatrains themselves—the measured feet and rhymes to which the outdoor ramble has come—manifest the shift:

> Indoors at last, the pages of *Time* are apt
> To open, and the illustrated mayor of New York,
> Given a glimpse of how and where I work,
> To note yet one more house that can be scrapped.
>
> Unwillingly I picture
> My walls weathering in the general view.
> It is not even as though the new
> Buildings did very much for architecture.
>
> Suppose they did. The sickness of our time requires
> That these as well be blasted in their prime.
> You would think the simple fact of having lasted
> Threatened our cities like mysterious fires.

In an entirely different key, the poet is here reviving the crisis that confronted him at the start of the poem, but observation is replaced by a more intense speculation. The massive volume of the world is parodically reduced to the pages of a weekly newsmagazine—a change that signals others. Where the first part of the poem is concerned with volume, or space (even as absence), this part is concerned with time. The female figure in the first part, whose "red-nailed hand" is a token of her role as Nature, is supplanted here by "the illustrated mayor" or governing male figure of Art. The involuntary memory is now an unwilling picture, and the imagined threat—to shelter, security, self—is more immediate than it was before. What is threatened is both a house ("where I live") and a way of life ("how and where I work"). There is every reason to think that Merrill is contemplating the fate of his own poetry, imagining it potentially "scrapped," or "weathering in the general view" to be replaced by newer, inferior models. His aesthetic standards, part of a tradition that has "lasted," are what is undermined by the corrosive but faddish "sickness of our time." How forcefully the third stanza enacts that threat by wrenching the rhymes from their proper end positions!

Having imagined the threat from outside, but without being able to console himself with any phrase like "Well, that is what time does," he now focuses even more sharply inward—on the poem itself and on the way in which language can both reflect and cause a collapse from within:

> There are certain phrases which to use in a poem
> Is like rubbing silver with quicksilver. Bright
> But facile, the glamour deadens overnight.
> For instance, how 'the sickness of our time'
>
> Enhances, then debases, what I feel.
> At my desk I swallow in a glass of water
> No longer cordial, scarcely wet, a pill
> They had told me not to take until much later.

It is a bitter pill he swallows—in a glass "No longer cordial" like the pousse-café drained earlier and "scarcely wet" with a poem's representational energy. The pill he takes corresponds to his earlier vow. In this case, the self-knowledge has to do not with his relation to experience but with his sense of art. At once a sedative and a stimulant, the pill induces a reverie of the Parisian interlude and its romance—the kind of dream that Pater called a finer memory, raised a little above itself and above ordinary retrospect. The final stanzas splice the two parts of the poem together in order to reach a conclusion tempered by both experience and art—a conclusion that proposes yet a new beginning:

> With the result that back into my imagination
> The city glides, like cities seen from the air,
> Mere smoke and sparkle to the passenger
> Having in mind another destination
>
> Which now is not that honey-slow descent
> Of the Champs-Elysées, her hand in his,
> But the dull need to make some kind of house
> Out of the life lived, out of the love spent.

Through the course of the poem, the city—whether as occasion or as emblem, whether discursive New York or dreamy Paris—has come to be identified with the speaker's own nature and his artistic options. What now seems an amalgam of the two cities glides into mind, this airborne passenger's train of thought, but it dissolves into "Mere smoke and sparkle." The glamour of a distant (in time) and idealized (in detail) Paris, he realizes, is an image for but not the purpose of the poem—by the pronominal switch ("her hand in *his*"), in fact, we see the memory depersonalized into an image. As a "destination," such a sweet descent to the Blessed Fields, while it may be a fate better than death, cannot finally satisfy one whose happiness, as Merrill put it in a previous poem, is "bound up with happenings." In one sense, the whole poem dramatizes a "recovery" from just such a temptation to the attenuated "sophistications of nostalgia." The underworld of memory is not the poet's home, and the rubble of contemporary reality can provide no refuge. Neither the present nor the past, then, is exclusively the subject of art; of neither material will the poet seek to "make some kind of house" or sense of himself. Rather, his "dull need" (a term with all the understatement of real and inescapable conviction) is for "the life lived," "the love spent." Those are very Proustian phrases—that one can have only what one no longer holds —but they also articulate a less rueful wisdom, and celebrate the sheltering presence of the past. In his remarks about "An Urban Convalescence," David Kalstone noted that in its research for durable images the poem itself comes to be—to have made—the "house," a "set of arrangements for survival," a new structure and tribute to what is "salvageable from the past."

Kalstone's reading helps to clarify the poem's largest intentions, and to identify the terms of its importance in Merrill's career. This poet's abiding subjects have been present from his earliest work, but "An Urban Convalescence" introduces, by its format and resolve, new ways of containing them. This is not a poem of the Broken Home, whose theme is dispossession, but of the Missing House, whose theme is self-possession. "An Urban Convalescence" is perhaps the most poised of a number of such poems; there are more extreme versions at either end of his career, poems that also address the question of how art stabilizes the passage of time. The last of his *First Poems*, "The House," would be one in which "deed and structure" are one, but the poem abandons that task—"we who homeless toward such houses wend / May find we have dwelt elsewhere"—for a sense of nature's vast maternal emptiness as a compensatory refuge. In *Braving the Elements*, "18 West 11th Street" confronts similar but explosive premises, and tries to restore to history's fragmented ruins the shape of its original dimensions. Similar to those two poems, but more successful than either, "An Urban Convalescence" seeks to free the poem from any constraints but those of the imagination itself, or from what Merrill calls with exquisite irony "the dull need." The poet works here to free himself of both the past and the present— the young woman in the cab and the old man in the crane— and to create for the poem its own moral and emotional standards. Such a convalescence is a paradoxical freedom, since it allows him a series of accommodations. By expanding the range of his voice and therefore of his consciousness, Merrill has been able to accommodate the past and the present, to accommodate the demands of Nature and Time within the confines of Art. For at the same time, he has sought to free the poem from stylistic bridles or pretenses. While myth may provide a bracing frame and autobiography the foreground of detail, neither dominates. Style, then, is an instrument of discovery and freedom, finally of reconciliation. The city that glides into the last stanzas—by now clearly seen as the infernal city of art's "material"—is abandoned in favor of "another destination" that the poet has "in mind." That "destination"—a word that neatly combines location and ambition—is the civilized domain of poetry itself, where a house and a life and a poem may come to stand for one another.

THE POEM as makeshift or eternal dwelling place, maze or monument, is a familiar, even a favorite one, of poets. *Water Street* makes use of that convention and of others. Throughout the book, poems take up the theme of art and love as sanctuaries. Death, too, is a fine and private place. In "Annie Hill's Grave," a casket "like a spaceship" bears her body to Necropolis, that "Land of our dreams" where she is reunited with her long dead husband who "lies in the next booth." In the rather eerie "Letter from Egypt," a boy's ancient golden tomb becomes a modern bridal pair's "first apartment." So, too, the glittering hotel's "packed public rooms" in "For Proust" are succeeded by the artist's own "one dim room without contour" in which the Ritz's fracas and fragrance will then be reimagined. There is, in all these poems, an easy correspondence between the timelessness of death and the immortality of art, between the space of a tomb and the expanse of the mind, effected by the poet's use of metaphors of liberating enclosure for both.

The tension between containment and release to be noted in such of Merrill's *First Poems* as "The Broken Bowl" whose "Spectrums, released, will speak / Of colder flowerings," is reworked in "Prism," a plaintive address by "a paperweight" —that is, by the crystal object and by the paper or burden of writing that weighs on the poet. The broken bowl's splinters had "cut structures in the air," made of the poem itself a "room for love's face." "Prism" is a less romantic, more perplexed account of artistic vocation. Like the prism itself, meaning to end up in "a maroon plush box, / Doze the old vaudeville out, of mind and object," the poet has instead

> lately taken up residence
> In a suite of chambers
> Windless, compact and sunny, ideal
> Lodging for the pituitary gland of Euclid
> If not for a "single gentleman (references)."

It is all "playful inconveniences" there, sliding floors and invisible walls, style's false insights and betrayals of outlook. Only rarely is it given to poet or prism "to see clearly." When, in other words, the prism becomes a mirror, it sees the poet as he does not want to see himself—spent, "a body / Unshaven, flung on the sofa," his eyes reflecting "years of vacancy." The "pea-sized funhouse" (a phrase that conflates the prism, the poet's room, and that old vaudeville of mind and object) becomes a glinting allegory of art, both a type and a parody of the revolving gem of stars above. But it is an allegory in which the human is belittled and forsaken. Merrill uses the same sort of image, the maze of perspectives, for love in "Poem of Summer's End," where the disorientations of heat and travel, the distractions of the sexual appetite, provide mean sidelights on a relationship. The setting here is a shabby room in an Italian inn. The poet is shown his lover's face, first in an "instructing" gloom, then in a revealing beam of light. Each is an "image blind with use, a clue," and love itself is seen—from the inside —as "that slow maze / So freely entered."

In the journey *Water Street* itself makes, between "An Urban Convalescence"—which David Kalstone calls a separation, "a poem which dismantles a life in New York City where life is continually dismantling itself"—and "A Tenancy," a conclusion that returns to the point of departure and settles the poet in a new house and renewed life, there are many excursions. Some are into the poet's past, others to foreign locales. On each, the question is that posed in "After Greece" (as it is in Elizabeth Bishop's "Questions of Travel"): "But where is home?" From "My country's warm, lit halls" of deceptive and entrapping familiarity, the poet seeks to escape, first by recalling a stay in Greece, then by dreaming of it:

> All through
> The countryside were old ideas
> Found lying open to the elements.
> Of the gods' houses only
> A minor premise here and there
> Would be balancing the heaven of fixed stars
> Upon a Doric capital.

The dream that allows him to "flee" makes of it a passage, or street, down which he returns to a "home" identified with memories purified to essentials. Where "passage" means entry, and "stanza" is stopping place or room, Merrill is working in *Water Street* with a limited but enriching set of interacting images. They recur and culminate in the book's final poem, "A Tenancy."

The word "tenancy" can mean either the period of a lease or the occupancy itself. Merrill's poem deals with both, with the span of a life and the plan of a house, with time and space, time *as* space. The occasion of the poem is his new occupancy of a house in Stonington, on the street of the book's *title* in every sense. But the subject of the poem, like that of "An Urban Convalescence," is self-possession and art's accommodations. The poem owes more than its subject to "An Urban Convalescence." Its format—the long free verse exposition that seems ruminative and improvisatory, tightening into crisp rhymed stanzas—not only follows the book's opening poem but seems quite intentionally to echo it, in order both to "frame" the book and to emphasize the continuities between the two poems. So, too, their plots are substantially the same: the initial casual detail (in "A Tenancy" it is "Something in the light") that prompts a deepening recollection; a depressed return through layers of time to the present moment; a further reverie that gradually emerges into a moralizing resolution. Even motifs of the earlier poem are repeated: the garland as emblem of time, the room as verse. But for all the notable similarities between the poems, there are important differences. Though its final lines are directed out toward a reader, are more "sociable" than those of "An Urban Convalescence," "A Tenancy" seems a more private, even elliptical one. To an extent, it is more overtly autobiographical than "An Urban Convalescence," which depends on generalized references and on mythical allusion, but the revelations (if that is what they are) are obscure. It is also more overtly a parable of Merrill's own poetic career but, while more difficult to decode, is less rich than "An Urban Convalescence."

The first sentence negotiates the exchange between present and past, and returns the poem to a time (1946) when he had first begun writing seriously. Having been demobilized, he tries on his old civilian clothes. The peacetime world demands of him a different sort of service:

> Something in the light of this March afternoon
> Recalls that first and dazzling one
> Of 1946. I sat elated
> In my old clothes, in the first of several
> Furnished rooms, head cocked for the kind of sound
> That is recognized only when heard.
> A fresh snowfall muffled the road, unplowed
> To leave blanker and brighter
> The bright, blank page turned overnight.

As the fable unfolds, this poetic room rented from Tradition is furnished with "ponderous *idées reçues*" and clichés like "the Real / Old-Fashioned Winter of my landlord's phrase." Gradually, "the more I looked," the objects in the room "grew shallower." This is a very idiosyncratic choice of words, especially in a stanza that starts (with "But") by signaling a change of mind. "Shallower" means not that the observer is, say, projecting his boredom onto the objects around him but that those objects—like the later "pebbles under water"—are growing diaphanous under his scrutiny, that they are revealed as themselves and are thereby able to reveal more than themselves. There is an influx of power, and "from within, ripples / Of heat." The "new radiance"—both willed and involuntary —rises to a pitch of memory and dream, the romantic sublime and literary allusion:

Brittle, sallow in the new radiance,
Time to set the last wreath floating out
Above the dead, to sweep up flowers. The dance
Had ended, it was light; the men looked tired
And awkward in their uniforms.
I sat, head thrown back, and with the dried stains
Of light on my own cheeks, proposed
This bargain with—say with the source of light:
That given a few years more
(Seven or ten or, what seemed vast, fifteen)
To spend in love, in a country not at war,
I would give in return
All I had. All? A little sun
Rose in my throat. The lease was drawn.

The setting—the end of a victory celebration—is clear enough
but not illuminating unless we are to imagine the end of the
poet's battle with recalcitrant material and circumstance. His
Faustian bargain is more significant. He hesitates to call it
diabolical, hesitates to name it at all, and settles for a figure of
speech: "—say with the source of light." Merrill's diffidence
in the face of the sublime is entirely characteristic. Years later,
in the very Faustian *Mirabell* (section 8.6), this same "SOURCE
OF LIGHT" is identified as "IMAGINATIVE POWER" and is said to
be "ROOTED IN THE LIVED LIFE." And so it is here. The bargain
struck, of course, is with himself. He finds the light to see by
—that is, his imaginative power—in the lived life, in the same
light that fills the room and is reflected from the windowpane
onto his face, like luminous tears. He asks then, for a term of
fifteen years, for love and peace, for emotional fulfillment and
stability, an *un*broken home. But the poem's "double seeing"
permits another interpretation. The span of time is that be-
tween his dedication to his art and the publication of this very
poem's account of it. And in his asking for "love, in a country

not at war," we can discern the subject of his first book and the title of his second. In return, he offers "All I had" and wonders how much that is or would be. I take the lump of a "little sun" that rises in his throat—like a rainbow's compact—to be an effective symbol both of the dawning of poetic song and also of the isolation and sacrifice demanded by that gift. What the tired men in uniform return to—homes, families, little sons— Merrill realizes he must renounce. His lease, drawn like a noose, is on what Yeats called the perfection of the work.

The single discrete line that returns the poem to the present —"I did not even feel the time expire"—also brings it to its crisis:

> I feel it though, today in this new room,
> Mine, with my things and thoughts, a view
> Of housetops, treetops, the walls bare.
> A changing light is deepening, is changing
> To a gilt ballroom chair a chair
> Bound to break under someone before long.
> I let the light change also me.
> The body that lived through that day
> And the sufficient love and relative peace
> Of those short years, is now not mine.
> Would it be called a soul?
> It knows at any rate,
> That when the light dies and the bell rings
> Its leaner veteran will rise to face
> Partners not recognized
> Until drunk young again and gowned in changing
> Flushes; and strains will rise,
> The bone-tipped baton beating, rapid, faint,
> From the street below, from my depressions—

These are difficult, elusive lines. They begin in a flat, assertive tone of self-possession: "Mine, my things and thoughts" have replaced the "ponderous *idées reçues*," even as the Latinate adjective and foreign phrase give way to plain speaking. Yet the "changing light" that is the poem's metaphor for the will to art is ambivalently celebrated, the nearly awkward inversions and the foreboding phrase "Bound to break" adding a markedly strained note. The tone of voice grows increasingly unsteady and sad. Even his ironic evaluation of his bargain and achievement—"sufficient time and relative peace"—is disclaimed. Of the body he no longer has—that is to say, of a life he has used up or outgrown—he asks "Would it be called a soul?" The best gloss of those puzzling lines is actually the poem that precedes "A Tenancy" in the book, the exquisite lyric "Swimming by Night." Its glimmering sketch of the poet as sorcerer's apprentice is one Merrill reuses several times in later work. In *The (Diblos) Notebook*, for instance, it is "the genie conjured up out of oneself," and in "The Thousand and Second Night" it is given its most explicit definition: "The soul, which in infancy could not be told from the body, came with age to resemble *a body one no longer had*, whose transports went far beyond what passes, now, for sensation." *Transport*, whether meant literally as metaphor itself or metaphorically as the move to a new house, is the subject of the poem, and it might be said that the Faust legend is paradoxically introduced in order to stress, not the speaker's eventual loss, but the poet's formidable soul-making. The last lines of this passage, which skillfully blend all prior military and musical motifs, are a final transport to summary. Again, it is the "lived life" that dominates, but in its secondary, Proustian meaning of memory or re-cognition rather than as experience.

The final three stanzas are more self-consciously direct in spite of some lingering questions. There are lurking, unresolved connotations to the three friends, who seem at first to have come to claim the bargain's cost, or to suggest other visitors, from Job's comforters to the magi. And the gift of wine and the use of the word "host" recall, though to no certain end, the religious streak in "An Urban Convalescence." But these are minor considerations. Clearly these good-natured, metrically alert stanzas are intended to conclude the poem and its retrospect on a note of balanced determination:

> From the doorbell which rings.
> One foot asleep, I hop
> To let my three friends in. They stamp
> Themselves free of the spring's
> Last snow—or so we hope.
>
> One has brought violets in a pot;
> The second, wine; the best,
> His open, empty hand. Now in the room
> The sun is shining like a lamp.
> I put the flowers where I need them most
>
> And then, not asking why they come,
> Invite the visitors to sit.
> If I am host at last
> It is of little more than my own past.
> May others be at home in it.

The amicability is evident at once. The dance that swirls through the earlier reverie is now parodied by the speaker's hopping and his friends' stamping. The muffling snowfall at the start of the poem has here melted into an easy image of renewal. And the synonymy of dwelling and art, of sheltering room and sustaining stanza, is memorably put in the lines "Now in the room / The sun is shining like a lamp," where by the comparison the "source of light" is domesticated to the poet's desk lamp. The last stanza settles the group in the room and the poet in his new house; it settles the poem and the entire book as well. Its open invitation, after all, points backward as well as forward, inviting the reader to reflect on the book's own con-

version *from* artifice to experience and *of* that experience into a
higher art. That has been accomplished not only by the evi-
dence in the book of Merrill's appropriation of his own life but
also by his recognition that imaginative power compensates for
most time and that the past can only be recovered by the
presence of art. That is, both the subject and the technique of
poetry are the "LIVED LIFE."

TWO POEMS in *Water Street* lay parent figures to rest with
equal parts of regret and relief. "Annie Hill's Grave" rather
briskly buries Merrill's grandmother, and "The Smile" con-
cerns an old man, associated with money, who "turned his face
and died" (the poem's title refers to his bedside set of false
teeth that are a mocking memento mori). These poems, by
implication, raise a subject that others deal with overtly: the
mixed feelings, the conscious yearnings and unconscious de-
sires, of the child. More often than not, that child is given a
typological rather than an autobiographical emphasis. The
combination of unwitting innocence, instinctual aplomb, and
sensible anarchy that characterizes a child's emotional life—at
least in literature—is turned to advantage in several poems and
usually with a portrait of the artist in mind. "The Lawn Fete
of Homunculus Artifex" is a nervous and unconvincing ex-
ample of this. "A Vision of the Garden" is a much better one.
On a frosted windowpane the child draws a face through whose
lines he beholds a winter garden so beautiful that the joyful
sigh it elicits clouds over the vision. Thus in outline the story
of the lost paradise is retold, and Merrill then draws the fitting
conclusion (as he had in "The Doodler") by linking the child's
inadvertent actions with the mature poet's "cold lines" of cal-
culated craft and with his lover's face, recognized now at last.
The inspiration and object of his art, in other words, are brought
together and allow him to recapture the garden's original vision

of transcendence. In such a poem—a brief and delicate lyric with considerable psychological, even philosophical ambitions —the figure of the child is doubly useful by bringing with it those associations it has been accumulating since Wordsworth's day. But what it gains in resonance it sometimes loses in immediacy. A poem like "The World and the Child," I think, is in its quieter way more impressive. Its astute control—and I should add that it is one of the few villanelles to include a convincing dramatic narrative—and the gradual amplification of its thematic terms (wisdom, love, pain) give it a haunting, nearly surreal quality, like certain songs by Mahler. What the child upstairs, "awake and wearied of," hears in the adult conversation downstairs is an accurate description of the poem itself: "mild variation, chilling theme." With no more than common experience and a few ordinary details—the click of a door, the hoot of an owl—Merrill succeeds in recreating the child's terrible loneliness and the world that is its cause and consolation.

This same disparity in technique and tone I have noted between the two short poems also sets apart the book's two longer poems that deal with the child. "Childlessness" is histrionic, lofty in conception but murky and perplexing to read. "Scenes of Childhood," on the other hand, with its clear succession of events and images, its shorter lines, its keen understanding of its own disclosures and equivocations, is a more conventional or straightforward poem and finally a superior one. This is largely a technical, not a thematic, unevenness: both poems deal with material that is profound and volatile. The evidently tortured emotional depths of "Childlessness" trouble its figural surface. Though there is, deliberately, little exposition, the plot is simple enough: the speaker is awakened by a winter storm, broods on his "childless" life in terms of the storm's abundant natural forces, then falls back into a nightmare of images impossible to construe except as a turmoil of unfixed guilt. How are we to read the first sentence, "The weather of this winter night, my dream-wife / Ranting and raining, wakes me"? That statement means he was asleep and was presumably dreaming before the action of the poem begins, and it therefore implies that a trace of the earlier dream (of the Family Life?) is shaping his now conscious sense of the scene. But that interpretation leaves too much unspoken. Part of the poet—the part, in fact, that wrote the poem—is married to Dream, that mysterious muse and queen of the night. That part of him is indifferent to the generative task. But another part is haunted by his grand refusal and has interiorized into his dream the endless cycle ("toddlers, holy dolls, dead ancestors") and a relentless guilt. For having fathered no children of his own, he feels condemned to remain ("In token of past servitude") his parents' child. Throughout the poem he tries, perceptibly or cryptically, to subvert that fate. By taking a maternal Nature as his "dream-wife," he ensures that his terrible arraignment will be in protective, nurturing hands. Later she is ambivalently called "the enchantress, masked as friend," and she unfurls bolts of a sunset whose exotic colors so remind one of art itself that when, at the end of the poem, the cloak "Has fallen onto the shoulders of my parents / Whom it is eating to the bone," the shirt of Nessus seems a son's crime as well as an artist's revenge.

The play of lights, the family romance, the emotional storm and stress, are all present again in "Scenes of Childhood." But "the primal / Figures" of the home movies replace the obscure, overwrought dream in "Childlessness," and there is, in this longer, more surely paced poem, a telling interplay between a rhetoric of conscious diagnosis and a diction of subconscious neurosis. The projector and screen—like Proust's magic lantern—are especially good images to contain these complexities. In fact, Merrill uses the film at key points all through his career —as technique (the newsreel rewound in "18 West 11th Street"), as subject (the work of Maya Deren running throughout the trilogy), and as symbol. In "Scenes of Childhood" the film shows its viewers—the poet and his mother—to themselves, in both senses. The projected scenes of the past show them as they were thirty years before, and those scenes introjected reveal to the poet past connections and his present relationships. The screening itself heightens the tension. The literally explosive film becomes a sort of play within the play, a tiny oedipal melodrama enacted *and* witnessed by its protagonists.

The poem's fifteen stanzas can be divided into two nearly equal sections. In the first eight stanzas, the poet and his mother are together, both in the room and in the film. In the next section, the poet is alone and meditating on those thoughts aroused by his heated encounter with himself and his past. The poem's sequence of encounter and meditation recalls that of "An Urban Convalescence"—though, of course, the pattern is one familiar from those great crisis poems by Wordsworth and Coleridge in which accident (a leech gatherer or lime tree bower) conspires with deep psychic currents to bring the poet to a new understanding. The opening four stanzas of "Scenes of Childhood" set the scene in a deliberate fashion—and for good reason. The film's jolting effect would have been diminished if it had started any earlier in the poem than it does. Merrill uses these preliminary lines, then, to create some anticipation. The tone here is fretted: the poet's eyes smart, his heart ready in the face of the buried life about to be revealed. He also introduces here several apparently incidental motifs whose significance will gradually emerge later in the poem. The most important of these are the interchangeable firefly and star—images for the whole dilemma, both artistic and human, of scale and perception. By the time the film itself comes to be described—and it is symbolically set in a pastoral world of nostalgia, an Edenic context of violation—it can move rapidly through its

frames of reference. Appropriately, it begins with the presiding
Fates — the three sisters who "Loom":

> With knowing smiles
> And beaded shrugs
>
> My mother and two aunts
> Loom on the screen. Their plucked
> Brows pucker, their arms encircle
> One another.
> Their ashen lips move.
> From the love seat's gloom
> A quiet chuckle escapes
> My white-haired mother
>
> To see in that final light
> A man's shadow mount
> Her dress. And now she is
> Advancing, sister-
> less, but followed by
> A fair child, or fury—
> Myself at four, in tears.
> I raise my fist,
>
> Strike, she kneels down. The man's
> Shadow afflicts us both.
> Her voice behind me says
> It might go slower.
> I work the dials, the film jams.
> Our headstrong old projector
> Glares at the scene which promptly
> Catches fire.

When one thinks of the tedious lengths to which the same old
story has been drawn out by so many novelists (and innumer-
able psychologists), the passage is remarkable for its concision

and suggestive powers. Its latent content is all quite manifest. The erotic triangle, operative violence, and mock apocalypse are superbly handled. It should not go unnoticed how Merrill inflects the climax by having the rhythm of the lines and the enjambments (perhaps by implication, the reel of film itself) wobble with their own intensity; and how he complicates the encounter by making his father—the cameraman, as his son is now—a type of the artist and by having his mother "chuckle" now to see herself "mounted" then.

The first section of the poem, its inventory of attachments and defiance so provocative but predictable, is really just a pretext for the poet's subsequent meditation—the primal figure, so to speak, on which he works a series of variations in the next seven stanzas. It is here, in an effort to frame the past by taking its mythic dimensions, that Merrill moves from history to imagination, from film to dream. By discovering, sometimes inadvertently, archetypal patterns his own life completes, the poet can liberate the self from its traumatic past by assimilating it into a timeless domain that is finally art itself. But there is a deep ambivalence in the act.

Alone, the screen or "field" of historical consciousness blacked out, he turns his attention to the "shining deeds" outside, some low and inconstant (fireflies), others "staying lit" (stars):

> There are nights we seem to ride
> With cross and crown
> Forth under them, through fumes,
> Coils, the whole rattling epic—
> Only to leap clear-eyed
> From eiderdown,
>
> Asleep to what we'd seen.

This is the first instance of the poem's transformation of private life into mythic pattern. The epic of dreamwork is not merely a child's crusade or Wagnerian saga. In fact, he was asleep to what he had actually seen: the cross and crown are obvious male and female symbols, and the fumes and coils through which he rides are the serpentine auroras of Wallace Stevens' great meditation on fate, "The Auroras of Autumn":

> This is where the serpent lives, the bodiless.
> His head is air. Beneath his tip at night
> Eyes open and fix on us in every sky.

Stevens' poem—which is not a model but a towering precedent and an aid to reading Merrill's poem—takes up ancestral themes and an infinite course, and in searching for "a time of innocence / As pure principle" for himself and his poetry, Stevens had returned to the figures of his parents, reading them into his own work. Merrill, too, is writing about origins, about the self's place in a larger scheme that can rouse feelings either of nostalgia or of terror. Throughout "Scenes of Childhood," the image of distant stars, and of the serpent or dragon shapes their constellations assume, is associated with the mother and with her powerful temptations. From "Medusa" in *First Poems* to the many references in "Ephraim," Merrill habitually links the *anima mundi* or ancient, ageless woman of the world with this polyvalent emblem. And as in "Auroras of Autumn," she is, immense and nearly transparent, "the purpose of the poem." The father, then, is linked with the opposing motif—those fireflies that were first mistaken "for stars, / For fates." Fireflies are functionally similar to the fire-breathing, draconic stars (those in the heavens and those in the film) but are inconsequential. And when they are described as "low, inconstant," it is possible that Merrill is passing judgment on his father's responsibility for the Broken Home. In lines that bring in yet another sort of lens or way of looking at things, Merrill remembers his father in such a way as to dismiss a rival:

Father already fading—
Who focused your life long
Through little frames,
Whose microscope, now deep
In purple velvet, first
Showed me the skulls of flies,
The fur, the flames

Etching the jaws—father:
Shrunken to our true size.

The last line refers to that moment, earlier in the poem, when fireflies were suddenly distinguished from stars. But something more is signaled. First, it is *our* true size: his the same as his father's. Second, our true size is life-size. As an adult accommodation with the past, these lines show some sympathy for and with the father. He stands guard, in this passage at least, against the encroaching, overwhelming power of the mother. Where she exaggerates and tempts to oblivion, he stabilizes and even comforts.

There follows from these mixed feelings a release or interlude. His mother distant, his father shrunken, the poet indulges in an idyll, a solitary wandering through a landscape of his own making: "Under fresh spells, cool web / And stinging song new-hatched / Each day, all summer." But this is interrupted, first by an image, then by language itself. When "A minute galaxy" of insects "needles" the poet, the reader sees circling a conflation of the two parental images. Fleeing, the poet runs "breathing / In and out the sun / And air I am." At the very point of his inspiration, of his avowal that he is out of nature, he realizes he has been betrayed by the overdetermined possibilities of words, and the spell is undone by what first induced it. The "Inaugural *Damn*" melts into the primal mother (or *dam*), at first a figure upstairs, and then an *ouroboros* shedding the Milky Way itself and tempting all us poor humans to abjure our claims to identity:

> The son and heir! In the dark
> It makes me catch my breath
> And hear, from upstairs, hers—
> That faintest hiss
> And slither, as of life
> Escaping into space,
> Having led its characters
> To the abyss
>
> Of night. Immensely still
> The heavens glisten. One broad
> Path of vague stars is floating
> Off, a shed skin
> Of all whose fine cold eyes
> First told us, locked in ours:
> You are the heroes without name
> Or origin.

These concluding stanzas are among the most resplendent in all of *Water Street* and can stand beside Stevens' idiom of an innocent earth, where

> The stars are putting on their glittering belts.
> They throw around their shoulders cloaks that flash
> Like a great shadow's last embellishment.

Stevens wanted true innocence as a pure principle both for the self-originated individual and for the poem of original power. The choking sense of dependence—that catches his poetic breath—is the burden of Merrill's lament here. To emphasize his dread of not having originated himself, the fall from that Edenic paradise of his artistic idyll recapitulates the jammed scenes of his childhood that had earlier caught fire. It is then that the poem undertakes its final struggle for freedom. The last stanza can be read several ways: interpretation is strained, I think, by the conflicting demands of closure and doubt. Is the power of Nature and the parent apotheosized, or are we meant to understand that the poet would shed his parent, shed the skin of common humanity? Does myth save us from the merely material, or do we make mock heroes of ourselves at the expense of true relationships? Both, perhaps. The poem has reached that extreme point where desire is identical with power. "Fine cold eye" is a chilling term for both the army of unalterable stars and the authority of parental priority. But why does Merrill shift from the first person he has used throughout the poem to the generalized plural ("us," "ours," "You") at the very moment when he wants to claim a distinction between dynasty and individuality? Because it is a common temptation, yes. Because in the face of the mother's power it links the poet again with his father, perhaps. But why do the heroic constellations call the child a hero without definition or deviation— that is, with absolute freedom? The lines would more properly be an admission made *by* the child *about* his parents. Yet the child, of course, was once a star—of the home movie and of his own dreams. And he can be a hero when in the anonymity of type he is no longer—or no longer considered—a Merrill. And further, as an artist, he can by his creative act entitle himself to power otherwise denied him as son and heir. Other poems in *Water Street* sought to house the past and to identify the enclosing shelter of memory with poetry itself. "Scenes of Childhood" is a more private and troubled attempt to do the same thing, substituting heroic status for security. More important, the poem introduces—in a more direct, if unsettled manner than any other poem in *Water Street*—a series of dilemmas Merrill confronts in later books with persistent anxiety but with increasing confidence.

ENDNOTE

1. When the poem was first published in the *Quarterly Review of Literature* (1960), 10(4):224–225), it was "a frail gold mask." The change may be an improvement, but it is also a presumably uncconscious echo of Elinor Wylie's "Sunset on the Spire," which ends "All that I / Could ever ask / Wears that sky / Like a thin gold mask." Merrill has kept the sense of the image, just reversed the time of day. He'd also used the same image as early as "Morning in the Grand Style," an uncollected poem published in the Winter 1948 issue of *Halcyon.*

RICHARD HOWARD

SAVING APPEARANCES

IN AN ESSAY about another poet's "regionalism," Richard Howard once proposed some definitions. "What a region finally suggests to a poet," he wrote, "is not new content but new possibilities in the treatment of convention." And the best regional poet is never a stay-at-home; there is "an incessant movement binding outer weather to inner, connecting space with events, history with theory. . . . The conventions of a place have given him a vocabulary in which to accommodate his action in whatever place it occurs, have given him a means of dealing importantly with the privations and privileges of a life." Given these generous terms, it might be proper to describe Howard himself as a "regionalist." Certainly he has staked out a territory, which in turn has given him a vocabulary. His region is not a *place*, but that place in our lives high culture occupies. It is the museum without walls and Borges' universal library combined. Howard's style, appropriately, is a highly literary or artificial one. It is adult, armchair, aphoristic, wrought, and ironic, the nimble language of a superior mind. It assumes—dangerously—that everything can be articulated and thereby understood. The features of this style are on display in all of his work: his skeptical but humane temperament and exuberant wit, his virtuosic syllabic schemes that lend to voice the appearance of verse, his learning that is neither embarrassed nor intimidating, his portrayal of the burden and prerogatives of the artistic sensibility. With their Wildean multiplication of personalities, his poems seek to demystify "private" experience by seeing it in terms of other relational models— political, historical, cultural, artistic. Paintings and photographs, books and letters, conversation and gossip—all the ways we depict and dramatize ourselves, at once revealing and stylizing the self, are Howard's "incessant movement" within his poems and among his books. In the very first poem of his first book, he advised, for survival's sake, to "seal yourself in layers of yourself." I want now not to peel back some of those layers, but to expose them.

The titular concerns of his three most important collections —*Subjects, Inventions,* and *Feelings*—suggest a shift from formality to intimacy, from exhibition to revelation, from generic events to specific experience. Yet at a time when other poets were shifting toward more openly autobiographical material and a more relaxed style, Howard went to the opposite extreme. Frost, Jarrell, Lowell—there are precedents for his dramatic monologues; and French poetry was the model for his homages to writers and painters. But no poet has made a career of them in quite the same way. And few have seemed to write so resolutely *against* the fashion of self-expression. No doubt he has done so because he felt the confessional mode was played out, or at least overexposed. And he may have shied from the Romantic "I" because of its associations with the visionary and sublime, the irrational or ecstatic, whereas he himself by nature and choice is a social and moral intelligence, concerned with limits—with the body, the shackling passions, quirks and flaws, wrong desires and bad faith. Certainly he is fascinated by psychology, and therefore by those ways that, in Browning's words, "Art may tell a truth / Obliquely, do the thing shall breed the thought." Obliquity, then, is his objective, however the self remains his subject. And that is why the *feelings* in Howard's poems are to be found where we are least accustomed by today's poets—though not by our reading of the past—to find them.

Howard's earliest songs of innocence and experience—in *Quantities* (1962) and *The Damages* (1967)—established the paradox of surfaces that is his obsessive theme. The best poems in that very first (and very Audenesque) book are those which recognize that "Even the most / Skillful mouths are / Merely the scars / Of love." And those scars speak, with a stoic self-denial, of the ways we must come to appreciate pain, to know both its price and its value. Finally, pain is not an occurrence but a condition. The surfaces of this fallen world are seen as emblems of loss in whose devices can be found the pathos of a remembered—or, more likely, imagined—joy. Our quiet virtues and gaudy vices are merely tokens of our original sin: dispossession. Our task—and it is Howard's *labor* and his *opus* —is the art of survival. Or, as he would say, the art of *sealing*, a word that means both to close up and to certify or authenticate. The self disguised as itself: loss is more: the paradox of surfaces. It's worth noting, too, that, through its Indo-European roots, the word *seal* is related to *pursue* and *persecute*. And from the beginning, by putting a mask on himself, by giving a characterized voice to others, by dramatizing hidden motives and emotions, Howard has been enabled to attack the self. Some of this seems almost like self-loathing; I'm thinking of poems like "Impersonations" or "At the Monument of Pierre Louÿs" in *Lining Up* (1984), but the strain runs through all his books. Even at its best or most impersonal, it is the most severe form of ironic self-consciousness.

The Damages sets about reckoning up the cost. It is a much more acute and intimate book than *Quantities*, and one often overlooked by commentators. More than before, here is Howard's unequivocal acceptance of the secular conditions of history and passion, though his concern in each case is with their consequences—that is to say, less with their presence in his life than with the absences they occasion. These poems are set in the realm of contingency, where *Dasein* is destiny, where necessary defeat becomes ironic triumph, where art is willed from what cannot be chosen. In such a world, once accepted, "Repetition is the only mode / That nature knows of memory." And to keep from merely repeating his memorials, Howard began—in "Bonnard: A Novel"—to objectify his memories by projecting them into situations with an independent life that was both *other* and *over*. In this poem, he takes the muted refinement of shades and textures in that painter's palette to sketch a possible grouping—each an aspect of himself—thus permitting him to argue rather than assert his discoveries. Those discoveries are only further definitions of his original dilemma, but now they sound achieved, and the poem's mild protagonist Charles-Xavier is given lines which both summarize and predict Howard's own accomplishment: "Beatitude teaches / nothing. To live without / happiness and not wither —/ *there* is an occupation, almost a profession."

The profession that has occupied his career since took its lead from that poem's technique, and resulted in the rightly honored but often misunderstood *Untitled Subjects* (1969), his closet drama with a cast of eminent Victorians—Scott, Ruskin, Thackeray, Jane Morris, and others. With its recurring characters and preoccupations, it should not be read as a series, or even as a sequence of monologues, but as a single Poem Without a Hero, in which the private lives of public figures function as extended metaphors—"lifelike but helpless, wonderful but dead"—in Howard's intricate meditation on time. The most plangent poem in the book is the final one, titled "1915," and originally called "A Pre-Raphaelite Ending." The speaker is the old Jane Morris, addressing her spinster daughter May. Wife to one genius and model for another, Jane sits now going through letters and mementos. She urges her daughter to save them, and in such tones that we must think *they* may save her. "I have nothing save them," she laments. "What survives," she has also said, "is the resistance we bring / to life."

> Moments come when the pattern
> is laid before us, plain. And then we know
> the limitations, accidentally
> repeated, are the stuff of life. They will
> return again, for
> they are just . . . ourselves.
> Then we know that this and none
> other will be our life. And so begins
> a long decay—we die from day to dream,
> and common speech we answer with a scream.

In the distance between those two rhymed words, *dream* and *scream*, lies the range of emotions that all the poems explore. And it is precisely the tension between them that gives the book its harried grandeur.

The poet's *levée* entertains its various speakers in order to explore the blurred distinction between the image (or present character) and the memory (or the past that character can recall), staged by those afflicted with art that depends upon both. *Findings* (1971), which is really just an extension and exegesis of *Untitled Subjects*, clarifies Howard's intentions in both books by emphasizing them as statement rather than as script. If, as he has his Robert Browning say in the poem "November, 1899," it is "hardest of all to endure what you / have not changed into," then we might say Howard has deliberately "changed into" his speakers the better to endure the artificial, though never arbitrary limitations that he calls "the stuff of life." Expression is exploitation; both are a version of *making do*, a temporizing gesture to stave off the void he knows as silence. Like Howard, these Victorians are compulsive doers and talkers, filling up all the empty spaces in their lives. The very length and bravado of these poems should lead one to suspect that the poet is engaged in a highly stylized—and so more poignant—defense against himself, as if to relive were to relieve. He might want to say, with Rimbaud, *"Je est un autre,"* but the effect is only to echo his exile.

The surface brilliance of *Untitled Subjects* blinded many critics to such paradoxes. The energies embodied there distracted readers from the sense of loss and helplessness at its heart—what he later calls "the life below the life," or the self beneath the character, the ghost inside the talking machine. And the book further confused its admirers into invoking the wrong origins for Howard's ends. To be sure, the ring of the book is Browningesque. But Browning's typical speaker is, say, an obscure rabbi or organist, whose poet is interested in exploring, under the guise of passion, the intellectual tactics of will. Howard's known and renowned artists are introjected voices to explore the passional tendencies of his own character—or rather, "characters." *Two-Part Inventions* (1974), his next and still best book, provides the true model. The six long poems in this book again deal with the generation that turned the century, a generation of outsized, parental figures, the last giants of the earth before modernism's imploded fragments. Here we have Hölderlin, Wilde and the old Whitman, Ibsen, Edith Wharton, Rodin, and an imaginary architect named Alessandro di Fiori, who seems a composite of Gordon Craig, Antonio Gaudí, Louis Tiffany, and a dash of Ezra Pound ("an ancient man who looked / exhausted by his own head of hair")—the type of the aged artist who has survived his art. But these poems are not cast as monologues, as before, but as dialogues, by his having released the implied listener in *Untitled Subjects*—the secret sharer. The poems are built behind the same scaffolding of facts, clearly lifted from their recondite sources, books Howard has consulted or translated or written, phrases forged together (though usually uncredited, unlike Marianne Moore's practice) from prose as different as Edward Fitzgerald's, Paul Valéry's, Northrop Frye's, E. M. Cioran's, or Howard's own book reviews. But the personalities here, split and gestured in intricately stage-managed confrontations, and supported by the elaborate rhetoric and polite formalities of an age past, achieve a heavy but powerful dramatic force. (Several of them have been performed as theater pieces.) And by inflecting their conversations into self-recognition scenes that insist "Knowledge is / not what you have but what you are," *Two-Part Inventions* recalls not Browning's dynamics of will but Henry James' moral drama of understanding. Like James', the intention of Richard Howard's art has been to dramatize the human heart and intelligence at their most difficult, their most lucid, their most *telling* points of convergence. Each of these enacted poems— these expenses of energy both exhausting and costly—moves toward what we have learned to call a Jamesian acceptance, a state of consciousness that Howard teaches us again is "that final / act which enables us to see clearly."

Two framing poems, on Hölderlin ("After the Facts") and Fiore ("A Natural Death"), are epistolary and seem the earliest composed (perhaps when Howard was first calculating his converted ambition) and the most studied. "After the Facts" involves a correspondence, initiated by curiosity and answered with caution, between a French matron and a German doctor, because of a childhood memory: a Stranger, to himself and the estate, madly wandering among the marbled gods around a moonlit pool, proclaiming the earth's divinity. Posed against that haunting image is the resulting condition: the hospitalized poet, once the "Master of our German Muse" and now "the witless Scardanelli," babbling in broken Italian that can no longer "recover itself into poetry." This reflection on the Romantic sensibility is resumed in what is probably the volume's most virtuosic poem, "A Natural Death," set in 1947 as a graduate student's report on her research into and eventual meeting with another "poor lost *Maestro*," Fiore. The innocent, industrious Cynthia tramps across the Continent to track down her subject's masterworks, only to find they were all made—like contemporary poems?—"too late to last," ruined by time's neglect or men's malice. And when, having learned how much of art is loss, she meets the old man in Paris and transcribes, here in the italics of shorthand, his last words, that loss is transfigured: *"the end of art   it is the recovery of paradise."* The news she brings him comes like death—death that affirmeth nothing, and therefore never lieth. And Fiore's final injunction is just the opposite of Jane Morris' panic to "save it all," though the sense of survival remains constant:

> *it is only when you have   given everything*
> *that you can give more   that you have more to*
> *give   it is inadmissable for a man to leave*
> *the trace of his passage upon earth   give it*
> *all back   the elements   the compassionate sea*
> *and the fire and the ground   and the growing*
> *air   as you described it   we must survive*
> *what we have made   it is not ours*

The acts of atonement an artist fashions of the life he destroys focus the other four poems as well. "A Phenomenon of Nature" re-imagines *When We Dead Awaken* back to its inspiration, exchanging the high Norwegian mountains for the cliffs of Capri, the deathly model Irene for an early romance with a poet named Sophie. Ibsen's lifelong theme—the betrayal of love—is here traced to the playwright's own vision of his art, just as in another poem, "The Lesson of the Master," Edith Wharton admits that "whatever we manage to do is merely / a modification / of what we have failed to do." The word that recurs in these titles is the cue: to discover the nature of things is finally Howard's purpose here, and authorizes his expansive, inclusive, novelistic dimensions: "Not fact but *finding* / is why I must write." The *ficelles* in all these poems are either women or homosexuals: sensual, submissive, predatory, canny, *natural*—the attraction of earth and the impulse that directs art's attempted escapes from the mundane. And the tension thus drawn out between them—at lengths that make quotation difficult—is the kind of delaying action that dominates Howard's manner. For his poems are, in their largest sense, protracted surrenders to silence, to the wordless void which is held distant by gorgeous gestures, by fencing with idiom. What is finally seen in these six poems is "the identity of fulfillment / with renunciation," which in its original sense means *to bring back word*. These poems of a survivor are messages of forfeiture and relinquishment, though never reluctantly spoken. What we learn in them is how "the passionate dead act within us," how an earth left godless by design is made divine by desire.

There are atonements too in *Fellow Feelings* (1976), where the poet is more *at one* with himself and with those fellows he shares his feelings with. The community is again of artists, but even more than before they are symptoms of the poet's own self-definition. In "Personal Values," for instance, Magritte's surreal compositions are recalled as the mediating "illustration" of a bathroom seizure's attendant distortions, a "more than fair / Copy of my condition." In one of the richest and more characteristic poems in the book, "Venetian Interior, 1889," Howard himself is the *cicerone* around Browning's Ca' Rezzonico, showing it off as another example of the illuminating darkness that Venice even now is sinking into, and that time keeps us in always, and of our duty (Howard is a poet who can speak to us of our duty) "to print earth so deep in memory / that a meaning reaches the surface." That, as I have suggested, is where Howard's meanings have always been, or always been sought, but what is different about *Fellow Feelings* is how the poet himself *surfaces* in these eighteen poems. Whether discussing his adoption as an infant in "Discarded" (the first of his fictions?), or divulging and debating his homosexuality, Howard is anxious to speak for himself—and sometimes so anxious to speak of himself that his tone grows impatient with a poem's ostensible occasion: "In any case or, to be casual, in mine. . . ."

One is aware of a narrowing. Howard's own special interests, rather than those of his ventriloquized Victorians, prevail —one of which is the grotesque, which aside from its (shall we say) picturesque qualities may attract this poet because it represents those areas of life most emphatically themselves, sources of energy that encourage comprehension but resist comparison. In this volume such poems as "From the Files of the Secret Police" and "Howard's Way" are perhaps too self-indulgent in this regard; and it is a tic that disfigures parts of his subsequent books as well. Other readers will be put off by his style whenever it hardens into a mannerism. In *Fellow Feelings* they may be disgruntled by "Compulsive Qualifications," which consists of answers to fourteen queries asked by an Idiot Questioner. Each section rings rather labored linguistic changes on the emotional depths implicit in the superficial things we say—a kind of Clichés and Their Relation to the Unconscious. One is tempted to describe the effort as Howard himself once spoke of Mark Strand's strategies: "a consideration of finality is his consistent project, sustained here by shifting the responsibility for the imminent wreck from 'the reaches of ourselves' to the ambiguity instinct in *language*." Though the tone seems at first particularly patronizing, one soon realizes that the poet is actually studying the morphology of human relationships, and the distance between the dumb questions and the "dazzling" answers is also a measure of the gap between love and knowledge, Eros and Psyche, and that the very compulsion in these qualifications is a sign of the frustration that the Word cannot be made flesh. Elsewhere, and incidentally, one might hesitate over his wordplay; but for the most part he uses it, and the paradoxes his puns so often uncover, to explode pretense and hypocrisy, the bourgeois obverse of paradox.

There are several major poems in *Fellow Feelings*. "Decades" is an ambitious evocation of his relationship to Hart Crane—a connection that may seem more a coincidence than a resemblance. In fact, the connection is merely the pretext rather than the motive for the poem, which is "a sidelong grammar of paternity," a family romance that quests for the solace of a dead poet-father. The need—it is both the homosexual's and the poet's, any poet's—"to choose / our fathers and to make our history," to marry the world in defiance of those Fathers from whom we can inherit only self-hatred, is the burden of this boldly autobiographical poem. It is a theme that also kindles "The Giant on Giant-Killing," Howard's gloss of a Randall Jarrell favorite, the bronze *David* of Donatello. Goliath is another of Howard's Victorians, the parent-as-destroyer for whom "the world came to an end because the sun broke *through*." David's innocence is an absence, a bronzed body as eternal in youth as in art, which demands to be seen, adored, surrendered to as an image of what time has taken. Goliath's ironic consolation is that Donatello's demure David will become Michelangelo's—the giant-killer become a giant, not unlike the fate of some poets.

If it were not for this Donatello statue, which stands in the Bargello, I would like to call Howard's intricate re-imaginings of paintings by Bellini, Simone Martini, Starnina, and others his Uffizi sequence. Instead, I shall call it his Florentine sequence. It begins in *Fellow Feelings* (though of course there are many earlier ekphrastic poems, like the formidable "The Chalk Cliffs of Rugen"), and stretches through his next two books, *Misgivings* (1979) and *Lining Up*. It is complemented by his series of apostrophes to Parisian luminaries photographed by Nadar—a more "modern" and spare sequence, tied to fact rather than released into speculation. The Nadar sequence starts out, or at least ends up as a history of fame, that commerce between an artist and his society. Photographs, even such painterly ones as Nadar took, seem the right medium in which to study celebrity. But the Florentine sequence is after more.

There is no smell of paint in these poems; he is concerned with design and intention, not technique. Or, as Kenneth Clark once observed, "the less an artifact interests our eye as imitation, the more it must delight our eye as pattern." The patterns Howard follows are those the paintings have helped him trace in his own experience. That is not to say that life imitates art, but that art initiates life. That vows are made for us—unconsciously by ourselves—is the Rilkean annunciation in the Simone Martini poem, "Vocational Guidance": "no dodging / the moment when you meet the Angel, / when he announces what you have known all along"—that having chosen life one must abide the choices life requires one to make. But this book's last words are its best, and come from one of Howard's best poems. "*Purgatory*, formerly *Paradise*" moralizes Giovanni Bellini's landscape idyll, itself the symbolic illustration of a medieval poem. Howard's poem is a meditation on degrees of confinement, the borders we share with the "community of pain" which the painting's figures form (and hence the displaced title). Even without the picture in our mind's eye, the poem has a mysterious and moving vitality of its own, quite apart from its ability to describe. We wander with the poet among self-enclosed images as he explains them, in an elusive act of faith in "a gold, given world." The painting is of a type known as a "Sacred Conversation." Anthony Hecht, who has himself written a poem on a similar object, once observed that what is hypnotic about such paintings is "their ability in some uncanny way to assimilate grief and even catastrophe into a view wholly benign and even serene and joyful." Howard's poem is not a joyful one, but there is a nearly serene resignation to it. The iconography of any "Sacred Conversation" is the Immaculate Conception, the mystery that celebrates humanity's ability to embody the divine. And Howard wants us to see things from the Virgin's perspective.

> All this she sees,
> the woman in black and white, bare-headed, alone.
> And we see it, the world without a Sacred Book,
> a world where neither the negligence of the rocks
> nor the endless care of the waters can prevail,
> but only that act by which a man wrests something
> out of death he knows will return there, to its home.
> Death is not home to us, even if home is death—
> why else are we here, free on our frail balcony
> while the world is bound in being? Patience is home,
> and suffering and change, the pang of things past, the prong
> of things to come. We bear our poverty within us.
> Out There it is . . . out there: God stays in his machine,
> and we—we breathe and live and are permitted here.

"Bellini's landscapes," Kenneth Clark wrote, "are the supreme instance of facts transfigured through love." If it is not love, finally, that Richard Howard brings to the facts of life, it is patience. And the "poverty" of the world—a metaphor we know from Wallace Stevens—is suffered so richly here that it seems to be its own redemption: these words brought back, bought back from silence. Occasionally, Howard bares the poverty that is within him. And always there is an excess for the eye to behold, a decorative carapace of style and material that can enchant as well as distract the reader. But neither that poverty nor that excess are Howard's true subject. The true subject, he would say, is not these facts but the *finding*, of the one within the other, each testing the other. He would say with one of his characters: I have nothing save them.

JOHN HOLLANDER

IN TIME AND PLACE

J OHN HOLLANDER has been a formidable presence in Amer-
ican literary life for a quarter century now. His work as
scholar, teacher, and editor is held in high esteem, and no critic
of poetry is his superior. Where many provide ingenious read-
ings of poems, he actually *listens* to a poem's inner workings
and secret harmonies, its encoded dialogue with other poems.
Vision and Resonance (1975) and *The Figure of Echo* (1981)
have more to teach about the way poems are put together, and
the ways that delight becomes instruction, than any books I
know. But his true importance is as a poet, and to judge by the
crudest measures—critical reckonings and anthology appear-
ances—Hollander's poems are either merely respected or to-
tally ignored. I suspect the reason is that many readers don't
know how to place him. They are uneasy about the "difficulty"
of his work. But is he any more difficult than several more
widely appreciated poets—say, John Ashbery or James Merrill?

Yes and no. Like the professional diver, every poet declares
a "degree of difficulty" that must then be factored into any
judgment of his performance. Merrill raises the lyric to a new
power and asks us to multiply autobiography by myth. Ashbery
deliberately leads us away from conventionalized "meanings"

and into a congeries of voices that daydream out loud. And each time we solve a poem by either, it becomes more puzzling. Hollander's poems are difficult in the same way—at once compelling and elusive—but their demands on a reader are of a different order.

Many of his critics have misprized the development and disciplines of Hollander's work either by repeating an early impression of him as an academic *flâneur* or by echoing R. P. Blackmur on Donne and finding him violent in his constructed emotions and private with actual secrecy of meaning. Over the years, Hollander has extended his poetic ideas far beyond the "easy" solutions offered by the metaphysical lyric or the verse epistle. This is one reason why the best—that is to say, the most challenging—of his recent books have been sequences. They are themselves elaborate interpretations that ask to be interpreted. Hollander *reads into* things, and the results require the sort of scrupulous pondering that dreams or scripture do. In short, his poems are parables, or models of experience. Borges, Kafka, and Wallace Stevens come to mind as avatars. Parables are among the least sparing or beautiful forms of poetry. They take away our feelings and give us better fictions instead. They analyze our consolations, harp on our debts and deceits. But the imaginative energy they bring to this task of disenchantment is itself a kind of compassion. Few poets are equal to it. Hollander, more than any of his peers, is writing this kind of demanding poetry. Again, like the diver twisting backward in the air, hovering impossibly in the sun before his plunge, the difficulties of a Hollander poem are formidable, and therefore exhilarating.

Though it will be catalogued under poetry, *In Time and Place* (1986) is actually a hybrid of verse and prose, the extremes on either side of "poetry." It is characteristic of Hollander to have situated himself at the extreme edges, for a longer view. One of his prose poems puts it this way: "We have, after all, to be grateful that our light lies broken in pieces: were we to have to live in the generality of it, without the beneficence of the shady (no matter how questionable now, always), it would be unbearable." Verse and prose, then, are the two shades from which he looks out on the bright confusions of our lives.

The book begins with a sequence of thirty-five short poems called "In Time." They resemble the texts for a lieder cycle, fragments of grief over lost love that gather into song. They turn on a broken marriage, the end of a life together, and so it's appropriate that they are all written in the so-called *In Memoriam* stanza, the ebb and flow of whose *abba* scheme continually loses and finds itself, pungently near the mark or plaintively far from it:

> And thus, as death serves as a hedge
> Around life, my imprisoned words
> (Yoked to the task, not caged like birds)
> Keep to the center, keep their edge.

The clipped stanzas and ironic elegance, even the bitter playfulness of these poems, serve both to control and to contour the deep emotion that is their pretext. And because they are closer to the bone than many of Hollander's earlier poems, there is even an occasional tentativeness.

None of the adulterous melodrama of betrayal and recrimination that mar so many contemporary poems of domestic life applies here. The tone is rather one of brave bewilderment: "For me the sentence has come first, / The verdict will emerge in time." Because he is a writer for whom the literature of the past is not a study but an instinct, it is likely that Hollander had Hardy in mind while writing "In Time." Like Hardy, he is writing about ghosts. First, about the ghost of the wife who has left him:

Even now, as whole cups of tears
Have dried into the usual air
And I may meet you here and there,
That spirit, moist with life, appears

Where someone else may bathe my wound
In the bright fountain of her smile,
Warming the darkness for a while
In a room shadowed but unmooned.

I see you even in the most
Guarded of places, in her bed
Fucking there with another ghost
Under the bedclothes of my head.

But by the end of the sequence, he realizes they have both
become ghosts: "Loss, swallowing its mystery, / Desire, feed-
ing on its end." The real lover is subsumed by the type, our
own personalities by the huge emotions stalking them. In ef-
fect, these are poems about all sorts of "Departures, losses,
even new / Emptyings of a partially / Refilled cup." The poet
is concerned here with what we make of nothing, how we
compensate and explain—until those explanations take the place
of a person and come to be called a poem.

FROM HERE he moves on to an exuberantly complex Nabokovian
fable about how we make ourselves up. "In Between" is the
book's prose interlude, in the form of a journal-notebook, that
book-before-the-book. Montaigne called his journal his *ar-
rière-boutique*, or back of the store. Hollander's witty, para-
noid narrator writes his in an invisible ink concocted of

dried tears, some sweat from this morning's fit of anxiety as
I peered through the half-open study door and saw the mess
of unanswered mail, a bit of fine white wine that had gone

beyond all hope and faith, and drops of remembered rain that had fallen once between two touching faces.

It is the very Ink of Experience, applied to each day's fresh page. In Hollander's fable of self-discovery, we are given a glimpse at the primal scene of writing, at those impulses that generate fiction and those fictions that empower life. Hollander's uncanny ability to make the allegorical real and the real allegorical is everywhere apparent, but let me cite one small episode to stand in for many. Here is his "description" of a room:

> There is the bed. There are someone else's shoes (and there is no proximate arrangement of two shoes which can avoid emblematic pathos, empty shoes—and perhaps hats—being the only memorials of presence we have now that are unfilled by body the way corpses are emptied of soul). There, the view of Rome on the far wall (a remembered purchase, an outgrown taste, a fantasy on remembered themes exhaled by remembered spots); there, the abandoned novel with the pages still turned down. (What had happened that afternoon that made one stop at "The Marquise chose not to go out, after all"?) All these things have minds of their own, tugging away at our consciousness of them, and doing much of our remembering for us.

The combination in that passage of philosophical aplomb, giddy inventiveness, and searching pathos is typical of Hollander's technique throughout. He looks high and low—to a pair of shoes or a novel—for his emblems of experience, and to each he brings the force of the others. The pair of shoes is seen with the intensity of van Gogh's picture of the same motif; the novel is mentioned because it prompted us back into life.

The highlight of the book is its third section, "In Place," a group of thirty—what? Prose poems? Fictions? I suspect Hollander himself would want them called *texts*. One of them, for instance—a teasing meditation on painterly conventions called "Dutch Interior"—begins this way:

> The light comes in from the window on the left, pearly and clear, but not if one is in the room that is in the picture. No indeed—from within, the light might seem more general, no matter where in the room the windows were, even as the contents of the room would cease to matter very much. The spotty globe, for example. . . .

If you squint at the passage, it looks more and more like poetry, and in fact with very little effort can be nudged into Hollander's favored, familiar hendecasyllabic lines:

> The light comes in from the window on the left,
> Pearly, clear, but not if one is in the room
> That's in the picture. No indeed—from within,
> The light might seem more general, no matter where
> The windows were, even as the room's contents
> Would cease to matter very much. The spotty. . . .

Why, then, do it as prose? One reason, undoubtedly, is the prompting of his material itself, which is what Aristotle called poetry's counterpart, rhetoric. Rhetoric is both setting and subject for Hollander, the very landscape of his imagination. Then, too, the particular texture and general effect of these pieces are to be distinguished from those of his poetry. Freed from the figurative and rhythmical strictures of verse, from everything that we mean by "time" in verse, Hollander can ply the rhetorical (i.e., dramatic and psychological) strategies of formal speech to render more exactly the give-and-take of the mind's serious play in thinking through its problems, both artificial and real. Prose—its format and flow—allows the poet to deal with experience abstracted to his ideas about it, whether those ideas be theories or memories. It is, finally, the mother tongue of parables.

The wonder of "In Place" is Hollander's ability to develop, distort, quicken, or upend our notion of a text and its responsibilities. Invoking the tropes of replacement (metaphor and metonymy) and the ploys of signifying (narration and designation), he has contrived a magic lantern of consciousness itself. Together, the texts convene a symposium on the economy of substitution, the dialectic of space and place, that is at once rhetorical and metaphysical: how things take place, how we find our places and figure out our lives, how the mistakes of imagination commute the sentence of speech. They are set in various defined, even overdetermined spaces: a drawer, a room, a building; the *paysage composé* of a farm or restaurant; a painting, a myth, an echo. They pose as derailed stories, world-weary travelogues, crackpot rationales, still-life ensembles, first impressions, or second thoughts. And they can be extremely funny. But they are usually studded with dark moral reminders —that nothing is got for nothing, that substitution both enhances and erases value, that language is both key and lock, that "the very breaking-up of the radiance that might have for ever remained a deep ground was what will always cause us to have embraced these discrete fragments—turning on and off, fading, ending in a border of darkness—as with the arms of our heart."

"Discrete fragments" is an appropriate but, at the same time, inadequate term for "In Place." Its dark borders define an uproarious and reverent center of joy in a fictionality that is the deep ground of myth and belief. One is tempted to go further and say that Hollander is here commemorating the orphic fragments of the visionary sublime, which now are scattered into the contingencies of everyday life and the way we talk about it. East of the word "Eden" was language, the fall into which alone gives us our grasp on transcendence:

John Hollander   309

And finally, there is something right about the vagrancy of the replacements. Nowhere can keep us for too long. Let us look at it this way: for want of the fruit the garden was lost, for want of the garden the places were gained, for want of the places new places arrived, for want of new places we dreamed and dreamed. We composed in the tiniest inner room all the chambers of the endless palace, opening on to each other, directly as well as indirectly, off unlit corridors, once entered and left, then lost, even if returned to at a later time and by a route that we could never have known to be circuitous. And each room a place of mistakenness, so much so that while we are in it, there is no way of getting it right. Once left, there is only what we say of it, which is never mistaken.

Hollander has taken some commonplaces and made them into the heart's own truth. The lucid difficulties of his work reward continual study. *In Time and Place* again demonstrates by its originality and élan that he is part conjurer and part philosopher, one of our language's true mythographers.

AMY CLAMPITT

THE MIRRORING MARRYINGS

WHEN AMY CLAMPITT'S *The Kingfisher* was published in 1983, reactions were as extravagent as the texture of the poems themselves. Those reactions came in two waves. The praise prompted a success; the success prompted attacks. About *The Kingfisher* and the books she has written since, opinions have been sharply divided: enthusiasts applaud their unfashionably rich rhetoric, their allusiveness and virtuosity, while detractors dismiss them as overstuffed and regressive. Because the two sides have been so insistent, their conflicting claims signal perhaps the most unusual debut in recent literary history. But because this is an old debate about American poetry, its resumption in this case was not a surprise. The oddly surprising factor was the poet's age. She was born in 1920, and even in a country with many famously belated debuts (by Whitman, Frost, Stevens), hers at sixty-three seemed remarkable. The further surprise is that *The Kingfisher* was not her first book.

She too had her long foreground. *Multitudes, Multitudes,* a full-length collection of twenty-six poems, was privately published in 1973. In retrospect, it may seem like a lost original, but actually it reads like a feebler, paler version of the book she published a decade later. All the poems in *Multitudes, Multitudes* are carefully dated at the bottom, and many go back to the mid- and late-sixties. Even then her style was recognizably her own. The syntactical sprawl, the glut of adjectives, the periphrasis and flurry of appositional phrases, the layering of references—all of these seem in place from the start. The same echoes of Hopkins, Stevens, and Keats that one hears in later books sound more faintly in this book too. One difference is the several character studies here, in the manner of Jarrell or early Lowell. They reflect Clampitt's still earlier efforts to write novels. In later books the impulse is reserved for personal poems of an affectionately comic note (like "Rain at Bellagio"), but this is also the ground from which her historical pastiches grew. In fact, the titles of many poems here might come from later books: "The Eve of All Souls," "The Skylarks of Mykonos," "Hera of Samos," "The Christmas Cactus." Her religious temperament, which seeks both to accommodate the world and transcend it, is even more strongly evident in these early poems, and focused here by the subject that has consistently animated her work: death. Because of this obsession—the fact and the idea of death—she is an obliquely "political" poet. If she deploys Greek mythology here, she also visits Attica prison. Her literary cast of mind never blinds her to Vietnam, or South Africa, or welfare hearings. But politics is only a trope for her larger sense that "nothing in the world is safely kept." Those ways in which laws, cultures, historical circumstance, injustice, or art, or love may shape and control us—these fascinate Clampitt from the beginning. Her concentration on details— odd bits of life or language—is finally her way to keep these huge forces in check. But by momentarily avoiding them, she allows them to rush into her poems with greater impact. This balance of restraint and engulfment gives all her work its peculiar strength.

Whatever *Multitudes, Multitudes* may have predicted, *The Kingfisher* announced a poet of lavish gifts. But they were unwanted gifts—or unwanted by those readers used to the workshop whimsy, the surreal bleats, and drab earnest verse that have been the stock-in-trade of younger American poets for two decades. It is true that there is a risky nostalgia in Clampitt's style, and in her partisans' reaction to it. "If a poet gets a large audience very quickly," T. S. Eliot once wrote, "that is a rather suspicious circumstance: for it leads us to fear that he is not really doing anything new, that he is only giving people what they are already used to, and therefore what they have already had from the poets of the previous generation." Some critics who disliked *The Kingfisher* took her for the New Formalism's extremist. But she is not, strictly speaking, an overly "formal" poet. She occasionally works in prescribed forms, though with less success than in more amiably free-form runs of rhythmical verse. It's her *rhetoric* the critics were actually scorning or admiring. And her rhetoric does recall, say, the stately grace of Richard Wilbur's poems of the 1950s. To some, her style marked a return to the sedate sort of poetry (the tag "academic" is usually attached to the complaint) dominant before Black Mountain and the Beats. But as I've said, this skirmish is a continuing one, and a useless one. The rhetorical range of American poetry has historically been a wide one, and nourished by its extremes. It is middlebrow writing —correct and empty—that has been the true enemy of both sides, and Clampitt has always written as if she had absorbed W. H. Auden's advice: "Be subtle, various, ornamental, clever, / And do not listen to those critics ever / Whose crude provincial gullets crave in books / Plain cooking made still plainer by plain cooks."

One gets the sense from Clampitt's poems of both attention paid and amplitude given; or as she puts in it one poem, of her being at once "earthbound" and "fired-up." Admittedly, what some find exuberantly literary, others find merely bookish; what seems complex and heightened to some will strike others as clotted or gassy; one reader's figured meaning is another's decoration. What is clear is that she has studied and learned a great deal—from the landscape and lifeblood of literature, as well as from the encyclopedia of the eye's observations. Clampitt is a virtuoso, and she has two of a virtuoso's faults, both easily blinked at. Her cadenzas are sometimes too heavily ornamented, so that her skill overwhelms her subject; and her program is too long. Her style is luxuriant, frisky, and "escapes / our mere totting-up." Stanzas, for this poet, are "little rooms / for turmoil to grow lucid in," and indeed her poems are each a series of refocusings: close-up and dissolve. Her effects are bold, often nervy, and buoyed both by tradition and by the community of solitaries. Wallace Stevens, in his "Adagia," said that "things seen are things as seen." A close observer of the natural world and of its "perishing residue / of pure sensation," Clampitt knows enough too to ask "What is real except / what's fabricated?" Her descriptions, then, are both; a sea-surface, for instance, is most itself when seen as something else: "this windsilver / rumpling as of oatfields, / a suede of shadow, / a nub, a nap, a mane of lustre / lithe as the slide / of muscle in its / sheath of skin."

The right word for Clampitt's style, of course, is *baroque*. That is to say, her poems are both intricate and full, their extensions defined by outsized syntactical gestures, by images and diction that introduce harmonic dissonances. This doesn't preclude a quiet dignity, but that is not the first note in her lyre. As in a baroque painting, the "action" of her poems is in the middle ground. The busy foreground pushes at a reader; her lines are crowded, overbright, and their extraneous detail sometimes makes them difficult to parse at first sight. The background of her poems, though, is softer, darker: traditional themes that structure and sustain the dramatic shape and force of her verse. It could be said she is a poet of light, light that separates and joins objects. One thinks of the atmospheric effects in her outdoor settings, or the firelit interiors of her nineteenth-century studies. And it is light, the fall and play of it, that figures so strongly in baroque art. Similarly, both the foreground and background of her poems are heavily allusive. Clampitt, like any baroque artist, pillages the art of the past. She looks at the world through language, so that what she sees is charged by the transforming power of metaphor. But—and this disturbs many readers—she looks at the world through art as well. It seems ridiculous to me that this art-about-art is so often deplored as etiolated and derivative in poetry; few object to it in, say, painting or music, perhaps because there it is recognized as a quintessential Romantic concern. Art models life, sets ideal or ironic standards, and so is a moral presence in poems—certainly in Clampitt's. It is her method to order, clarify, and illuminate experience. Art is to the poet what ideas are to the philosopher.

"It is a privilege to see so / much confusion," said Marianne Moore. By "confusion" she meant the world's own welter, its facts, artifacts, curios, and contradictions. And by "privilege" she meant their moral ordering. Clampitt is a poet in the mold of Moore. Some of the poems in *The Kingfisher* even sound like Moore—"Times Square Water Music," "Good Friday," "Marginal Employment," and the appropriately named "Exmoor." But it is not that studied resemblance that attracts me so much as a deeper affinity: the curiosity and exuberance both poets share, their shrewd moralism, a disposition to view things through the spectacles of language, their love of (in Clampitt's phrase) "the ramifying / happenstance, the mirroring / marryings of all likeness." To have, for instance, Moore's

"A Grave" in mind while reading Clampitt's "Beach Glass" is helpful. The same setting and point of view, the same indeterminate "you" addressed, the same thematic concerns—the sea as a "collector" and a grave, the ocean in which (here is Moore's conclusion) "dropped things are bound to sink—/ in which if they turn and twist, it is neither with volition nor consciousness." Of course the details are different. As she walks along her beach, Clampitt's eye is quicker than Moore's, more capacious, less sententious. What Moore notices are gorgeous or dire anomalies, timeless and detached in their moment of having been noticed. By contrast, Clampitt's details—"last night's / beer cans, spilt oil, the coughed-up / residue of plastic"—tend always to implicate some human drama behind them. This adds depth to a poem without narrative detours. And in her more deliberate way, she moves from the smaller particular to the grander generalization. The bits of beach glass she comes upon—the amber of Budweiser, chrysoprase of Gallo, lapis of Milk of Magnesia—are charming for their sea-changes. But she goes on to make her point about the stuff of human making. The myth of the engulfed cathedral is as much a part of these lines as is the religion of commercialism; and all of it is reduced to the Nothing that is everything is this poet's mind. It is a poem that turns back in on itself, on its "looking":

> The process
> goes on forever: they come from sand,
> they go back to gravel,
> along with the treasuries
> of Murano, the buttressed
> astonishments of Chartres,
> which even now are readying
> for being turned over and over as gravely
> and gradually as an intellect
> engaged in the hazardous

redefinition of structures
no one has yet looked at.

The word that literally sticks out in that final stanza—"gravely"—
is her nod to Moore's poem; and her sense of intellectual
"redefinition" is both a tribute paid and a sly statement of her
own terms.

When the English edition of *The Kingfisher* appeared in
1984, Faber had changed her into a different, and lesser poet
for the British audience. It makes a certain sense to have
deleted very local poems about life in New York City; they
may not travel well. But also gone were some of the best poems
in the book—its entire last section, in fact, some long and
difficult poems that show more powerfully than many others
how historical her imagination is. Part of that history is per-
sonal. Earlier poems that have set her parents to rest—
"Beethoven, Opus 111" and "A Procession at Candlemas"—
are part of her ambivalent project in this book to come to
terms with her own past. The several poems about her Iowa
childhood present a very mixed image, and some crucial motifs.
In most of them, a real or imaged "habitat of magic" (a phrase
from "The Quarry") that is safe, enclosed, aloof from the
immensities of the Midwest plains which are most often de-
scribed in terms of water: "only waves / of chlorophyll in
motion, the darkened jetsam / of bur oaks, a serpentine of
willows / along the hollows—a flux / that waterlogs the mind."
That same flux looms in "The Woodlot." The child-poet's eye
looks for lines, for "fine manners." But it was barbed wire or
nodes of evergreen and maple that "gave the prairie grid / what
little personality it had." While the tantrums of big weather
blow over here, the child is drawn elsewhere:

Deep in it, under
appletrees like figures in a ritual, violets

Amy Clampitt   317

are thick, a blue cellarhole
of pure astonishment.
                    It is
the earliest memory. Before it,
I/you, whatever that conundrum may yet
prove to be, amounts to nothing.

"Astonishment" is a key word in Clampitt's vocabulary, and
may account for her heaping of terms, as a way to understand
and praise what stuns her. Or, it being her "earliest memory,"
an attempt to retrieve a primal image (the mother's breast,
someone would suggest), or to compensate for a speechless
wonder. But what fascinates me about this moment in "The
Woodlot" is that the word "astonishment" comes from the
same root that gives us "tornado," so that beneath the surface
of the poem, beneath that apparent sharp contrast, her fear and
her refuge from that fear are the same emotion. This is a
peculiar but entirely characteristic maneuver on Clampitt's part.

"Imago" is the fullest version of these contrasts and mirror-
ings in *The Kingfisher*. It is a poem about growing up, and
about growing away. The poem's term for this is "unfathoma-
ble evolvings." Her choice of adjective is apt, because the met-
aphor of the sea—and the sensation of *flux*—is everywhere,
as an image for the vast waterless plains of Iowa, and for her
unconscious yearnings ("A thirst for something definite so
dense / it feels like drowning"). The portrait of the child here
begins by juxtaposing two sorts of stories she is given: the tall
tales of the western migration, and the fairy tales she reads on
her own: Indians and merfolk. An image from the first—an
infant daughter's headstone, "so small it might be playing
house"—leads into the fabled palace the young girl is reading
about in her farmhouse parlor. The severe and formless Iowa
of Grant Wood and of provincial expectations is contrasted in

the child's imagination with the "hard and handsome," dark and mysterious world of European culture:

> the abysm of history,
> a slough to be pulled out of
> any way you could. Antiquity, the backward
> suction of the dark, amounted to a knothole
> you plugged with straw, old rags, pages
> ripped from last year's Sears Roebuck catalog,
> anything, to ward off the blizzard.

A knothole through which forbidden pleasures might leak into the staid Iowa farmhouse is, of course, also the child's peephole, and similar to the cellarhole in "The Woodlot"—her access to astonishment. It is "the Italy / of urns and cypresses" that lures her, as it had Keats; a world theatrical and even lurid. At this point in the poem the knothole looks back at her from

> a pair of masks whose look, at even
> this remove, could drill through bone:
> the tragic howl, the comic rictus,
> eyeholes that stare out of the crypt
> of what no grownup is ever heard to speak of.

But the last stanza, the longest in the poem, abruptly changes the tone of the poem. We are back home, on prayer meeting night. Here Clampitt plays with two meanings of "born-again." There are the worshipful revivalists surrounding her. And then there is herself, as if reborn through the eyehole into a new knowledge. Rather than speak autobiographically, she introduces a luna moth, after its metamorphosis from caterpillar "the emblem / of the born-again." The earlier knotholes next become the eyeholes on the luna moth's wing—the imago, both moth and totemic image of the unconscious—that predictably draws the child away to the East and to Art, as in the fairy tale the child had been reading about "the merfolk who revert to foam, / eyeing at a distance the lit pavilions / that seduced her, their tailed child, / into the palaces of metamorphosis." That she is drawn *underwater* is Clampitt's way of mingling the terms and fortunes of her two opposed states.

She can also move these terms beyond the personal. All her angles—topographical, political, memorial—are manifestations of her concern for how men have lived with themselves in time. The six poems of *The Kingfisher*'s final section confirm this, and in a harrowing way. Never journalistic, never strident or self-righteous ("The purest art has slept with turpitude, / we all pay taxes"), they explore the causes and the cost of human suffering. One, "The Dahlia Gardens," is especially disturbing. It tells the story of Norman Morrison, a young Quaker activist who immolated himself in front of the Pentagon in 1965—another kind of terrible, emblematic moth in this book. It is a story that might have been rendered with the sentimentality of much political poetry. Instead, Clampitt makes it strange and urgent. Minds—those of bureaucrats and of martyrs—fill up with darkness:

> overland, the inching caravans
> the blacked-out troop trains
> convoys through ruined villages
> along the Mekong
>
> merging
> with the hydrocarbon-dark, headlight-inflamed Potomac
>
> the little lights   the candles
> flickering on Christmas eve
> the one light left burning
> in a front hallway   kerosene-

lit windows in the pitch dark
of back-country roads.

That darkness is a terrible energy. In one version it is oil:

. . . hydrocarbon unearthed
and peeled away, process by process,
in stages not unlike the stages
of revelation, to a gaseous plume
that burns like a bush. . . .

In another, fanaticism:

Hermaphrodite of pity and violence, the chambered
pistil and the sword-bearing archangel,
scapegoat and self-appointed avenger, contend,
embrace, are one. He strikes the match.

The poet works to unite "system with system into one terrible
mandala."

METAPHOR is the figure of speech that embodies change, and
even violence, and it is change and process, borders and shore-
lines, in-between states, "the unrest whose home—*our* / home
—is motion," that are central to *What the Light Was Like*
(1985). The poems in this book are grouped into five sections
that move from "The Shore" to "The Hinterland" to "The
Metropolis," and back again. What changes is not just the
locale, but the register and the vantage, and the way turmoils
are contained. We start in a cottage on the Maine coast, then
move to (and because it is the scene of her past, revisit) an Iowa
farmhouse on the inland sea, then to an apartment on Manhattan
island. Each is a marginal existence, a fugitive vision. The book
opens with "A Baroque Sunburst," ends at nightfall, and in
between flicker images of light and dark. Those images, along

with a crosshatching of allusions and themes, and its bracing structure, make this the most unified and resolute of all her books.

A familiar narrative device for this poet—one she shares with Elizabeth Bishop, A. R. Ammons, and others—is the ramble, during which unconsidered trifles are snatched up as symbols. Her favorites are her plucky city adventures and her walks in Maine, along its bogs and tidal flats, a shoreline that stands between solid familiarity and oceanic flux. The opening of "Low Tide at Schoodic" can stand in for her method in all these poems, whereby abstractions and images are allegorically loaded onto the plain object of meditation. The move here from surf to still tidepool, the movement of both the water and the walker, is brilliantly told in terms of a palace revolution:

Force, just here, rolls up
pomaded into vast blue curls
fit for the Sun King, then crumples
to a stuff of ruffs and kerchiefs
over ruined doorposts, the rubble
of an overthrow no one remembers
except through cooled
extrapolation—tunnels
underneath the granite,
the simmering moat, the darkened sill
we walk on now,
prowling the planar windowpanes of tidepools
for glimpses of kelp's ribboned whips,
the dead men's fingers.

This book also includes versions of *The Kingfisher*'s more ambitious poems. Poems here about the death of Clampitt's brother echo earlier poems about her parents; the title poem, about the death at sea of a Maine fisherman and how "the iridescence / of his last perception, charring, gave way to unreversed, / irrevocable dark," is a muted echo of the more anguished and searching poem "The Dahlia Gardens." But other poems here—"Black Buttercups" and "A Curfew" particularly—have a more urgent, personal, and thereby affecting note to them. The title poem reminds us "that what you love most is the same as what you're / most afraid of—God, / in a word." As before, it is love that draws Clampitt to the world's "wallowing and glitter," and it is fear that pulls her back from a vision of that world as a manifestation of dark, unknowable will.

The book's literal and figurative centerpiece is "Voyages," a sequence of eight poems subtitled "A Homage to John Keats," in part a costume drama drawn from Keats' letters and poems and from biographies of the poet, and in part a displaced study of these same themes of love and fear. It is nearly impossible not to draw an appealing portrait of Keats. Even so, Clampitt's pastiche is strikingly successful, circling as it does Keats' "own recurring dream of being warm," of the "fine weather, health, Books, a contented Mind" that animated and eluded his short life. "Voyages" is also an extraordinary act of literary self-definition. The ways she identifies her own writing with Keats' —with his lush impetuosity, his taste for grandeur, his regard for the literature of the past as "a Refuge and a Passion"—are illuminating.

But with good reason she concentrates more on Keats' life than on his work, and previous poems in the book forge stronger links between the two poets. We think of Clampitt's dead younger brother (to whose memory her book is dedicated) when she speaks of Keats' beloved Tom. We think of her own early prairie life when Keats contemplates his brother George's emigration to the wilds of America. The loss of both brothers to the cold immensities is several times contrasted with the warm, feminine indoors which nurtures the poet in "that imaginary place, that stanza / where nothing at all had happened," and prompts him, in turn, to open the casement window on the real: "The cold outside was real. / Dying was real . . ."

But it is not only the "continual allegory" of Keats' life that Clampitt is appropriating for herself as a way to make her turmoil lucid. She is interested, her footnote says, in "the powerful way in which literature can become a link with times and places, and with minds, otherwise remote." To that end, having joined herself to Keats, she enjoins a subsequent line of poets—Walt Whitman, Hart Crane, Wallace Stevens, and Osip Mandelstam—in which she means to take her place. All of them are poets of immensities: Whitman and Crane, of the sea; Stevens, of the auroras; and Mandelstam, of the cold. All of them countered their fears with trust in a redemptive art, their sense of engulfment with the imagination's posthumous whispers out of time. Clampitt's daring here is, in Pound's phrase, to have gathered from the air a live tradition, her voice one with theirs:

> How clannish
> the whole hand-to-hand, cliffhanging trade,
>
> the gradual letdown, the hempen slither,
> precarious basketload of sea drift
> gathered at Margate or at Barnegat:
> along Paumanok's liquid rim, the dirges,
> nostalgia for the foam: *the bottom of*
> *the sea is cruel.* The chaff, the scum
> of the impalpable confined in stanzas,
>
> a shut-in's hunger for the bodiless
> enkindlings of the aurora—all that
> traffic in the perilous. That summer,
> orphaned of sublimity, he'd settled for
> the way an oatfield's stalks and blades

checcquered his writing tablet with their
quivering. But after, back in Hampstead,

the samphire-gatherer's mimic god-deliverer
still bled metonymy: an ordinary field of
barley turned to alien corn's inland sea-
surfaces, and onto every prairie rolling,
sans the samphire trade's frail craft, un-
basketed, undid the casement of the homesick,
stared once more, and called an image home.

"Life," remarked Wallace Stevens, "is not people and scene but
thought and feeling." "Voyages" is both. It is a poem whose
livelihood trades in character sketch and minutely observed
setting, but whose life is what it thinks of them and how it
invokes and quickens our feeling about them.

CLAMPITT herself has said that her third book, *Archaic Figure*
(1987), "differs from *The Kingfisher* and *What the Light Was
Like* rather more than either of those books differed from the
other." But because her talent has unfolded rather than devel-
oped, I prefer to view the book as the third panel of a triptych.
Many poems in all three books could go in any of the collec-
tions. The entire last section of *Archaic Figure* is largely left-
overs. But the earlier parts of this book complete the large-
scaled self-portrait and historical inquiry that the triptych un-
dertakes. The autobiographical intimacies of *The Kingfisher*
dramatize a sequence of private initiations into womanhood,
and the literary homages in *What the Light Was Like* are a
process of affiliation. Those two movements, simultaneously
away from and into the self, are here combined into the poet's
studies of *women artists*—George Eliot, Margaret Fuller,
Dorothy Wordsworth. None led an untroubled life, none is

what we would call a triumphant artist. They are apt choices, then, for what Clampitt says the book's central concern is: "the experience of women, as individuals and as a part of human history." For this poet, that experience has been a very mixed one.

Two figures dominate the book. One, its figurehead on the dust jacket, is a headless female statue from a votive group in the Heraeum of Samos (now in East Berlin), by the sculptor Geneleos from about 560 B.C. The delicate figure, with her tresses and gathered, pleated chiton, is called *Orinthe,* or "Little Bird." The opening, the titular or dedicatory poem of the book, "Archaic Figure," broods on this figure—the austere, elusive virgin beyond time—"that saw—or so to us it seems —/ with unexampled clarity to the black core / of what we are, of everything we were to be, / have since become." The other and opposing figure is Medusa. She might also be considered, in the long run, a headless figure, but we most often think of her *as a head*—in this instance, one that completes the headless statute of Orinthe. The Medusa could be thought of as the female counterpart of the Minotaur: monstrous because the most "human" part of the person is bestial, murderous, irrational. Clampitt's monster is, typically, more pathetic. She stands as an emblem of the body itself, or of the fallen body, subjected to time and brute force:

> The tentacles, the brazen phiz whose glare
> stands every fibril of the mind on end—
> lust looked at backward as it were,
> an antique scare tactic, either self-protection
> or a libel on the sex whose periodic
> blossom hangs in ungathered garland
> from the horned clockwork of the moon:
> as cause or consequence, or both, hysteric
> symptoms no doubt figure here. She'd been

a beauty till Poseidon, in a flagrant
trespass, closed with her on Athena's temple floor.

She is a sympathetic but still forbidding figure throughout
the book, as in later poems she is associated first with Athena,
and later with the slightly grotesque George Eliot. She may as
well be the presiding force in the long poem "An Anatomy of
Migraine"—the modern pathological manifestation of the old
myth? It is not just horrific pain, the very pain of existence
itself, that she represents, though she is the constant reminder
in this book that "we are animals, mire-born, / mud-cumbered,
chilled and full of fear." In the poem "Hippocrene" she is said
to be the "harbinger of going under, / of death by water." The
indirect reference is to Virginia Woolf; to those headaches and
depressions that signaled the onset of her fatal madness. The
motif of drowning goes back to her earliest poems, and if we
make the appropriate connections, it is possible to see Orinthe
and Medusa as embodiments of the two principles—restraint
and engulfment—that have fascinated Clampitt's imagination
in all four books.

I want to take these connections one step further. "The
Nereids of Seriphos" in *Archaic Figure* makes an explicit link
between the Greek landscape that Clampitt is drawn to and the
Midwest plains of her childhood. They are both, let us call
them, elemental landscapes, and they are joined by others in
her books, notably by the Maine coastline. There is a blessed
indifference, a cruel sanctity to these places, and they may
continually be contrasted with the doomed happiness and plen-
itude of both the nineteenth-century households she re-imag-
ines and the Manhattan apartment and blocks where she dwells.
The latter world is an interior one, cozy but crossed with
upheaval and destruction: one she identifies herself with. The
other is outdoors, vast, an image of eternity: one she has fled
but revisits. Both are part of what she calls "this / botched,

cumbersome, much-mended, / not unsatisfactory thing" that is existence itself. The mixed state, the middle ground: it is here Clampitt's poems mark their boundaries, replenishing themselves to soothe an old uneasiness, pushing against and beyond the scramble of natural facts and human history toward the calm of ideas about life. And those ideas, in their turn, are lit by the light of her style—a light "that's always shifting—from / a nimbus gone beserk / to a single gorget, a cathedral train of blinking, or / the fogbound shroud / that can turn anywhere into a nowhere."

ANTHONY HECHT

ANATOMIES OF MELANCHOLY

> Then praise was for a kind of art
> Whereof there is no school;
> There the unlettered instinct rides
> In all its bodily skill.

A T ONE point in a poem about his childhood, Anthony
Hecht takes a small inventory. It is a poet's inventory,
whereby gift is symbol, image conjures image, and a present
predicts the future.

> Here is the microscope one had as a child,
> The Christmas gift of some forgotten uncle.
> Here is the slide with a drop of cider vinegar
> As clear as gin, clear as your early mind.
> Look down, being most careful not to see
> Your own eye in the mirror underneath,
> Which will appear, unless your view is right,
> As a darkness on the face of the first waters.
> When all is silvery and brilliant, look:
> The long, thin, darting shapes, the flagellates,
> Rat-tailed, ambitious, lash themselves along—
> Those humble, floating ones, those simple cells
> Content to be borne on whatever tide,
> Trustful, the very image of consent—
> These are the frail, unlikely origins,
> Scarcely perceived, of all you shall become.

The kind of research that goes on here is twofold. The poem these lines are part of, the astonishing "Green: An Epistle," is itself a *recherche*, a finely detailed Proustian recovery of lost time, both an historical project and a personal obsession. And the passage also describes a literal research that peers into a world that makes itself manifest in the shapes and colors and rhythms of words. In fact, these lines comprise a miniature allegory of origins—of any lyric poet's "unlikely origins." But it is how this allegory is fractioned, into a darkness and two impulses, that most intrigues me, because it goes to the heart of Hecht's work. That primal darkness, first of all. That it is the very image of the poet's own eye echoes Emerson: "The blank we see in Nature is in our own eye." And it is crucial to remember how often Hecht takes this darkness as his subject. Few contemporary poets have so persistently and so strikingly come to terms with evil and violence in history, or what we literally call *human nature*. And throughout his four collections are occasions of madness, paranoia, catatonia, hallucination, and dream; there are exile, plague, miscarriage, murder, genocide. Indeed, the intricate trelliswork of his stanzas— some of them feats of engineering not seen since the seventeenth century—and the grandiloquent diction that are the hallmarks of Hecht's style seem at odds with such subjects: too composed.

"In each art," Richard Wilbur once wrote (Hecht quotes the sentence in his 1966 essay "On the Methods and Ambitions of Poetry"), "the difficulty of the form is a substitute for the difficulty of direct apprehension and expression of the object." Elaborate schemes, then, substitute for painstaking analysis. And in general that is true of Hecht. It is true as well that he seeks to dramatize both the difficulty and the apprehension by means of his style. Sharply contrasting tones of voice—lambent figures and Latinate turns suddenly giving way to slang— are used not just to color his poems, but to structure them. His poems continually favor such sorts of doubleness—paired per-spectives, sentiment cut with cynicism, moral standards under-cut by doubt. Some poems depend on abruptly juxtaposed points of view. Others work with the dynamics of motion and stasis. "The Cost" is one: a young Italian couple race on their Vespa around Trajan's Column. Theirs is a world—or a mo-ment in the world—of "weight and speed," "risks and tilts," "the spin / And dazzled rinse of air," "their headlong lurch and flatulent racket." What they circle is, in a sense, the image in stone of themselves: the spiraling bas-relief of the emperor's troops, long since motes of dust like those the latter-day mo-torcycle kicks up. The couple's very motion depends on their *not* thinking of the difference. Self-consciousness, or what Hecht here calls "unbodied thought," is entropy.

Or, to return to the terms in the allegory I began with, we have two shapes, two forms of stylistic life, two modes of being —the flagellates and the simple cells. I want in this essay to look through the other end of the microscope; to look back at Hecht's work through these contrasting impulses, and to find the eye of the poet in the darkness visible. And, though I will want to make connections with other poems of his, I want to take one poem as my "slide"—one of Hecht's most familiar and successful poems, "A Hill," first published in *The New Yorker* in February 1964, and collected in *The Hard Hours*.

In Italy, where this sort of thing can occur,
I had a vision once—though you understand
It was nothing at all like Dante's, or the visions of saints,
And perhaps not a vision at all. I was with some friends,
Picking my way through a warm sunlit piazza
In the early morning. A clear fretwork of shadows
From huge umbrellas littered the pavement and made
A sort of lucent shallows in which was moored
A small navy of carts. Books, coins, old maps,

Anthony Hecht 331

Cheap landscapes and ugly religious prints
Were all on sale. The colors and noise
Like the flying hands were gestures of exultation,
So that even the bargaining
Rose to the ear like a voluble godliness.
And then when it happened, the noises suddenly stopped,
And it got darker; pushcarts and people dissolved
And even the great Farnese Palace itself
Was gone, for all its marble; in its place
Was a hill, mole-colored and bare. It was very cold,
Close to freezing, with a promise of snow.
The trees were like old ironwork gathered for scrap
Outside a factory wall. There was no wind,
And the only sound for a while was the little click
Of ice as it broke in the mud under my feet.
I saw a piece of ribbon snagged on a hedge,
But no other sign of life. And then I heard
What seemed the crack of a rifle. A hunter, I guessed;
At least I was not alone. But just after that
Came the soft and papery crash
Of a great branch somewhere unseen falling to earth.

And that was all, except for the cold and silence
That promised to last forever, like the hill.
Then prices came through, and fingers, and I was restored
To the sunlight and my friends. But for more than a week
I was scared by the plain bitterness of what I had seen.
All this happened about ten years ago,
And it hasn't troubled me since, but at last, today,
I remembered that hill; it lies just to the left
Of the road north of Poughkeepsie; and as a boy
I stood before it for hours in wintertime.

The poem is animated—urged, structured, and colored—by
all of the contrasts I have mentioned, and by the "painful

doubleness" its displacements enact. It stands with a group of poems central to Hecht's achievement—among them "Coming Home," "Apprehensions," "The Grapes," "The Short End," and "The Venetian Vespers"—that are essentially anatomies of melancholy. They are poems richer in incident and memory than others. They seem to cast a wider net and into deeper waters. But their purpose is peculiar. That purpose can be seen all the more clearly when a poem with the opposite motive— "Peripeteia" would be my example—is placed beside this group. *Peripeteia* is Aristotle's term for the reversal of fortune or intention on which the action in a drama turns, and in Hecht's poem it is an extraordinary turn of events. The poet is alone— that is, he feels a "mild relief that no one there knows me"— in a theater that is filling with people before a play. He is, he says, "a connoisseur of loneliness," and his "cool, drawn-out anticipation" this night is less for the play to be performed than for a long-running "stillness" before the curtain rises. Even without knowing that the play is to be *The Tempest*, we might have guessed this poet to be a sort of Prospero (or Shakespeare) in contented exile (or retirement), enisled in loneliness, his island (or "isolation") his work, his muse a miraculous daughter:

> Each of us is miraculously alone
> In calm, invulnerable isolation,
> Neither a neighbor nor a fellow but,
> As at the beginning and end, a single soul,
> With all the sweet and sour of loneliness.
> I, as a connoisseur of loneliness,
> Savor it richly, and set it down
> In an endless umber landscape, a stubble field
> Under a lilac, electric, storm-flushed sky,
> Where, in companionship with worthless stones,
> Mica-flecked, or at best some rusty quartz,

Anthony Hecht   333

> I stood in childhood, waiting for things to mend.
> A useful discipline, perhaps. One that might lead
> To solitary, self-denying work
> That issues in something harmless, like a poem,
> Governed by laws that stand for other laws.
> Both of which aim, through kindred disciplines,
> At the soul's knowledge and habiliment.

The image of the child standing, waiting, alone in an empty field—as the man he became is waiting in the theater—will bring at once to mind the child in "A Hill." But whereas the latter poem ends with the forlorn child, "Peripeteia" starts there, with some complacency, and then with an astonishing turn of the poem's fortunes moves on to quite another stage of "self-granted freedom." The play begins, unfolds its plot. By a sly and implicit irony, Hecht may mean for us to understand that his speaker has gradually fallen asleep, and that the play resumes in his dream. But no matter. The see-through magic of theater or dreams or desire itself comes to the same thing, as suddenly

> Leaving a stunned and gap-mouthed Ferdinand,
> Father and faery pageant, she, even she,
> Miraculous Miranda, steps from the stage,
> Moves up the aisle to my seat, where she stops,
> Smiles gently, seriously, and takes my hand
> And leads me out of the theater, into a night
> As luminous as noon, more deeply real,
> Simply because of her hand, than any dream
> Shakespeare or I or anyone ever dreamed.

The eyes widen. The lush rhetoric, the sweetness at once improbable and inevitable, the whole panoply of redemption and enchantment have a truly Shakespearean resonance in Hecht's redaction. But, as I say, this is an unusual gesture. The group of poems of which I take "A Hill" to be representative does the work of disenchantment.

I WANT to start at the most literal level of reading: the biographical. All of these anatomies of melancholy seem the most autobiographical of Hecht's poems, even when they include the added displacement of characterized voices and plots. That might just make them the more identifiable as dreams. Like "Peripeteia," "A Hill" calls itself a vision or dream. And it seems more of a private poem than a personal one. Its juxtaposition of images—piazza and hill—is evidently charged with private associations and meant to operate both within the poem and on the reader as dream-work will. The images are not superimposed, but displaced, the one by the other, the later by the earlier—and both recalled, as if by an analysand, a decade later. The poem cannot be read as any simple alternation of manifest and latent meanings. The action here is the emergence of a suppressed memory. The poem itself does not offer any elaboration or explanation. But the reader who remembers a bit of Hecht's biography may have some clues. The Roman setting, for instance. During the Second World War, Hecht served in the Army, in both Europe and Japan, and returned home to a slow and difficult period of readjustment. "Like most others who saw any combat at all," he writes, "I experienced a very pronounced and fully conscious sense of guilt at surviving when others, including friends, had not." Then, in 1951, he was awarded the first Prix de Rome writing fellowship ever granted by the American Academy in Rome, and he returned to Europe. Rome, then, carried for the poet a sense of triumph and guilt. And it is not just the burden of history or of artistic tradition (mention of the Farnese Palace focuses that) that presses on the poet until, like Dante, he faints at the intensity of his own imagining, but the fact that Rome is where he has been *sent*, as if in luxurious exile, that makes it appropriate as a scene of instruction.

And what of the hill, the infernal landscape? Poughkeepsie? Perhaps. A state of soul? More likely. And with its factory wall and hunter, it is a landscape out of Auden as well. Let us say it is actual *and* literary, psychological *and* metaphysical. And with only slightly altered topography it recurs in several other poems. It serves an overtly symbolic function in such poems as "Exile," which is dedicated to Joseph Brodsky:

> Vacant parade grounds swept by the winter wind,
> A pile of worn-out tires crowning a knoll,
> The purplish clinkers near the cinder blocks
> That support the steps of an abandoned church
> Still moored to a telephone pole, this sullen place
> Is *terra deserta*, Joseph, this is Egypt.

Or, in his nasty, brutal, long poem "The Short End," when Shirley turns away from the Live Entombment and faces another kind of death-in-life:

> A grizzled landscape, burdock and thistle-choked,
> A gnarled, barbed-wire barricade of brambles,
> All thorn and needle-sharp hostility,
> The dead weeds wicker-brittle, raffia-pale,
> The curled oak leaves a deep tobacco brown,
> The sad rouge of old bricks, chips of cement
> From broken masonry, a stubble field
> Like a mangy lion's pelt of withered grass.
> Off in the distance a thoroughly dead tree,
> Peeled of its bark, sapless, an armature
> Of well-groomed, military, silver-gray.
> And other leafless trees, their smallest twigs
> Incising a sky the color of a bruise.

It is the same bleakness, out of Kafka or Beckett, and its props grow familiar: the ruined building, the tree, the military echo. The apparent sound of a rifle-shot (what he first *thinks* he hears is more important than what it turns out to be—a dead and no golden bough) in "A Hill" brings to mind other allusions to the Second World War. The execution in " 'More Light! More Light!' " The soldier-orphan in part III of "The Venetian Vespers." Or in "Still Life," where the exquisitely rendered natural detail of a misted landscape before dawn gives way to light—and to a sudden memory:

> As in a water-surface I behold
> The first, soft, peach decree
> Of light, its pale, inaudible commands.
> I stand beneath a pine-tree in the cold,
> Just before dawn, somewhere in Germany,
> A cold, wet, Garand rifle in my hands.

Such memories hover over the landscape of "A Hill." But for Hecht himself, though he rigorously excluded them from the poem, there are specific personal associations. In a letter to me, he once explained:

As for "A Hill," it is the nearest I was able to come in that early book to what Eliot somewhere describes as an obsessive image or symbol—something from deep in our psychic life that carries a special burden of meaning and feeling for us. In my poem I am really writing about a pronounced feeling of loneliness and abandonment in childhood, which I associate with a cold and unpeopled landscape. My childhood was doubtless much better than that of many, but my brother was born epileptic when I was just over two, and from then on all attention was, very properly, focused on him. I have always felt that desolation, that hell itself, is most powerfully expressed in an uninhabited natural landscape at its bleakest.

The most direct poetic version of these same events is "Apprehensions." (The title alone indicates the poem's mix of fear and guilt, understanding and arrest, and a dreaded anticipation of the future.) The poem recounts his brother's "grave and secret malady," its effect and that of the stockmarket crash on his family, and his father's attempted suicide (a double failure which is linked, by a stolen barbiturate, with the brother's illness). But those events, convulsive in themselves, seem the background to the primary relationship in the poem, that between the young Hecht and his Fräulein, "a Teutonic governess / Replete with the curious thumb-print of her race, / That special relish for inflicted pain." The world of this childhood, this poem, is one "made of violent oppositions," which the child could placate only by "mute docility." The pain inflicted is linked, finally, to the Holocaust and the war; even more eerily, during the dream reunion at the poem's end, Hecht associates himself with this figure, a witch out of Grimm, a foster mother. In fact, through the whole poem in some strange way this menacing Fräulein stands in for the child's mother, who is barely mentioned. The sense of abandonment, loneliness, and cruelty in the child's home life is balanced—or compensated for—in the poem by two gifts, two modes of apprehension, a book and a vision, both of them associated with the creative imagination and thereby with the poet's later vocation. The *Book of Knowledge* gave him encyclopedic access to the treasury of the world's stories; a minutely detailed vision out the apartment window—whereby a taxicab, and then the street, and the city, and then the continent are held and transfigured in the transfiguring eye of the artist—gave him a sense of some other available power. In a young life marked by what he calls "elisions," these experiences are fulfilling. But they *are* compensatory: fugitive, fragmentary, the stuff of romance, in every sense imaginary. To put this poem side by side with "A Hill" is to be struck with the similarity between the *Book of Knowledge* and the Farnese Palace, the Manhattan avenue and the Roman piazza—a world of figures apprehended there. The child standing alone in front of the open window is a type of the solipsist, the artist; he is "superbly happy" because he is alone. (Freud defined melancholia as regressive narcissism.) But this is a rare indulgence of Hecht's, and not altogether to be trusted. It is most likely a screen memory. The child standing alone in front of the hill is perhaps a screen memory too. A hill, a mound or barrow, may be a tomb, and this poem's genre is less the dream-vision than the elegy, perhaps an elegy for the self. A hill is also traditionally a symbol of the mother. It is where the dead abide, and entrance to the otherworld, the matrix. My guess is that the mother is the unspoken, unacknowledged but looming presence in "A Hill," or at least in the second part of the poem—its landscape the mother's body— where a primal world supplants the busy, bright masculine Roman scene. And I suspect the figure of the mother is the focus of those feelings of fear and guilt, abandonment and loneliness in so many of Hecht's poems. His own account substitutes his brother, but he is the occasion, not the cause. The opening of "The Venetian Vespers"—a poem set in a water-borne city—connects "the stale water and glass / In the upstairs room when somebody had died" (the somebody, it soon emerges, is the child's mother) with

> those first precocious hints of hell
> Those intuitions of living desolation
> That last a lifetime. They were never, for me,
> Some desert place that humans had avoided
> In which I could get lost, to which I might
> In dreams condemn myself—a wilderness

Natural but alien and unpitying.
They were instead those derelict waste places
Abandoned by mankind as of no worth,
Frequented, if at all, by the dispossessed,
Nocturnal shapes, the crippled and the shamed.

In fact, some lines later, the speaker associates his mother's death with the image of "underwater globes, / Mercury seed-pearls"—Mercury the hermetic psychopomp to the dead. Another poem, "The Grapes," makes a similar association. The speaker now is a no-longer-young chambermaid, an antitype to the Fräulein. (In this poem, has Hecht cast himself, under the name of Marc-Antoine, as her neglected lover?) Her experience of the vision-of-the-hill is a daydream, an image generated by a magazine article, the image of a sole survivor of a crash, adrift in a rubber boat in mid-Pacific, "that blank / Untroubled waste." And her disenchantment comes when she happens to be gazing.

Gazing down at a crystal bowl of grapes
In ice-water. They were green grapes, or, rather,
They were a sort of pure, unblemished jade,
Like turbulent ocean water, with misted skins,
Their own pale, smoky sweat, or tiny frost.

Again, the underwater globes; something—a whole world—drowned and distant. The maid in "The Grapes" is mourning her own life, but the pattern persists, poem to poem. The most frightening appearance of the mother in all of Hecht's books comes in "Behold the Lilies of the Field," where, from the couch in a psychiatrist's office, the speaker relates a vivid fantasy of having attended at the flaying of a Roman emperor by his barbarian captors:

When they were done, hours later,
The skin was turned over to one of their saddle-makers

To be tanned and stuffed and sewn. And for what?
A hideous life-sized doll, filled out with straw,
In the skin of the Roman Emperor, Valerian,
With blanks of mother-of-pearl under the eyelids,
And painted shells that had been prepared beforehand
For the fingernails and toenails,
Roughly cross-stitched on the inseam of the legs
And up the back to the center of the head,
Swung in the wind on a rope from the palace flag-pole;
And young girls were brought there by their mothers
To be told about the male anatomy.
His death had taken hours.
They were very patient.
And with him passed away the honor of Rome.

In the end, I was ransomed. Mother paid for me.

This nasty little oedipal fantasy and its erotic violence—an impulse that fascinates and horrifies this poet—stand at one extreme of the group of poems I am discussing. "A Hill" stands at the other. Neither poem, nor any of those between, can be reduced to a textbook formula. I do not mean to *solve* the poem, to pluck the heart out of its mystery, but only to suggest that its mysterious force derives in part from such pressures. Besides, when I invoke the word "mother," I mean it to stand in for the source of light and love, as well as the Queen of the Night. She is the preconscious. She is memory. She is the muse. The sense of abandonment makes the poet invert her sustaining warmth into a lifeless cold, the pit of hell. In other poems it is a grave for Jews. In "The Short End," whose remote, admonitory parent-figures are George Rose and Miss McIntosh, it is a coffin for George Rose whose "otherworldliness" leads to a lesson that *love* and *bitterness* are the same. None of these anatomies of melancholy offers the reader—as distinct from their protagonists—any easy lesson. Indeed, what

I want to suggest is the probing complex of emotions—the controlled disorder, painful doubleness—that drives the poem and is pursued through an intertexture of images that touches, obscurely or overtly, most of the major poems in Hecht's work.

MELANCHOLY IS Hecht's keynote, especially in *The Hard Hours*, whose first poem is "A Hill" and whose epigraph is "*Al that joye is went away.*" Darkness and suffering suffuse the book. Its ironies curdle into cynicism; its wrenching horrors are dwelt upon. I wonder if the book's many victims aren't projections of the poet himself; if the sufferings of wartime Europe don't find their subjective correlative in the poet's own. There are also references in the book that puzzle. "Adam," for instance, is a poem addressed to one of his sons by his first marriage. It is a poem with the book's title in it ("Adam, there will be / Many hard hours, / As an old poem says, / Hours of loneliness"). Its concluding stanza is peculiar, except in the usual metaphoric way:

> Think of the summer rain
> Or seedpearls of the mist;
> Seeing the beaded leaf,
> Try to remember me.
> From far away
> I send my blessing out
> To circle the great globe.
> It shall reach you yet.

(Watery seedpearls, globe . . . already the central cluster of images has been invoked.) Likewise, "A Letter" ends ominously:

> There is not much else to tell.
> One tries one's best to continue as before
> Doing some little good.

> But I would have you know that all is not well
>   With a man dead set to ignore
> The endless repetitions of his own murmurous blood.

I have asked the poet what lay behind such lines—behind the entire book, really—and he answered in a letter that I quote now with his permission:

At the termination of five-and-a-half years of a painfully unhappy and unsuccessful marriage, a separation settlement was made, followed by a divorce, which required of my ex-wife that she live within 150 miles of New York City, so that I should be able to see the children on a regular basis. I must add that, while the marriage had been an unhappy one virtually from the start, its failure was a terrible blow to my self-esteem, and it was not I who sought to terminate it. When it was over I invested all my frustrated familial feelings on the two boys whom I saw, like most divorced fathers, on weekends, making those days unhealthily emotional, and completely without any ease or naturalness. In a way, I resented this arrangement: I had a job to perform during the week (teaching at Bard in those years) and such spare time as I had was devoted entirely to the children, who were pretty young in those days, the younger one still in diapers when all this began. So I had no private life of my own, and consequently invested too much emotional capital in the children. I was the more inclined to do so because I knew their mother to be completely irresponsible with regard to them. Then one day she told me, as I was delivering the children to her at the end of a weekend, that she had fallen in love with a Belgian, and that while I could legally prevent her from moving to Europe, as this man wished her to do, if she were forced to stay in this country she would be very unhappy, and if she were very unhappy, the children would be very unhappy. There was, of course, no argument to counter this. I had asked my lawyer, before the separation papers were drawn up, whether it would be possible for me to obtain custody of the children. He told me that it was virtually impossible, and in those days he was right. So she took the children off to Belgium, and I sank into a very deep depression. I felt no incentive even to get out of bed in the morning. I don't believe I thought in terms of suicide, but neither did life seem to hold out any attractions whatever. My doctor was worried about me, and suggested that I commit myself to a hospital, chiefly, he said, for the administration of medication. It was Thorazine, and some other drug the name of which I no longer recall. I was there for three months, toward the end of which time I was allowed to go out during the days. Lowell was particularly kind to me during this period. The hospital was called Gracie Square Hospital, and there were some public pay phones on my floor, on which incoming calls to patients would be carried. Anyone could pick up a phone when it rang, and then page in a loud shout whomever the call was for. It was the custom of the patients to announce, in a loud and cheerful voice, on picking up the phone: "Crazy Square." Many of the patients were on electric shock; it had been agreed before I went in that I would be treated solely with medication, and this was observed. And the medication did indeed control the depression. What would have been a grim three months was, while by no means cheerful, yet remarkably endurable. The only thing I remember complaining about—it was pointless, of course, to complain about the food or routine—was the pictures. The plain bare walls were occasionally "enlivened" by framed pieces of cloth with arbitrary patterns on them, things that might have been drapes or upholstery. The chief point about them was that they were non-representational, and would not remind any patient of anything that carried an emotional burden.

This memoir is all the more moving for its dispassionate and at times even witty tone. The "frustrated familial feelings" should by now be familiar ones. Hecht's own childhood feelings of abandonment are first recklessly overcompensated for, and then sadly reinforced when his own children are taken away. The subsequent breakdown is as marked a contrast to his frenetic life before the children left as is the contrast of moods in "A Hill." And the symptoms of his resulting depression have also made their way into later poems. But there are two details in this letter that I want to draw particular attention to. One is that pun, "Crazy Square." Even when drugged and confined, the poet's ear is attuned to the incongruous, to the play of words—as if, even when sliding around, language could still hold its meanings together. The other is his complaint about the hospital "art." The very words he uses here recall phrases in "A Hill"—"the plain bare walls" echoing "a hill, mole-colored and bare," and "I was scared by the plain bitterness of what I had seen." I will suggest that what he is looking at has a great deal to do with "A Hill," and ask a reader to keep in mind this letter's memory of Hecht's complaint about those nonpicturing pictures. Ironically, their "function"—not to stir any old emotional burdens in a patient—had the effect of rousing Hecht. The burden they may have carried to him is a factor of their resemblance to the hill in his poem.

IN HIS essay "On the Methods and Ambitions of Poetry," Hecht talks about the homage a poem pays to "the natural world, from which it derives and which it strives to imitate. And there is in nature a superfluity, an excess of texture which plays no necessary part in the natural economy." *Excess of texture* neatly defines that aspect of Hecht's own style we register as baroque. I say an aspect because he turns to it— turns it on, even—usually as a deliberate thematic maneuver.

There are swags of it in "The Venetian Vespers," for instance.
The poem's speaker, like the child in "Apprehensions," is look-
ing out his window:

> Here is a sky determined to maintain
> The reputation of Tiepolo,
> A moving vision of a shapely mist,
> Full of the splendor of the insubstantial.
> Against a diorama of palest blue
> Cloud-curds, cloud-stacks, cloud-bushes sun themselves.
> Giant confections, impossible meringues,
> Soft coral reefs and powdery tumuli
> Pass in august processions and calm herds.
> Great stadiums, grandstands and amphitheaters,
> The tufted, opulent litters of the gods
> They seem; or laundered bunting, well-dressed wigs,
> Harvests of milk-white, Chinese peonies
> That visibly rebuke our stinginess.
> For all their ghostly presences, they take on
> A colorful nobility at evening.
> Off to the east the sky begins to turn
> Lilac so pale it seems a mood of gray,
> Gradually, like the death of virtuous men.
> Streaks of electrum richly underline
> The slow, flat-bottomed hulls, those floated lobes
> Between which quills and spokes of light fan out
> Into carnelian reds and nectarines,
> Nearing a citron brilliance at the center,
> The searing furnace of the glory hole
> That fires and fuses clouds of muscatel
> With pencilings of gold. I look and look,
> As though I could be saved simply by looking . . . .

And of course he cannot be saved: the grandeur is a delusion,
and its excess a measure of his own inabilities. Everywhere is

seems and *like*. Left behind, but behind it all, is thin air. The empurpled passage stands as both tribute to and accusation of the imagination. Trope is a contrivance, a twisting, a turning aside.

Readers in the past have missed Hecht's canny relationship to such gold pencilings. "Somebody's Life," a pair of unrhymed sonnets, is a sly satire on this impulse of art. A poet sits atop a cliff, overlooking the sea and rocks. In an attitude of sublimity he "Felt himself claimed by such rash opulence: / There were the lofty figures of his soul." The poem then goes on to ask a more serious question, "Was this the secret / Gaudery of self-love, or a bloodbidden, / Involuntary homage to the world?" (That last phrase an involuntary allusion to the essay published eleven years earlier?) In any case, the poem avoids a direct answer, as if thereby to acknowledge there is none, and instead juxtaposes the actual and the figurative:

> As it happens, he was doomed never to know.
> At times in darkened rooms he thought he heard
> The soft ruckus of patiently torn paper,
> The sea's own noise, the elderly slop and suck
> Of hopeless glottals. Once, in a bad dream,
> He saw himself stranded on the wet flats,
> As limp as kelp, among putrescent crabs.
> But to the very finish he remembered
> The flash and force, the crests, the heraldry,
> Those casual epergnes towering up
> Like Easter trinkets of the tzarevitch.

Again the notion of salvation; "epergne," or glass serving dish, is from a French word meaning "to save," and the mention of "Easter trinkets" hints at resurrection, though the tsarevitch, like the poet in his own dream, is doomed.

The extravagance of the high style in a Hecht poem should signal some unknowing desperation, some pride before a fall.

It often verges toward a Latinate diction, and the added syllables give a kind of tumbling motion to the rhythm. Or appositional phrases and clauses are heaped up for momentum's sake. There is a brilliantly colored blur, a manic rush. One hears it, sees it, at the beginning of "A Hill":

> A clear fretwork of shadows
> From huge umbrellas littered the pavement and made
> A sort of lucent shallows in which was moored
> A small navy of carts. Books, coins, old maps,
> Cheap landscapes and ugly religious prints
> Were all on sale. The colors and noise
> Like the flying hands were gestures of exultation,
> So that even the bargaining
> Rose to the ear like a voluble godliness.

The language here is loaded with emptiness: "shallows," "gestures," the bogus art. At this pitch of exultation, the vision occurs. It is, first of all, a transformation scene, the world's flapping backdrops revealed as *teatrum mundi*. When Hecht says the "pushcarts and people dissolved / And even the great Farnese Palace itself / Was gone, for all its marble," certainly we are meant to hear the echo of Prospero's lines:

> And, like the baseless fabric of this vision,
> The cloud-capp'd towers, the gorgeous palaces,
> The solemn temples, the great globe itself,
> Yea, all which it inherit, shall dissolve
> And, like this insubstantial pageant faded,
> Leave not a rack behind. We are such stuff
> As dreams are made on, and our little life
> Is rounded with a sleep. Sir, I am vex'd,—
> Bear with my weakness—my old brain is troubled.

What at the start is proposed as "real," the Italian setting, is described in language charged with metaphor, color, allusion, artifice. The "vision" that intrudes is described as starkly, as naturalistically as possible. A shred of ribbon, a distant crack . . . these are all that remain. And a whole series of contrasts is stressed: palace and hill, Rome and Poughkeepsie, commotion and stillness, warmth and cold, adult and child, lucent shallows and dark depths, sensual consciousness and numbed instinctual memory. The plain style of the poem's second half befits the stillness, the "cold and silence." And what is crucial to understand is that this deflation or disenchantment that works to mock the high style and reveal the insubstantiality of metaphor in fact accords with Hecht's own sense of the true art of poetry. In the essay I've already quoted from, he begins by asserting that "art serves to arrest action rather than promote it, and to invite instead a state of aesthetic contemplation." Twice in this poem its action is arrested, first by the scarifying vision, and a decade later by a sudden memory. And the poem then ends abruptly, even melodramatically, as if further to arrest the action of interpretation. The speaker reverts to childhood, and stands—as, in a sense, the reader does too—before the hill in winter, blank as a page. The clarification and connections we might expect to follow are omitted. But the point of the poem, what the reader is invited to contemplate, is not really the explication of personal experience, but an understanding of the competing forces of experience itself—forces that are embodied in the poem's contrasting styles. The poem ends with an image, not a moral. The tense of the last line could as well have been changed from the historical past to the present indicative—"It is winter. I am standing, for hours, before it"—to underscore the fact he is describing a condition rather than an occurrence. Hecht's essay on poetic methods concludes with what may as well be the final word on "A Hill": "in allowing us to contemplate, even within a single poem, such diversity of experience, both the good and the bad, brought into tenuous balance through all the manifold devices of art, the spirit is set at ease by a kind of katharsis, in which we are brought to acknowledge that this is the way things are. . . ."

That last catch phrase, by which Rolfe Humphries called his translation of Lucretius' *De Rerum Natura*, brings me to a final observation about Hecht's anatomies of melancholy. Though his imposing rhetoric often belies it, Hecht is by temperament closer to Frost than to Stevens, and like Frost a poet in the line of Lucretius, who wrote, as he says at the head of Book IV of his epic, "clear verse about dark things." Lucretius was a poet of violence and profound melancholy, of intellectual rigor and imaginative grandeur. He searched in his poem the ground and limits of human life, its instability and monotony, and celebrated its mechanism—those principles of Strife and Love by which nature decays and regenerates, unraveling by night what was woven by day, and out of which we make our ideas (like Death Wish and Life Force), and gods (like Mars and Venus Genetrix), our fantasies and our metaphors. In *Three Philosophical Poets*, from which Hecht drew the epigraph and orphic title of his first book *A Summoning of Stones*, George Santayana summarizes Lucretius' philosophical perspective and his poetic method:

> Naturalism is a philosophy of observation, and of an imagination that extends the observable; all the sights and sounds of nature enter into it, and lend it their directness, pungency, and coercive stress. At the same time, naturalism is an intellectual philosophy; it divines substance behind appearance, continuity behind change, law behind fortune. It therefore attaches all those sights and sounds to a hidden background that connects and explains them. So understood, nature has a depth as well as surface, force and necessity as well as sensuous variety. . . . Unapproachably vivid, relentless, direct in detail, he is unflinchingly grand and serious in his grouping of the facts. It is the truth that absorbs him and

carries him along. He wishes us to be convinced and sobered by the fact, by the overwhelming evidence of thing after thing, raining down upon us, all bearing witness with one voice to the nature of the world.

That description comes as close to Hecht's purposes too as any critic can. He is a contemplative rather than a lyrical poet. A steady contemplation of things in their order and worth—the facts of his own life, the course of history, the archive of myth and belief—is his goal. And it is, in Santayana's phrase, the truth that absorbs him and carries him along: a wary, circumscribed, but certain knowledge on which are erected love's monuments, and hope's ideal cities, and all the bright, revolving orders of the imagination. But he indulges their excesses precisely in order to test and often to undermine them. They are his rough magic, and he will abjure them.